Praise for the author

To state that my heart and mind were deeply moved by **Finding Grace: journeys of grief, courage and healing** seems an understatement. Jane's writings inspire deep reflection of one's own grief journey. Her intricate weaving of her own story, the stories of 19 other bereaved families and the wisdom of the finest of philosophers reads like a lovely mosaic. I have been searching for that one piece of literature that would speak to the hearts of all bereaved families and now I have found this in **Finding Grace.**

   Kristin Glenn, Outreach Director of 3 Hopeful Hearts, Fort Collins, Colorado

Nicolet's **Finding Grace** is a deeply thoughtful guide for navigating the storms and anguish of grief. Her honest and powerful spiritual insights into the grieving process offer ways to intentionally navigate the darkest of times. I highly recommend **Finding Grace** as a wonderful resource for chaplains and grief counselors as well as anyone experiencing loss.

   Pat Slentz, Spiritual Director and retired Hospice Chaplain

Jane Nicolet has created a work which posits a unique relationship between grace and grief, suggesting that grace can exist inside and around the landmines that so often sabotage the healing path of bereavement. For over 35 years I have counseled grief-stricken clients who have struggled to survive a variety of overwhelming losses. I regret that Nicolet's **Finding Grace** was not yet available to me as a guide and inspiration. I encourage therapists of all disciplines to add this book to their repertoire of materials for work with survivors of loss.

Nadine L. Thomsen, Licensed Psychologist

In **Letters for Grace**, this journey of a mother through the most painful of experiences, offered to me an even greater understanding of the journey we all must take - to survive what we may never understand. Jane Nicolet shares powerful insights and shares them in language that is authentic and beautiful. This is a book we all should read.

Leonard Urban, author of God is Fainting

Any parent who has lost a child will relate to the heart-wrenching grief so masterfully portrayed in **Letters for Grace**. Through her grueling journey of healing, Jane Nicolet writes from a place of frailty to forgiveness, eventually finding gifts in the grieving process. I've read thousands of stories of loss and grief and have rarely found such a gifted writer, authentically baring her soul with brilliant use of metaphors and poetry.

LeAnn Thieman, author of Chicken Soup for the Mother and Son Soul

Finding Grace

journeys of grief, courage and healing

Jane Nicolet

Author of <u>Letters for Grace</u>

BALBOA
PRESS

A DIVISION OF HAY HOUSE

This book is a work of non-fiction. Unless otherwise noted, the author
and the publisher make no explicit guarantees as to the accuracy of
the information contained in this book and in some cases, names
of people and places have been altered to protect their privacy.

Balboa Press books may be ordered through booksellers or by contacting:

Balboa Press
A Division of Hay House
1663 Liberty Drive
Bloomington, IN 47403
www.balboapress.com
1 (877) 407-4847

Because of the dynamic nature of the Internet, any web addresses or
links contained in this book may have changed since publication and
may no longer be valid. The views expressed in this work are solely those
of the author and do not necessarily reflect the views of the publisher,
and the publisher hereby disclaims any responsibility for them.

The author of this book does not dispense medical advice or prescribe the use
of any technique as a form of treatment for physical, emotional, or medical
problems without the advice of a physician, either directly or indirectly. The
intent of the author is only to offer information of a general nature to help
you in your quest for emotional and spiritual well-being. In the event you use
any of the information in this book for yourself, which is your constitutional
right, the author and the publisher assume no responsibility for your actions.

Any people depicted in stock imagery provided by Getty Images are
models, and such images are being used for illustrative purposes only.
Certain stock imagery © Getty Images.

Print information available on the last page.

ISBN: 978-1-9822-1064-9 (sc)
ISBN: 978-1-9822-1066-3 (hc)
ISBN: 978-1-9822-1065-6 (e)

Library of Congress Control Number: 2018910065

Balboa Press rev. date: 10/24/2018

Acknowledgments

There are many voices, sharing their stories and their courage, interlaced and resting tenderly within the pages of this book. My very sincere and public thank you goes to every family who interviewed with me. You each granted me precious time to listen to the details of your worst nightmares. I continue to feel honored by your trust in me. You granted me an intimate look into your heart-felt grief, helped me to hear the calls of your own grace, and allowed me to share it all with our common human family. I will never forget the power of your spirits, your capacity for love, and your ability to have faith in what lies beyond. You are grace personified.

A special thank you goes to El, an extraordinary friend and skilled, thoughtful representative, who said yes, over drinks and burgers, to helping me launch my writing into the wider world.

Notes:

The following booklist is offered as both a thank you to its authors and a gathering of ideas for any who are striving to move beyond a life in grief, or supporting another who is living in the midst of despair. Studying each one of these books has helped me, in abundant ways, to focus my life into the hope of the possible.

Dyer, Wayne. (1989). You'll See It When You Believe It. New York, NY: Harper Collins.

Dyer, Wayne. (1992). Real Magic. New York, NY: Harper Collins.

Gonzales, Laurence. (2012). Surviving Survival. New York, NY: W.W. Norton & Co, Inc.

Kumar, Sameet. (2003). Grieving Mindfully. Oakland, CA: New Harbinger Publications

Palmer, Parker. (2008). The Promise of Paradox. San Francisco, CA: Jossey-Bass.

Singer, Michael A. (2007). The untethered soul: the journey beyond yourself. Oakland, CA: New Harbinger Publications, Inc.

Tolle, Eckhart. (2003). Stillness Speaks. Novato, CA: New World Library and Vancouver, Canada: Namaste Publishing.

Contents

Parents tell their stories

In Dedication

To daughter, Leslie, always a source
of Grace in this world.
Your very presence reminds me that life is
worth living because love abounds.

And to Matthew, my source of Grace in life beyond.
You are always my son . . . always alive within me.

Preface: waiting for the call

I opened my eyes again, for at least the fifth time, and watched the newest early morning light play across my bedroom doorway. Finally giving in to the morning's sleepless reality, I simply stare at the familiar. This stillness, poised for something I can't yet name, reminds me I'm a woman in waiting. No longer gainfully employed, I live with time on my hands and restless spaces in my mind. "Relax," I murmur to myself. "Be patient; stay aware; whatever it is will be right in front of you." And soon it was – in the form of a warm summer morning's 5k and two women who said yes to a writing project that became my passion, a mission which would challenge and move me toward gracious love, compassion and peace in ways unexpected.

Introduction: finding Grace

Nothing lasts forever. As much as we may construct our lives so that the people, places and things we love and depend on are safely secure with us while our own journey unfolds, the fact is, like we, they must all dissolve in their own time. We humans and our endeavors, like the energy from which we come, inevitably experience transformations. What we love and need as well as what we fear and avoid, our very selves, simply can't last as first created. Change is our forever . . . a natural state. The issue is that what is most *natural* is also often felt as loss; still, with all their complexities in hand, change and loss will most surely find their way into our lives. The changes any loss brings neither signal the end of life's richness, nor any shortsighted promises for hope and peace. Instead, they serve to interrupt its flow, to challenge its assumptions and demand an accounting of what we consider to be most important in our life.

Dependent on the many iterations of change and loss in a life – how small or large they may appear, how challenging, even overwhelming they may become – every loss serves as an entry point into some manner of grief. As a natural response to suffering losses, it comes unbidden. Whether difficult change is unplanned or expected, merely annoying or totally devastating, we humans fight to avoid the fallout until grief leaves us no choice. Then, when its full force descends, it is suffered, and in time and a variety of ways, endured. The fires of profound loss burn fiercely. They have the power to reduce to ashes the unnecessary trivia of one's life while also lighting a path to reclamation. And when we finally awaken to continuing a life beyond grief's darkly hot and painful place, a glimpse of the transformative gift hidden within loss is waiting: gracious whispers, calling to us, assuring that this is the time for evolution. Our personal transformation is more than survival of the fire; it is the work of reclaiming a space of mercy and forgiveness, of hope in the imagined – the place where Grace resides.

Finding Grace: journeys of grief, courage and healing, was born in moments of personal pilgrimage when I became more available and open to the voice of Grace through the grieving lives of others. I had accepted that I was meant to write another book. But it wasn't until I met and listened to the conviction of two women sponsoring that August morning's 5K event – two special people who were in the midst of a life's work of supporting others through profound loss and grief – that I understood the focus for my next book. I was meant to immerse myself in Grace – open myself to all its possible signs, accept its place in the human heart, and begin conversations about its power and possibilities. And I was meant to do that while listening to the heart-achingly poignant stories of the bereaved. I made a commitment to walk into the lives of others, listen to, write and share their stories. I trusted that when I looked up from my writing, I would discover patches of blue – spaces where dark clouds parted and the light and love of Grace flowed into the brokenness of irreversibly altered lives. And as I watched and listened, it happened . . . through faith and mystery, thoughtful reflection and community, ritual and legacy, and always, compassion.

Ultimately, this book is meant to open doorways to finding personal meaning within the interconnections of grief and Grace, and to discovering ways to navigate that tender and significant space between grief's despairing and Grace's transformative healing. In part, this book is about the irretrievable loss suffered by bereaved parents. In part, it is about the courage, choices and pathways to healing of so many who journey through their individual versions of unwelcome loss and gracious transformations. And, in part, it is about the sacred paradox found when grief and Grace share the same heart space. <u>Finding</u>

<u>Grace</u> does not claim to have all the definitive answers about reconstructing the many faces of grief into Grace. It doesn't promise any magic, assuring that one will automatically be ready to hear a Grace call as soon as misery pays a visit; but, by retelling authentic stories of bereavement, reflecting on revealed questions and imagined possibilities, and detailing unique perspectives about finding healing within loss, this book does promise to bring Grace-inspired conversations into a grieving life.

the call of Grace

> *"I have spent my days stringing and
> unstringing my instrument while the song
> I came to sing remains unsung."*
> Rabindranath Tagore

*Grace calls out to our hearts when grief's dark power
threatens; and when we let it, its whispers of promised mercy
and peace breathe hope into our despair. It challenges us to
muster the courage to open our hearts even more widely, to
make a trusting move from no to yes, even when the doubt and
indecision of maybes won't easily stand aside.* I reread what
I've just drafted and know it is a central core of this book
meant to highlight the intricate interconnections between
grief and Grace. But locked and blocked, I sit yet again,
staring at the screen, chin in hand. The same place I've
been for weeks . . . more like months, if truth be told. The
maybe place holds me hostage – maybe readers won't want
to hear any of my story; maybe I shouldn't write about
how grief almost ended me; maybe having the author
also be a bereaved mother is too . . . self-absorbed, too
personal; maybe what I've been sensing really isn't Matt
leading me forward. Maybe I haven't actually been called
to write this book after all.

I've begged the Grace muse to whisper just the right
words to a mind thirsty for the courage to hear and believe
her own voice. And for weeks, a variety of words and

ideas appeared and played on pages, only to be discarded as too thin, too vague, just not good enough. I've lost my voice. Nothing I've written gives this idea – Grace calling us beyond grief – the clarity and comfort it deserves. I'm frozen in place, struck dumb by my inability to describe what I thought I'm meant to do.

I cover my eyes with cupped hands, shutting out the screen for a few blessed moments and lean back. Another break, my well-used delaying tactic, shakes me out of my chair and pushes me down to the kitchen. Reaching for the refrigerator door my eyes fix on the magnetized saying that I always keep there as a reminder. I take in the familiar words with a big breath, stand quietly, relax my shoulders into a more normal position and utter a quiet word of thanks. The irony of walking past these words for weeks and only now really seeing them again is not lost on me; it slaps me awake. I've just gotten a call from Grace in the form of a refrigerator magnet: "Be Truthful, Gentle, And Fearless." Gandhi's words spill over to remind me what I've neglected: to detach from my analyzing, worried ego and the need to control this outcome; to accept this task and trust my inner heart's voice; to fearlessly, gently, speak the truth I've come to understand.

Questions still pepper my new resolve, but I trust they will encounter their answers when the time is right. Maybe that's what this project is all about – trusting that the dynamic, healing energy of Grace moments are just steps ahead. I start back up to my office, with fresh perspective and new hope, to begin again.

"You experience grief when you experience any change in your relationship to the world. . . ."
Sameet Kumar: <u>Grieving Mindfully</u>

Before Grace can take center stage, her antithesis, grief, needs to be acknowledged. These each emanate from love – the love of ourselves, of others, and of the world we've come to understand and accept as ours; and, they both are able to hold dynamic space within the human heart. One is triggered by an unacceptable loss of something deeply loved and the other by the desire to re-establish healing spaces for love to flourish.

Grief answers to different names, many of which refer to where we express love – our hearts: we suffer through heavy hearts, heartache, heartbreak and broken heartedness. Though most often understood as bereavement, grief is not limited to loss through death. It can come alive in us through a move, a job change or loss, a divorce, life-altering illness, aging, care-giving, death of a pet, an unanticipated end to a beloved life . . . and the list goes on. Despite grief being a conceptual presence rather than a material entity, we identify and feel grief as sensations, impressions and actions – a pounding hammer to our damaged, vulnerable nail. It is the powerful reaction to the loss of what we've grown to love and believe belongs in our life. Anything that separates us from such a love has the power to elicit grief. According to Kumar (<u>Grieving Mindfully</u>), grief happens to us systemically – physically, emotionally, mentally, spiritually and interpersonally. He calls it a "black hole" with the power to plant the seeds of misery that, if we aren't careful, we might easily find ourselves sowing for the rest of our lives.

Most of what we understand about the grief of unwelcome change and accompanying loss comes from those belief systems, cultural traditions and family rituals and messages we've taken to heart. Here's how I once understood grief events: 1) unexpected and unpleasant change easily leads us to experience the loss of something critically important, something we believe is precious; 2) loss is bad because it messes with the intricate and intimate balance we have with our own reality; 3) losing what we love is so painful we are thrown into grieving; and 4) grief leaves us mired in hopelessness and heartbreak because that's what it always does. Generally, by this last statement I had stopped intellectualizing grief and had begun to emotionally move into the miserable cycle I most wanted to avoid.

Just for the next few moments, free yourself to open into another series of ideas that I discovered after my own son's death was actually more accurate: 1) change and loss are an acknowledged part of the natural flow of all life; 2) unexpected change and accompanying loss are inescapable; 3) our relationships and the objects of our love will inevitably evolve and/or disappear over time leaving us to face grief within our lifetime; and 4) how we decide to intentionally process the irrevocable losses we encounter has the power to create the lifestyle we lead during grief and beyond. Living powerlessly within inevitable grief is not a done deal, a hand dealt to us without our permission. We have choices, optional hands to fan out and study.

I finally spread out my own optional hand when all else was dark. The cards of my life journey lay there, bathed in a light I'd not noticed before – one that helped me more clearly see my present, sense a future, and then tentatively set in motion the charting of another path. This pathway's various tracks and channels all were lit with a common message: *Let go! You don't have to dwell indefinitely in suffering.* I followed the pathway as it continued: *When the hottest fires of grief begin to abate, courageously and tenderly rouse yourself to notice the changes in your spirit, your body, and your heart. For within those spaces come deeper breaths, calmer thoughts and kinder memories.* When I sensed my own softening, a slight shift of my heart, opening to more than despair, I began to pay attention.

During these moments Grace is as close as grief. It calls in this gentler time, asking us to accept what is, to be present in the *Now* of life, and to remain patient, allowing grief to simply exist within us. Without our resistance to its presence, grief will begin to move through and beyond, leaving room for the Grace whispers of our hearts. Surrendering to a Grace call takes strength. But once done, we can gradually notice the power, the trust and hope essential for us to participate in our own evolution – moving beyond dark into light, beyond pain into peace, beyond resistance into surrender.

> **"The most beautiful thing we can experience is the mysterious."**
> Albert Einstein

Grace, like grief, is as vast, complex and individually intricate as the human experience. It is a tender word, not in a frail or breakable way, but in an intimately benevolent way. Grace is rife with meaning, a conceptual presence defined through synonyms, metaphors and personal examples. It's an abstraction, an idea that comes alive within the swirl of individual philosophies, varied worship styles and personal experiences. An extrasensory component, more mystical than material, Grace is felt and described through our senses and impressions in subtle and finely tuned ways, often beyond our conscious thought. Grace, once accepted, becomes an interacting character in our lives ... another living, available presence. At its essence, Grace is love – pure and accessible.

Depending on who's doing the explaining, Grace is credited with increasing energy, nurturing creativity, transforming emotions, relaxing mind and body, pouring out forgiveness, and providing hope and courage to any and all who are open to its blessings. It's considered synonymous with spiritual mercy, loving compassion, healing transformation, and God's unearned, unconditional salvation. Metaphorically, it's representative of a life jacket, a gift from the soul, a savior and guide, balance within disorder, a blessed pathway out of pain, . . . the light at the end of the tunnel.

The powerful possibilities of Grace are obscured when we relegate it to just another vocabulary word. We can only make use of its gifts by understanding it is more than any one word. It appears most alive in extraordinary, often complicated experiences beyond the tangible. Catching a Grace moment requires awareness, the willingness to awaken to a personal truth – either something important is wrong and needs our attention, or we have been surprised awake by the clarity and beauty of a blessing that surrounds us. When we can intentionally admit we need to pay attention, flashes of Grace events come alive in and through us. A weight lifting from our mind and heart, an unexpected assurance that all will be well regardless of the clamor around us, experiencing relief or gratitude, smiling for no particular reason other than it just feels good, handling the pesky and tough details of life's daily reality more gently and hopefully – these are the stuff of Grace moving through our individual lives, whether or not we've learned to call it by name.

The power of Grace is most easily visible and magnified within community – those loving exchanges and essential connections and interactions among humankind. It is at work in the ready smiles of willing strangers who help one another; in the quiet, nonjudgmental listening of a friend; in the hope of a picket line and positive outcomes of a nonviolent demonstration; in heartfelt tears born of forgiveness; in apologies and thankfulness given without expectation; in authentically lived humility; in the selfless work of volunteering; in a joyful return or an unselfish departure; and in the tender intimacy of giving your fearless, difficult truth to another. We may not always know what to call them, but we know these moments when we see and feel them; they are loving, sacred experiences.

> *"When you fully accept you don't know, you give up struggling to find answers . . . and that is when a greater intelligence can operate through you."*
> Eckhart Tolle: <u>Stillness Speaks</u>

It's taken years of tamping my own ego down, but I've finally come to understand Grace whispers as uniquely personal, intimate, soul-driven experiences. They are held within that spiritually-intelligent part of us originally sparked by the divine. When it senses we are open to our own needs, Grace wells up from our souls to enter our heart spaces and begin its whispering. I think of it moving throughout my heart, seeking out those places that long for it most and eventually coming to rest close to the darkness that is grief. I first became aware of it many years ago as a distraught teen; Grace flowed into a shadowed place in my heart and, unwittingly, I benefitted from its call. Even though I didn't understand then what had happened, how I let go to surrender shame into acceptance, I gratefully welcomed the gift. And then, clueless teenager that I was, I simply moved on to let life happen as it would. Throughout its ordinary and commonplace events, I rarely thought about that earlier transformational experience. Instead, I maintained a lifestyle balance by using my usual prescription: letting the ebb and flow of physical, emotional, human and cultural realities direct my thinking and interacting.

I welcomed the familiar, those most comfortable, practiced options to guide my decisions, and believed all things would unfold as they must. As a young adult I prepared myself to handle all that came my way – education, love, marriage, profession, children, change, losses, joys, happiness, pain – by using those ways I had accepted as true to absorb the inevitable weight of disappointment, sadness, anxiety, and even depression. Overall, I was an independent, a stoic, who learned to judiciously circle around all I experienced in order to enjoy, deny, ignore or rail against their impact on me. I was an ice skater skimming the surface, watching for expected pits in the ice and skirting them when I could, stumbling along when I couldn't.

Then, in middle age, unexpected and heartbreaking reality slammed me to the ice and I realized that I didn't have the skills to pick myself up and navigate to stable ground. My son, Matthew, died and a few years later, his step-father left our marriage. The precarious balance I had learned to appreciate, evaporated. Everything I believed true – the love, safety and trust of it all – wasn't. Adrift in unfamiliar, risky territory, I lost my way. I closed into myself tightly, resisting with all my might the miserable reality of my life. I had run out of options for my next moves. If I was to stay upright, something had to change. I had to accept that the lifestyle I had loved would never return to me; my life would never be the same again. Out of viable alternatives, I stopped begging for the assurances of comfortable answers and surrendered to the unknown.

> *"Help is inherent in the call, and we either seek it and have a hand in the proceedings, or . . . are pushed from behind by the soul's tough love."*
> Gregg Levoy: <u>Callings</u>

Ah, "the soul's tough love" – an intriguing and daunting idea to consider. I vision my soul doing some heaving lifting, pushing me to be accountable for and present in my own life. I'm pretty sure our soul's Grace knows when to step up and when to step back. When loss triggers grief in us it feels impossible to listen to anything beyond the sound of our own hearts breaking. And Grace stands by, waiting for us to notice there's more to hear. Grief professionals make distinctions between different levels of grief, naming them acute and subtle. Acute grief, often early in the process, is characterized by periods of intense and all-consuming distress. Subtle grief, available as time progresses, gives the bereaved some times of relative calm, the in-between moments when sorrow abates to the point we can think about something alive and vital, still present in our lives. Hearing a call for renewal from within is muted during despairing, acute periods of grieving. But Grace is patient. When the time is right and we're again present to our life, it will surface, calling to us and offering just the right questions to challenge and gentle us back to the living.

Calls will come. When that happens we have choices: we can be too mired in distress to hear a call; we can be awake to a call and purposely accept, neglect or deny it; we can be confused by a call, shake our head, but continue to listen; we can be closed to a call, hoping the push from deep inside somehow fades away. The whole idea of hearing, let alone answering a call is tricky in a world where, for many, noise is a welcome distraction.

Still, calls will come and with them also come questions, doubt and cynicism. We're listening for a voice out of . . . where? What's supposed to happen? Am I going to hear an actual, divine voice and magically know what to do? Am I supposed to sense something? Do I see or hear someone call in a dream? Can I open a book and find perfectly appropriate passages that will jump off the page at me? Will random song lyrics deliver the menu to forgiving myself? If I tune into a religious service or to some self-help speaker could I get the recipe for lessening my suffering? Will a friend's words over coffee give me a spiritual direction? Really . . . a little help here.

And the answers come: to all our questions, Yes! Just be present to your daily life because calls and answers are everywhere we turn. They are the air we breathe, the steps we take, the decisions we make, the integral pieces ready and willing to fill in and clarify the puzzling lives we lead. We don't have to physically go anywhere special to experience them, because . . . wait for it . . . calls and their answers live within us. YOU – the divine force within and around you – are what you seek. Your own inner spark of the sacred assigns you as the challenger, the healer, the forgiver, the inspiration and origin of your own soul's tough love. We will finally understand the sacred power of Grace when we accept it is real, accessible and waiting patiently within.

"Your greatest gift lies beyond the door named fear."
Sufi saying

"Generally, people won't pursue their callings until the fear of doing so is finally exceeded by the pain of not doing so . . . Too many of us, it seems, have cultivated the ability to live with the unacceptable . . . ." Author Gregg Levoy, in Callings speaks to one of the reasons I didn't welcome a call at first; I knew the price it was going to exact. What's left when I've kicked "unacceptable" out? It holds fear – that understanding that we'll have to surrender to something untested while giving up things important to the world we already know: a belief, a relationship, a position, long-held anger, an exciting but dangerous drama, an accepted lifestyle . . . and more. Grief in league with its ever-present sidekicks, fear, misery, anger, guilt and depression, hold us in a short-sighted prison. What we see, hear and feel become limited by the boundaries we've built around ourselves – our own status quo. Hearing, let alone listening for the whispers that question what we've submitted to, no matter how loving and lovely it might sound in theory, feels unrealistic and naïve to the incarcerated mind and heart. As long as we sanction our self-imposed prison walls, a calling voice only threatens to confuse the very delicate balance between the past we know and the charted future we believe that past must surely bring.

It doesn't make listening any easier that calls essentially come in the form of questions. Who needs another message that leaves us wondering, that tells us it's time to take the left instead of that right turn that looked pretty good earlier? Well, actually, we do. The irritating truth is that the most annoying and thorniest questions are the juiciest ones. They're the intriguing calls that drive us into blind alleys, seemingly with no way out, until we become quiet enough to calmly sit in our own uncomfortable presence for a while. Then, lo and behold – just ahead is a personal map and flashlight. My blind alley experience led me into a kind of internal call and response, a dialogue with the caller within – myself.

After I grew past my irritation and realized I actually had something important to say to myself, I began to grudgingly participate in the conversation. The questions that became most important for me were: What makes life worth living? What are you afraid of? What do you have to lose if you let go of the pain you're in and free fall into the unexplored? What is there to gain? I had to be brutally honest and shine some light on my own truth. Then, and only then did I start to get serious about finding my way out of the dark. Answering my own questions triggered changes in my patterns of thinking and behaving until I fell into another lifestyle. And my biggest take away turned out to be a bit of a paradox: what I gained from what I most feared – opening my heart to feel again, to consent to the unknown – has been far more merciful than accepting life within the familiar shadows of deep grief.

M. Kipp in <u>Daily Love: Growing in Grace</u> posits that Grace shows itself as soon as we decide to let go of what we can't control. Trusting that Grace is real requires that kind of surrender: to gather enough courage to move steadily toward uncharted territory. Because Grace essentially inhabits an ethereal dimension, welcoming it requires we climb toward the personal, reflective, inner, "greater intelligence" that Eckhart Tolle (Stillness Speaks) believes is available to all of us. But we have to buy into that idea or there is little chance of being able to hear its call. Surrendering to the existence and invisible power of Grace comes before all else. If we're to hear our own, very personal invitation for change we must detach from the need to hold on tightly to ideas, things, relationships and desires – just because right now they are all we know. Repeat after me: *"I trust there is an inner, loving place where wisdom, strength and peace exist. Grace lives in me."* Now, continue repeating it because believing that Grace is not only an external gift – given from a divine space outside us – but also an internal presence, is key to experiencing a Grace call.

> *"The heart is the place through which*
> *energy flows to sustain you.*
> *This energy inspires you and raises you. It is*
> *the strength that carries you through life."*
> Michael Singer: The Untethered Soul

Literally, our physical hearts have a pulsing, energetic memory. Singer shares how this muscle can hold tight when we tell it to: "When loss strikes . . . our hearts try to push it all away. But if we close around the pain, to control it somehow, we stop it from passing through." He goes on to posit that when we've stopped our hearts from releasing the despairing emotions that hold us tied to misery, we've given them the permission to resurface in our lives, over and over. This same heart, our emotional and spiritual essence, is the core of who we are; it beats within us as the dynamic source of our lifeblood, the nucleus of our interacting selves, the tether anchoring our spirits to our bodies. As a conduit between our spiritual and physical selves, the heart consistently delivers vital, soulful information. Within the spaces of its chambers live the significant, ever-present, emotional conversations grief and Grace wish to hold with us. We take those conversations *to heart* as living messages meant to direct our musings, our understandings, our beliefs and resulting behaviors, focusing us toward distress or restoration.

During disheartening times, the grief messages are often first heard, felt and absorbed. When that happens all the disquiet and misery they carry settle quickly and deeply, before we're barely aware of their power. Even without our intentional permission, grief begins to rule the emotional chambers of our hearts, soon moving into our physical selves to stay, visiting over and over. It isn't until we sense and allow the shift into subtle grief that we can begin to finally make our break – easing our spiritual, mental, emotional and, eventually, physical selves out of grief's grip. Then, free to interact within gentler heart spaces, we're open to hear the whispers of different conversations, with Grace in the lead.

Though I absolutely know that heart housekeeping is critical to clearing space for a Grace call, I still recognize my own fallibility. I can backslide. Sometimes I'm caught off guard by crisis: life begins to unravel and before I realize it I'm already at the end of a quickly fraying rope. Then

I take Grace's call, and often, in my perfectly imperfect humanness, I'll return to my old demand: Grace save me. I race around a while with my hair on fire, heart hardening with angst and fear, and expect a tidy solution – maybe another, strong length of rope easily within my grasp, to tie me to safer, more habitual and familiar ideas. But they will only return me to the known, the customary solutions, the ongoing cycle. Luckily, instead of quickly handing me a rope to tie my heart back into its former shape, Grace directs me toward another path, away from the familiar.

A delicate, intimate balance exists when my heart and Grace share a call and response. The search and find mission I started after Matthew died taught me that healing pathways come in many shapes and lengths, and may be only heartbeats away. Now I realize that when crises come, after I've finally softened, begun to unclench my heart, fully heard and trusted the music of my own soul's call through Grace, I'm free to move beyond the fear, to put out my own fires and let go of the fraying rope. And then comes surrender – a blessed time when my heart stops asking, "why did this happen to me?" and instead welcomes the potential, the imaginings of what's beyond.

"Practice makes Graceful"
Sarah Kaufman: <u>The Art of Grace</u>

The documented science of physicality and the practice of Grace hold me fascinated. Here is Grace, operating at a physical level and teaching us vital, visible lessons. Corporal grace is attached to movement, to how one's body operates in different situations. Evidently a person's physical grace depends on billions of cells in the brain all working together. When our brains are intact, it seems we can be as physically graceful as we want to be. It is a matter of practice. What might look like physical poetry is born of repetition – a habit of doing over and over, and over again until the desired has become spontaneous. One simply becomes more graceful, more grace-filled, by thoughtfully and repeatedly moving. Grace, like grief, tells us if we're practitioners, we'll adapt their intrinsic traits and dispositions into our daily living. The healthier and kinder of the two, Grace, calls us to quiet our minds, soften our hearts and surrender to the gracious opportunity of coming to peace with our fear and pain, and then to hang in there long enough for that practice to become our ongoing reality. The restorative power of Grace is in its ability to open each of us to something that presents as both divinely inspired and beautifully real.

An oft-quoted Cherokee parable about human behavior uses the fight between two wolves, one good and one, dangerous, to predict an end result. These wolves metaphorically represent internal characteristics within all of us. Contained in the menacing wolf are the qualities of fear, self-pity, blame, rage, the locked heart and self-absorbed ego. In the admirable wolf are hope, loving kindness, peace of mind, mercy and good will. These opposing forces spar daily within us all. When asked which wolf/characteristics will survive and thrive, the parable tells us the survivor will always be the one we feed.

Grief and Grace are my antithetical wolves of this native legend. Each has the power to impact, even rule our bodies, minds and hearts to direct the lifestyle we choose. When grief is inadvertently or purposely fed, we accept as true the thoughts and feelings of anxiety, anger, guilt, suspicion, depression and despair; when we consciously feed Grace, we operate in the love of hope, joy, serenity, compassion, forgiveness and generosity. Integral to the human condition, they reside side by side, always ready to vie for our heart spaces. The one we practice living, through feeding it to our thoughts and feelings, our beliefs, intentions and behaviors, will be the one with whom we endure . . . or thrive, day by day.

"Acceptance of the unacceptable is the greatest source of grace in this world."
Eckhart Tolle: <u>Stillness Speaks</u>

Believe and see. Contrary to a generally-held cultural message, we don't have to *see* Grace as a physical reality before we can *believe* in its powerful presence. The opposite is what gives Grace life. *Once we believe* in the capacity and truth of grace-filled moments, *we will witness* their transformative power at work in our lives. Whether it becomes our reality through organized religious worship, experiences within spiritual, sacred traditions and practices, or the personal, often unexpected encounters with the ethereal, Grace is our way out – of the grief that layers itself onto loss . . . and our way in – to surrendering into new ways of thinking, feeling and responding to hopelessness and despair. We practice our way into Grace-filled living when we absolutely believe the message of our reclaimed hearts: you are a divinely-loved soul who deserves the unshakeable love, the laugh-out-loud joy and awe-inspiring forgiveness and peace that finding and living with Grace offers. When our grieving, demanding intellect surrenders and our hearts soften and open, the soul's deep and gracious calls can be heard coming through a grateful heart . . . and then life changes.

amazing Grace

"I didn't lose God at all . . . though I got really angry with Him. He's the only reason I survived." With both awe and calm acceptance, Cathy says of her struggle: "I lost my purpose . . . and then one day, God just gave me peace."
(*I Know Some Day I'll See Them Again:*
Michael and James' stories)

I'm just a few streets from the bustle of downtown; finished with my errand, I'm headed out of town toward home. I'm a little lost. The small street I choose on my way to eventually find the interstate seems out of place – so quiet even though it's still so close to the noise of an awakening city. It was the incongruity of it that caught my eye – the stark white wood in the midst of concrete, the white picket fence around its lot, the compactness and composure of its space. And its marquee. I pull over and stop the car, wanting to give its message my full attention. To the right of this small church, written on the free-standing signboard, I've found one fundamental recipe for hearing the call of Grace in the midst of bitter, hopeless grief: *Worry ends where Faith begins*

I grew up a child of this kind of church, a pupil of its traditional teachings, a believer in its merciful, powerful God. And it was during that time I first encountered the concept called Grace. So as a youngster, if I understood Grace at all it was as a quality wrapped within the same arms that held the beliefs of my early religious education. Grace continues to own a vital, long standing and sustaining place in traditional religious messages: loss and deep grief are compassionately held and more easily understood and endured through a connection to God's mercy, which is an ever-present and freely given gift. Healing enters misfortune and sorrow when the Divine is a present force in the life of the grieving. Consequently, when I began this project – gathering grief stories and exploring the interconnections between grief and Grace – before I even began my first interview, those initial teachings told me I could expect to hear the name of God echoed throughout the many narratives of profound loss.

Worry ends where Faith begins. These five simple words speak of human journeys that we all eventually come to understand are anything but simplistic. Frankly, though I might have longed for it, I've found no evidence of neat, straight lines connecting the worried certainty of loss and grief to the amazing grace promised through faith. Grieving is a messy business. Encased in our humanity, we imperfectly wander and busily blunder through complex, time consuming and personally unique pathways, attempting to navigate those places where travel is painful. And it was examples of those kinds of human experiences – complex, consuming and unique – that I encountered through thirteen months of interviewing other parents whose children have died. Over that time in conversation with the bereaved who were working to maneuver through grief's muddied and chaotic panorama I discovered examples of a patient and persevering belief in the healing and amazing Grace gained within a God-centered faith. Though anything but simplistic, religious constancy surfaced as one integral way to move toward finding Grace within a grief-filled landscape.

"Amazing Grace! how sweet the sound that sav'd a wretch like me! I once was lost, but now am found, Was blind, but now I see. T'was grace that taught my heart to fear, And grace my fears reliev'd; How precious did that grace appear The hour I first believ'd!"

"Amazing Grace" stanzas 1 and 2

These words, found within one of the most beloved of all Christian hymns, was first heard in 1773. John Newton, former slave ship captain turned clergy and poet, composed the famous "Amazing Grace" lyrics after experiencing a conversion event. He heard a call from Grace through the echoed cries of those many souls he carried into slavery. Eventually Newton left the slave trade to preach and live the salvation messages of the God he believed found, and eventually saved him. I grew up singing this song when grace, faith and God were linked and spoken of together. It was the first song I thought of when I was planning a memorial service for my own son, Matthew, because its confident melodic line and the promises of its lyrics had always seemed both uplifting and dependable. And, then, I needed that; then, I longed for Newton's faith – the promised direct connection from heartache to an eventual place of peace. Newton was telling his own salvation story in clear declarations of faith and redemption: Grace is available; the faithful find it when they believe.

During my interviews, traditionally-embraced faith experiences surrounding peace within grief emerged in a myriad of ways . . . and each was absolutely dependent on the believer who shared his/her story. The various paths of assurance each followed depended on elements like background, age, gender, earlier religious experiences, community support structures and length of time since the child's loss. But in each and every case where God was brought into our conversation, I listened to the unfolding of a gamut of emotions . . . from wondering and confusion, to hope, a patient knowing, and immense gratitude. Someone's child was dead, questions needed answers, and attempts to understand a new reality, within a faith-based context, took a variety of paths.

> *"Nothing else in the world matters*
> *but the kindness of grace,*
> *God's gift to suffering mortals."*
> Jack Keroac

Not all parents who talked of God in their interview were either able or ready to identify Him or His religious community of believers as their most simple path to healing. Melinda, once devout, talks of her confusion about God's place in her grieving life. And before our time is over, she also shares her enduring hope that she might again know the same sweet and assuring faith she wants for her children.

> *Melinda talks about her anger toward the*
> *God she sent prayers to daily, the God she*
> *believed was benevolent and loving, the God she*
> *thought had the power to change the outcome;*

"I felt I was doing everything that needed to be done," she says of her prayer life. Even though Melinda wants her kids to have the "childlike" faith she once had, she says Derek Earl's death has taken that kind of faith from her. "I can't un-know what I know," Melinda reflects. Derek still died, they still grieve, and all the ugly what if and why questions remain. She recalls continuing to go to church after both an earlier miscarriage and Derek Earl's death in an attempt to feel the spirit move within her again. She describes the picture of her leaving her car far back in the parking lot so that during her walk toward the front doors of the church she could intentionally, like Ironman, put on pieces of armor, one by one, to protect her before she enters the service. In time, she decided to no longer attend a church. She's afraid she might never experience that deep faith she once loved, but Melinda is also hopeful . . . that (in time and with the right circumstances) she will again regain her belief.
(For Everything a Time: Derek's story)

The story of Scarlett's stillbirth portrays the ebb and flow of parents striving for balance. Being rooted in God-centered traditions does not automatically assure there will be no anger, confusion or challenge as they navigate their worst nightmare. Like Melinda, Ashleigh lives with questions:

"I was destined to be her mom," Ashleigh asserts. She continues talking about how, at first, she is so angry at God. "I have such an interesting

> *relationship with God because . . . I choose to believe in Him and I choose to believe Scarlett is in a better place with Him. At the same time . . . I'm so angry that this could happen because I grew up believing that if you love God and praise Him – if you're a good person, you'll be rewarded and good things will come your way."* She goes on to express the tender, agonizing question to God: *"What lesson are you trying to teach me?"*

Ashleigh's last words as I leave the interview are about assured love and the hope it brings in the midst of deep pain. She recounts how compassionate and generous it was that the hospital chaplain came by their room to offer them consolation, and to bring a blessing for their daughter. The parents gratefully accept this opportunity to listen to the words of a familiar, comforting hymn of faith, "May the Lord, Mighty God":

> *"May the Lord, Mighty God, Bless and keep you forever.*
>
> *Grant you peace, perfect peace; Courage in every endeavor.*
>
> *Lift up your eyes and see God's face. And his grace forever.*
>
> *May the Lord, Mighty God, Bless and keep you forever."*

God resurfaces in Parshad's final letter to his daughter:

> *"Dear Scarlett,*
>
> *Your mom and I only got to be with you for a very short time, and while your life might not fit the traditional picture of what we are used to seeing, I know that your life was picture perfect.*
> *Even though it hurts me that we can't spend more time together, I know that your life was a divine design by God and that he must know what is best. I know you are with God now, and that gives me comfort.*
> *We love you so much Scarlett and we will not forget you. . .*
>
> *I love you.*
> *Your Dad"*
>
> (*Scarlett's Story*)

Like Melinda and Ashleigh, I not only experienced an incredible array of emotions but also found myself asking faith-based questions after the death of my child. For many years I worked at discerning how the God I once trusted could now have a place in the life of this heartbroken, angry, bereaved mother. It took time but I did come to a gentler understanding of God's place in my bereavement. I live in more hope that Newton's faith-filled view of the power of amazing Grace found and wrapped itself around my son at his end. Writing these lines about the meeting between Matt and the Divine gave me a different kind of peace.

My dear son,

My thinking about the place God, soul, spirit and grace have in my life has morphed and grown in complexity over this tempestuous journey since your death ten years ago this month. I'm no longer angry at God. Though I still admit to confusion about how your death fits as a piece in the puzzle that is religion, God no longer gets blamed for your death – or for me outliving my child. I believe you and God met along the way and had come to terms together; I smile to think about how that conversation, full of intellectual wonder and unqualified love, might have unfolded. Now, any of my concerns really no longer apply.

(from <u>Letters for Grace</u>: Matt's story)

Cathy's narratives encompass the loss of two adult sons. She describes herself as a woman of faith who struggled to understand the place of God during the times and resulting fallout of both sons' deaths. She now credits God's grace and a loving community for her ability to move forward.

Cathy's loss stories highlight the fact that grief and the chaos that surrounds it often make healing seem impossible. People in deep grief can lose themselves. She talks openly about losing her purpose after each of the boys' deaths, and the downward, pain-filled spiral she experienced; somehow she had to learn how to climb out of its grip. It was finding an intentional reason to continue to live that saves her today. "I always felt like I messed up," Cathy admits. But she goes on to say that her faith is returning even stronger because she believes she's starting to understand God's purpose for her. "I didn't lose God at all . . . though I got really angry with Him. . . He's the only reason I survived." She feels more at peace when she is able to give to others and her faith shines stronger when she feels needed. With both awe and calm acceptance, Cathy says of her struggle: "I lost my purpose . . . and then one day, God just gave me peace."

Finally, Cathy takes a moment to think about how her experiences with profound loss might be helpful to others. "Remember the good stuff," she advises, and find people who are like minded to share your experiences. Most importantly, according to Cathy, "trust God." Cathy states with concern, "I don't know how people lose their children without the hope that they're going to see them some day." She goes on to talk about her sons by saying that sometimes she still can't comprehend that they are really gone. Then she says with assurance that there are other times when she can see them, up there in heaven, running around on streets of gold, happy and at peace, seeing her mom and dad, her brothers and cousins – all those she has loved and already lost. "They're happy. I know some day I'll see them again."

(*I know some day I'll see them again*:
Michael and James' stories)

Patrick and Erin intentionally embrace their faith in God and their religious community to move forward after the heart-aching loss of Isaac James. In God's time their family was graced with the entrance of another new life. With the safe arrival of baby daughter, Gabrielle, also comes healing and a measure of closure for the couple who credit their God and His loving followers as blessed messengers of the ongoing Grace in their lives.

> *"To be honest," Patrick reveals, "if you don't have faith, I don't know how you can go through this. It is so hard." Erin continues, "God put . . . people in our path that He knew we were going to need." After highlighting the kindness and help of Patrick's boss during this difficult time, the couple talks more about the importance of their Christian faith and their church home. Though they are fairly new to the church when they lose Isaac, the congregation richly blesses them with an outpouring of support. "Our families are wonderful," Erin asserts, "but I could not have imagined going through that without our church family."*
>
> *Early in 2016, Patrick and Erin learn they are again pregnant. They recall this pregnancy as an "amazing emotional roller coaster." Every day they feel pricked by the pins and needles of anxiety and worry. And with gratitude and guarded anticipation also comes some guilt. Erin recalls: "I felt really guilty when I did get pregnant with her . . . that I think people are going to forget about Isaac now." In preparation*

for a next child after Isaac's loss, Erin shares
with Patrick a name she believes should be given
to their next child – Gabriel. The biblically
historical angel, Gabriel, whose name means
"God is my strength," serves as a messenger
from the Lord. Erin and Patrick feel the promise,
strength and hope of their chosen name. Though
they were originally expecting a Gabriel, the new
parents are delighted to welcome a baby girl,
Gabrielle . . ."
(Our child in heaven: Isaac's story)

Delivered grace for God's people has long been the foundation for countless faith-based conversations and conversions involving healing and salvation after inevitable, heart-aching loss. I watched and listened to the unfolding of various ways the call of Grace was experienced within the expressed faith traditions and practices of the bereaved. In every interview where faith took center stage and parents had been able to gain a believer's acceptance of their child's passing, trust in a power greater than themselves and their circumstances, held true. Some, in hope, continue to search their hearts, souls and the faith-based landscape for encounters with the Divine; others have gratefully found themselves lifted toward healing. And in each of those realities, Grace has been a willing companion.

"The Lord has promis'd good to me,
His word my hope secures;
He will my shield and portion be
As long as life endures."
"Amazing Grace," stanza 4

Dan and Ginny speak of the comfort they've experienced in their surrender into the promises of God. There is no doubt that His loving strength has fueled and become theirs, and best of all . . . Kelby is waiting.

> *"Our faith is so much stronger," Dan states. He and Ginny have a God-centered marriage where prayer, surrendering problems into God's hands, and knowing that you will see your child again are unfailing, living truths. They acknowledge the natural and very real struggles a couple faces when their child dies. They know their own tragedy severely tested their strength as a couple but with time and work, they found themselves again. Ginny smiles, "I've always been so proud of us. We didn't give up on each other. And every day is one day closer to my son who I will spend eternity with." She looks over at Dan who gives her a small smile: "We both will."*
>
> (*Love beyond loss:* Kelby's story)

The long, varied and intricate pathways these parents traveled were illuminated by the light of their own unique, faith journeys. They were all, in one way or another, looking for relief – that precious space where the dark clouds of grief are parted by a light powered through moments of God's grace. His promised, unconditional love, the gifts of time and a supportive community of like believers, the hope of renewed faith, the courage to try again and continue forward, and the unquestioning trust that their children will be waiting for them, all surfaced as essential keys in the stories of this reflection.

Those who absolutely believed they were, and are still held in the caring arms of God, know Grace as assured, extraordinary and enduring. And for them, that faith has made all the difference.

> *". . . through the hands of such of these God*
> *speaks, and from behind their eyes*
> *he smiles upon the Earth."*
> Kahlil Gilbran

finding Grace in the mystery

With a slight smile, Dan voices his truth: "There are
times I've just kind of felt her presence – like this little
shimmering light that I can perceive and feel and see.
There are times when I feel really connected. . . ."
(*An exceptional, loving force*: Johanna's story)

"How do you define Grace?" I asked, taking another
sip of coffee. I was after a picture of Grace in its fullness –
beyond my childhood training, within and outside of
theological constructs, apart from the dictionary and
thesaurus – so I was posing this same question to lots of
people . . . some embroiled in the grieving process, and
others, on the periphery of grief's assaults. Responses had
been coming in various forms. One portrait, seen in the
amazing Grace essay, was Grace as a freely-given, divine
favor from God, and through Him, readily available to
each of the faithful. This time, my question brings another
picture into focus and I am reminded of something I've
read recently. In Grieving Mindfully, Kumar writes that
for some, spirituality means finding Grace while growing
closer to God. Then he goes on to conjecture that the
spiritual can also be identified by a secular journey – one
moving toward self-realization and personal authenticity.
Using my same question, same timeframe, same variety
of people, today's conversation highlights that type of
event – an individual, personal experience that walks us

into Grace . . . an encounter dependent on the consent of the heart.

She looked at me, clearly surprised at my question, and then glanced away to gather her thoughts. She's a church-goer in her middle years who has been acquainted with worry and sadness . . . so I admit to expecting a God-centered answer. Instead I follow her down a more indirect path – one filled with wonderings. Her response starts as a thoughtful silence, followed by measured, personal reflections on a few experiences; it culminated in a variety of interesting synonyms targeting her feelings about Grace. It was a fascinating kind of time travel, moving me from one lane of understanding – where there had been a focused connection to time and tradition – into others, apart from specifically physical or sacred settings. She shared her heart and spirit, weaving emotions into ideas, wrapping them all around her own personally unique understanding of the goodness of life. Her perceptions of Grace came alive within intimate, heartfelt events of her life where the unexpected and mysterious emerged. Though Grace is always available when we call on it, it also appears that gracious happenings find us, even when we're barely aware they could be possible.

> *"The best and most beautiful things in the*
> *world cannot be seen, nor touched . . .*
> *but are felt in the heart."*
> Helen Keller

During a variety of discussions with the many who shared their grief with me, reported ethereal events were sometimes called spiritual. Other times there seemed no term for them – only a wave of a hand, a rapt smile, and a reference to something peace-filled and beautiful, often beyond our humble, human comprehension. The power of the mystical surfaced throughout conversations and unfolded within a variety of examples:

- using practices like meditation, mindfulness study, prayer and contemplation as meaningful ways to become aware of life-altering, ethereal communications;
- surrounding oneself within the beauty of nature and interacting physically, emotionally and spiritually in natural settings;
- becoming aware of the souls/spirits of lost loved ones as well as angels and guides who are present to lead the bereaved toward more gracious and compassionate healing places;
- being in just the right place to hear loving words at just the right time, given by others in community with the grieving; and
- being in the company of the dying to hear unexpected, honest, joyful and fearless messages.

Storytellers welcomed Grace moments into their personal lives through each of these. And with every account came the belief that something mysterious, unexpected . . . even miraculous, had touched them.

> *"Maybe a vision means seeing into what's*
> *more real than anything else."*
> Brian McLaren: We Make The Road By Walking

I'm across the table from Greg, not knowing exactly what to expect. It's only my second interview and I'm still finding my way through interacting with others as they share information about the most difficult time in their lives. These moments with a still-grieving father is my first encounter with this newest pathway into the forgiveness and comfort of Grace. His story evolves and he recounts the unexpected and transformational encounters with the *"something"* he now believes is *"out there."*

> *As our interview winds down, some personal anecdotes Greg shared earlier lead me to steer our conversation more deeply into situations he has used to learn and grow through his grief. Two very personal accounts indicate that he realizes he has been touched by a power beyond the world we know. "Flashes" of a mysterious presence and irrefutable happenings lead him to know "something's out there." His first description is of a time when his son surprised and amazed him with a tender revelation. Greg remembers his son of four or five telling his parents that when he was up in heaven, he saw them. The boy confidently shared that he knew he was meant to come and be with them because they seemed so sad. Greg shares this simple, moving story with tears shimmering in his eyes. How wonderful that the second gift, his son, given to him at a time when grief filled his life, always knew he was meant for Greg.*
>
> *His next, equally powerful story surrounds his mother's death. Loved ones had been called in anticipation of Greg's mother's passing. They gathered together, spending time with her and*

each other, as they waited. Hours before her death, he remembers her excitedly calling out to the family – she was seeing someone or something she wanted them to witness with her. As they surrounded her, asking what she wanted them to look at, she indicated a space where no one stood. Looking at each other, they questioned her more. What were they supposed to be seeing? Who was there? Happy and alert, she smiled and joyously declared she was looking at Marie. Greg is quick to note that his mom had no trouble knowing who was physically present in the room; she recognized all the names and faces of her loved ones. Marie, as an unseen presence, neither frightened nor confused his mother. Instead it seemed to give her both joy and peace.

Again tears fill Greg's eyes as he recalls the beautiful memory of his mother finally coming face to face with the grandchild she had never had the opportunity to meet. And, how amazing it is that this first meeting takes place when Marie's father is in the room with them both. It has been said that when one is in the presence of real healing, there is a grace that hangs in that moment. Greg's story is healing grace in action.

(Her sweetest gift: Marie's story)

Leanna recounts the heartbreaking story of the suicide of her adult son, Grant. After Grant's death, examples of a sacred connection between mother and son unfold in beautiful and unexpected ways.

Leanna affirms that she has repeatedly experienced ethereal events, letting her know in profound ways that her son is always close, always bringing her gifts. Not long after Grant's death, Leanna began to hear her son's voice, feel his breath close to her. Her dreams are vivid and regular for about two years after his passing; all of her senses are engaged during those dreams as she and Grant directly communicate. She keeps a journal during this time of exceptional dreams and remembers that once her son told her, "Mom, our bond can never be broken. I'm always with you."

Over the years since Grant's death, his mother is certain he has been a real and sacred presence in her life . . . and not only in her dreams. She sets the stage by sharing how she and Grant loved to watch meteor showers together. In August, 2016, Leanna and Tom (Grant's stepfather) are looking forward to watching a predicted, fantastic meteor shower. Unfortunately, that night they note that thick clouds have gathered and believing there will be no way for them to enjoy the celestial show, they go to bed instead. In the early morning, the couple is awakened by a clatter from another room and when Leanna checks, she discovers that a photo book has "fallen" from a shelf. But it is as if the book has been plucked from its spot and dropped purposely on the floor because all of the photos in front of and close to the book remain in their places, undisturbed. And it is

*then that Leanna recognizes her latest gift from
Grant – the noise that awakens her to discover
a beautifully clear sky. She and Tom go outside
to enjoy the brilliance of light streaking across
the horizon and celebrate the wonder and joy of
Grant's presence with them.*

*(Remembering Grant through the whisper
of wings:* Grant's story)

In moments when we heed a sacred call from within, we
are invited into quiet, to listen closely and let gracious
messages speak. Being presented with a completed, fully-
understood picture of any life lost too soon may be too
much to ever expect, no matter how long or hard we
search. But discovering peace and mercy within what we
are given is an incredibly precious gift.

Elizabeth, a passionate, spiritual person, narrates
the story of Hollis, her second son, who succumbs to
Cancer after a valiant battle. Her memories are filled with
examples of the inexplicable.

*Throughout Elizabeth's storytelling, she
pauses to share with a kind of wonder, various
circumstances that have unexpectedly tied people
and events together; on one level they seem to
be random occurrences, but somehow when
she considers the coincidences in more depth,
they feel ethereal – as if a life force beyond her
knowing has stepped in to create connections for
her at just the right moment, for just the right
reasons. Her first example detailed the dream
her husband, John, had before his son's birth,*

identifying Hollis as a possible reincarnation of John's dead, younger brother, Raymond. As she stops to consider the factual similarities between life events of both Raymond and Hollis, Elizabeth surprises herself with their various connections. This is just one illustration of how she feels touched by circumstances beyond her full understanding, leading her to acknowledge that life unfolds beyond simple coincidences.

Another life-altering account comes after her son's death. Three days after Hollis' passing, Elizabeth and John are driving back from Texas to Colorado for his burial. As they travel through Austin, Elizabeth notices a very little house on the side of the road with what appears to be a statue of a Buddhist Monk on its porch. Next to the house is a long, blue building with only one word on it – Moonlight. Elizabeth, who shares that Hollis had become a Buddhist near the end of his life, feels strongly that she is meant to stop the car, turn around and return to the place where she first glimpsed the house. The statue turns out to be an actual monk and she and John take the opportunity to meet him and the others who live in their small monastery. After hearing Elizabeth's story about Hollis and his interest in Buddhism, the monks graciously perform a Buddhist ceremony in his honor. It is here in her story when Elizabeth refers to a recovered poem, "The Night Sky," she's found in Hollis' effects. "Moonlight" not only names the building next to

*the monastery, it also appears in her son's own
poetic words found in his personal journal.*

The year after Hollis' death, Elizabeth again senses her son's creative and collaborative presence. She believes that together they are meant to produce something new.

> *"He gave me a song," Elizabeth declares with assurance. In 2012, mother and son, collaborated during one of those ethereal opportunities on a song she composed called "Walk in Light." Hope and belief unite in remembrance of a life very much alive in the hearts of those who will always love him. "He makes me laugh still," Elizabeth affirms as she talks about her son. She feels healing every time she senses his presence. (Her saint who walked in light: Hollis' story)*

> **"Love is what we were born with.
> Fear is what we learned here.
> The spiritual journey is the relinquishment,
> or unlearning, of fear and the acceptance
> of love back into our hearts."**
> *Marianne Williamson*

My visit with Lindsay and Scott brings me a new awareness of the longing some experience when they open their hearts to the intricate joys and sorrows of impending parenthood. They are a compassionate couple who tell me about their stillborn daughter, Lauren Grace. Their positive belief that every one of their lost children remains connected to them helps each to more peacefully live within their healing journey.

The couple considers the part the ethereal plays in their lives. "Scott is soulful," Lindsay says, and then calls herself spiritual. She goes on to voice that their three heartbreaking, unfulfilled pregnancies and all the complications attached to them "tests every belief you have to your core." Both Lindsay and Scott are open to the possibility of a power beyond their known world. Tears appear again as Lindsay shares the story of an inspired message from Lauren after her stillbirth, delivered to her by an online friend, another bereaved mother who Lindsay discovers is also a medium. According to this messenger, Lauren was insistent that Lindsay understand that her tiny daughter knew she was loved: "she wants you to know she knows." In a voice thick with emotion, Lindsay recalls how healing that conversation was for her. She affirms, "You have a connection with your children even if they don't walk the earth."

(The power of tiny miracles: Lauren's story)

Dan, who lives his life as both a bereaved and proud father speaks of his Johanna with love and gratefulness. He calls his daughter an extraordinary, amazing force. And though she no longer inhabits this life plane with him, she is by his side daily.

When I asked Dan to talk about what his daughter might be saying to him today, he first acknowledges the strength he feels from her. Her ethereal visits remind him that living fully means staying open and mindful in interactions with others, and that great joy comes from connecting with all living and non-living beings. Just surviving is not good enough; there must be something more for a life to be well lived.

Dan realizes that enduring with hope and in grace allows one to remain open to, as well as learn from what is offered from beyond what we know or fully understand . . . and to keep the loving connection between father and daughter gloriously alive. He talks about his time with Johanna: "She visits me periodically. She has focused my spirituality and has given me the greatest gift of all, knowledge about the interconnections of all things and insight into the indivisibility of our Spirit as we journey beyond our mortality. I know . . . that sometime after I pass on I will meet up with her again." But until that day, Dan gratefully celebrates the gifts Johanna gives him daily as he moves forward, creating a life beyond suffering: "She gives me the strength to endure, to grow, and energizes my commitment as a physician to care, truly care, for others."

(An exceptional, loving force: Johanna's story)

Parents, Taia and Dion, made the purposeful decision to weave their consummate love for their lost child, Lyla Hope, into their grief with the intention of transforming their own life patterns of thinking and feeling. Instead of accepting heartache, they lovingly embrace and practice living wholeheartedly.

"We don't practice a specific religion, but . . . I believe we are spiritual people. I believe there is something higher, bigger and better than us. We totally believe she is with us here today," Taia declares with a smile. Millie, her oldest, and Lyla seem to share a special bond. She recalls Millie's twenty-week ultrasound check with a kind of awe. First, Taia reveals, she could feel Lyla in the car with her and Dion as they travel to another ultrasound, this time for Lyla's unborn sister, Millie. At the hospital they find themselves in the exact same room with the exact same tech and the exact same doctor as two years earlier, but this time there is a very different outcome. This daughter is thriving.

Another example is a story Millie reports to Taia that "just stopped me in my tracks." She and her daughter are returning home when Millie says, "Mommy, I've been here before." After some questions, it becomes clear to Taia that her two-year old isn't talking about a street or their neighborhood, but about something much larger and more important. Millie tells her, "No . . . I came here before and you named me Lyla and then I came back and you named me Millie." The mystical nature of this conversation is both comforting and stunning. Taia continues that Millie also remembers that Lyla visited her as a baby to tickle her and make her laugh. Now, six-year old Millie is most happy to tell anyone about her big sister. The ethereal, the unexplainable, accepted and shared clearly and

simply by their child, is an ongoing reminder to Dion and Taia that Lyla's spirit is an ever-present reality in their family circle. "She is with us," Taia states with simple eloquence.
(She is always with us: Lyla's story*)*

In most all sacred, meditative disciplines the key to moving within the mystery of the ethereal is to relax and release whatever false securities hold us prisoner to a grieving reality. At the core, in the very heart of this letting go, is trust – the surety that there is more to this world than the concrete and readily tangible so often touted as our only true reality. The long and varied pathways the grievers of these stories explored contain the mysterious, the transcendent and miraculous. Restorative moments surfaced, helping to describe, even define, each unique experience. And as the transforming power and light of Grace appeared, hearts opened to re-imagined lives, moving beyond the confining boundaries of unsettled confusion, despair and suffering. Within these ethereal settings, Elizabeth's words come alive: *"I'm still trying to figure out this whole existence thing we get to share here. I just think we're supposed to learn how to get through it all with love."*

"I do not at all understand the mystery of grace –
only that it meets us where we are but
does not leave us where it found us."
Anne Lamott

Grace in the Now: time, transition and transformation

Lindsay and Josh take time together, while hospital personnel persist with a question that haunts them throughout all the hours to follow: "Are you ready yet . . .?" She and Josh, enveloped in inconsolable grief, desperately want time to make the critical decisions that will last as memories the rest of their lives.
(*Where love blooms:* Ella's story)

I'm looking at the calendar when I hear that special ring tone, set to remind me I'm 30 minutes away from an appointment. Yep – that's life: events scheduled according to a variety of time frames and set to different bells and whistles. Grabbing a jacket, I hesitate long enough to hear myself mumbling: "So, Jane, are you ready for this step? It's bound to lead to a different way of us relating; I just hope she's able to hear and understand." I head out the door, aware that now might be just the right time.

"Are we there yet?" Depending on why it's asked and who's doing the asking, this familiar question and all the meaning it carries with it can make us smile or roll our eyes or even cringe. During different times in my life I've responded all of those ways, but during one long and very critical time, that question carried the power to haunt me. I recall meeting with caring and well-meaning friends when bereavement hovered closely around me. I let their questions – the ones I'd heard often, asked with genuine concern – play out in my mind again: "How are you doing?" "Are you getting out more?" "Feeling better? stronger?" "Are things easier?" In other words: *Are you there yet* – back to that place where you existed before it happened? I learned to hate those questions, posed with such sincerity, unwittingly asking me to do the impossible: cycle back to a time before profound grief, to be who I used to be, to behave as if no longer touched by the unrelenting burdens of deep despair. I know they meant well. But in their discomfort I feel them urge me to hurry up and heal – operate within the familiar patterns I practiced before grief held me captive. How do I tell friends in ways they can understand that they are expecting the impossible? Because the truth is, once profound grief takes up residence in you, time is meaningless; there is no returning to that accustomed place before it.

It's taken time, finding Grace in the chaos of the ever-present demands of . . . well, time. Saving space in our lives to note, process, even celebrate compassionate and peace-filled moments aren't expected, or even understood ways to operate in our fast-paced culture. But, without doubt, taming the part time plays in the unfolding of our days and nights is fundamental to allowing Grace into the core of our grief. It turns out that everyone else's ideas about the time one should take existing on the dark roller coaster of grief only brings a griever alarm and dismay. Evidently, somewhere, an inexorable ticking clock, marking a fixed timetable of expected behaviors, starts its countdown soon after grief strikes. Check any professional literature that studies the grieving process. Their messages are clear: real time is only in the present, the now. It is madness to schedule healing; there is no timetable for grief. Each individual grief event follows its own uniquely individual pathway. And when the bereaved are able to hold space for authentic encounters with grief's despair, the ticking clock loses its power. Finding Grace becomes the *Now* – pathways leading into acceptance and surrender.

> *"Time isn't precious at all, because it is an illusion.*
> *What you perceive as precious is not time but*
> *the one point that is out of time: the Now."*
> Eckhart Tolle: The Power of Now

Regardless of Tolle's admonition that time is only a human-inspired illusion, we have taught ourselves, obsessively, to use it as a punctuation mark for most every life experience. Whether calling for patience or demanding hurry, we have learned to regard time as both a promised healer and an impatient taskmaster. But, using time to organize and judge our progress toward or away from anything, especially grief, is a tenuous and dangerous proposition at best. Intentionally or not, by doing so we make the agreement with ourselves to turn over of our most important thinking, feeling and healing opportunities to an artificially-constructed ideal. Though we recognize time never concerns itself with the human condition, we still slavishly follow it, work tirelessly to manipulate it, and give it enormous power in the design of our lives. Time delivers its demands and without noticing it, we relinquish *Now*.

What is the *Now*? As soon as I pose this question to myself, I know there is only one way to get to an answer. I look up, take my hands off the keyboard and move back, resting into the chair, and begin to drink in, really experience without time's distraction, my *Now*. I wake myself into a scene where I decide to participate and be fully aware. Encircling me is the constructive energy of sights, sounds, textures, movements, and even in pockets, the stillness of inertia; all of it the authentic, positive and negative vitality of the minutes I intentionally direct my mind and heart to appraise and appreciate. I understand my job is to value the experiences and relationships of the here and now. And, sure enough, because I'm not reliving events already past or busily constructing new ones, I notice a quiet opening within me . . . and contained within that, the subtle whispers of possible connections and understandings. This newfound *Now* space is alive with awareness and vulnerability, and if I'm ready, an opportunity to intentionally, truthfully encounter my present reality. Just sitting, letting a calm pulse around me, brings time to gently accept . . . grief's place in my life, its many fears I've inadvertently nourished and the joys and hopes I've neglected. And with each surrender, I move closer to a reinvented future.

Grace is most present in our *Now* – those thoughts, emotions, experiences and relationships of our right here, right now reality. So, let's say we accept that the present is our healthiest place to live and deal with our grief. Now what? Do we just learn how to live in a more aware state of life? Listen more? Hope more? Expect more? Yes, all of that . . . and beyond. Because next come those transitions we weren't able to notice before. With senses ready to tune into and acknowledge other realities beyond misery, we approach our life differently. Transitions are our doorways from one time period, one experience, one feeling, one belief . . . into another. Immersed within the focus and calm of a grace-filled *Now,* grievers can begin to note the variety of pathways available to turn us toward redefining and reconstructing our very identity. My earlier coffee time with my friend, answering her latest "Are you there yet?" questions turned out to be a valuable alternative pathway for our ongoing relationship. She listened and responded in ways that let me know she finally understood that the *there* I'm headed is no longer the one she had always thought best for me – for us. And for me, telling my truth brought the gracious awareness that I had actually opened a new door into transition.

> *"Time is too slow for those who wait;*
> *too swift for those who fear;*
> *too long for those who grieve; too*
> *short for those who rejoice . . ."*
> Shakespeare

Experiences centering on time and transitions signaling movement toward transformation surfaced continually throughout my various grief conversations. Some of these events presented as heart-achingly common challenges, others as unusual occurrences; some came as surprises, either helpful or fear-filled; and some reportedly led the way into healing. No matter the experience, each was unforgettable for the storyteller and integral to the story. Everything, whether in beauty and joy or complexity and sorrow, can characterize its description, even its definition, in the language of time. And though it is always our clearest channel into acceptance, a *Now* reality steeped in acute grief, also holds great pain.

When one is marking time living in a *Now* of hope or loss, the significance of each moment is magnified, etched in one's memory. Melinda talks about the importance of time in their story:

> *"We spent probably more time preparing and trying than we did actually being pregnant."* . . . *"When you're trying to make a baby, it doesn't just go month by month; it's week by week, and sometimes even day by day."* The summer of 2011 finds them pregnant and waiting again . . . The couple includes friends and family in their hopes and dreams for their new baby. But much too soon, it's over. After their miscarriage, and time used for more planning and fertility treatments, they discover they are pregnant again. But this time they decide to wait before giving others their news. They hold their unborn close to their hearts, joyously loving it while also keeping the fact of another pregnancy to themselves. It seemed wise and somehow safer to wait. The time was finally right: *"We thought we were safe."* Only 2 ½ weeks later, Derek Earl, their beloved son, is stillborn. Since they hadn't shared their joy and anticipation with others, they found themselves alone in their grief. *"It wasn't real for anyone else,"* Trey states, *"and he's really not real to them now."*
>
> (*For everything a time:* Derek's story)

Lindsay and Josh live through the ever-present questions that parents facing a stillbirth must answer. In their case, this time of acute grief, their *Now* is all too real, so much so that they are unable to notice this timeframe as anything other than a harsh and unbending taskmaster. And, at its end, as only a wretched memory.

The room is quiet, the nurse silent, until finally Lindsay asks for information. The nurse's answer comes: "I'm looking for the heartbeat.". . . "It was such a shock. I think I just started screaming . . . crying . . . and all they said to me was 'You have to go to the hospital and have your baby out.'" Lindsay and Josh take time together, trying to find enough balance to make the first of many decisions to come. The couple must now think through and decide about delivery options – C-Section or Vaginal birth. Together they discuss their thoughts and feelings, while hospital personnel persist with a question that haunts them throughout all the hours to follow: "Are you ready yet to . . .?" Lindsay feels pushed to do something immediately but she and Josh, enveloped in inconsolable grief, desperately want time to make the critical decisions that will last as memories the rest of their lives.

Frustrated by the seemingly arbitrary and insensitive time frames, they hold their ground, wanting any decisions to honor their daughter. After taking precious time, the parents make the call for an induced labor and natural birth. "The more we sat and just cried, we came to the decision we owed it to her to have her naturally . . . to go through the process." Lindsay is given drugs to start her labor and the waiting begins. And, all the while, the questions that must have answers keep coming: Are you ready yet to tell us if you want pictures? Are you ready to have us invite in a chaplain? Are you ready to tell us if you want an autopsy? Are you ready yet to tell us what you want us to do with your daughter's body – what funeral home to use? Have you decided about cremation? Burial? Lindsay expresses her pain in a quiet voice as tears continue to fall: "It's the saddest thing to be in labor and know you're delivering a dead baby. When you lose a baby, you won't have any memories except bad ones."

(*Where love blooms:* Ella's story)

Though we may be continually reminded that the construct of time is only an illusion, that *Now* can feel as fresh and jagged as the grief in which it lives. When all we can do is wait for time to hand us something horrid, it's powerful presence is overwhelming. Parshad, Scarlett's dad, talks about how time stood still.

Back in the medical facility the couple's decisions begin. They opt to stay and deliver (their stillborn child) as quickly as possible. . . . Parshad asks for another ultrasound. "Maybe it will be a miracle; maybe she will be alive." This ultrasound, like the others, shows no heartbeat. And then a bit of light appears: they discover their obstetrician, Dr. H, has returned to check on them. She understands Ashleigh's concerns about the time in waiting and they decide that a C-Section will be performed. But even though the strength and love of family and friends are available, Parshad recalls this particular time as "utterly by yourself." In the quiet of that outside hallway, he waits during the longest five minutes of his life before permission to join Ashleigh during the epidural is granted. "It's a very strange moment; I'll never forget. You've lost your child; your wife's on a surgery bed in the next room . . . and you're utterly by yourself. It was a moment in time that just stood still."

(Scarlett's Story)

"Light precedes every transition. Whether at the end of a tunnel, through a crack in the door or the flash of an idea, it is always there, heralding a new beginning."
Teresa Tsalaky: The Transition Witness

Transitions materialize in the lives of the grieving as acute grief settles into something less intense and the rigidity and hopelessness of timing expectations abate. Author, C. S. Lewis, in A Grief Observed, talks about transitions as subtle changes that are already in play before we actually notice them. They enter our conscious *Now*, the space where time slides away, when we recognize the opening of the possible. And, though those interviewed rarely have a name for these changes, they surface in interviews through heartfelt sighs, smiles and individual examples of lives moving into clearer, less-shadowed realities.

Cathy shares a time of transition when she courageously admits her feelings of guilt to her son and experiences his unexpected forgiveness. Her ability to move forward, to think beyond the darkness of a grieving, conscience-stricken mother allows Cathy to think about the possibility of fashioning a new beginning.

During those last months when James was living with them, she was called for jury duty. As she thinks back to the instructions of the District Attorney, those familiar words take on new and terrible significance. You (jury members) must find him "guilty beyond a shadow of a doubt . . . have an open heart and know that it is up to me (the DA) to prove him guilty." Tears fill Cathy's eyes as she bravely faces her guilt: As I heard the DA, I knew that "everything I told him (James) in the jailhouse (all those years ago) was wrong. I went home feeling so guilty." She follows with the conversation she had soon after with James: "I looked in his eyes and said, 'I'm so sorry. If it wouldn't have been for me you probably wouldn't have been in prison most of your life.'" But her son affectionately replies, "It's OK Mom. It turned me around. I was going the wrong direction. It helped me. You don't have anything to be sorry for." Cathy's voice is gentle and filled with awe, "He was so gracious to forgive me."
(I know some day I'll see him again: James' story)

"The wound is the place where light enters you."
Rumi

Chris and Emily speak of significant transitions that helped them slowly but inevitably move into a new pathway toward healing.

> *The first anniversary of Carter's stillbirth is shared by the new family together. At 3:04 am on July 21, 2008, Chris, Emily and new baby, Clara, all happen to be awake and out of bed at the same time. Looking at the clock, the parents note it is the same time as their son's birth. Later that morning, the three attend "Carter's church," where his ashes lie interred, to commemorate his ongoing place in their growing family. After church the family travels into the foothills together to picnic, play and soak in the natural beauty around them.*
>
> *And things continue to change. Emily can still recall when she first noticed herself feeling differently. "I remember the first day I was laughing and had a good time at work and I felt kind of normal again and then all of a sudden . . . I felt like . . . Oh wait! Is it ok to be happy and laughing? And then you realize your son would want you to be happy and not be in this weird place forever." She pauses and then gently shares that in these last few years she has been able to finally accept the past with a more grateful heart.*

And from transitions like these come transformation – moving with grateful hearts toward a refashioned time where gracious experiences of openness, beauty and inspiration abide.

This afternoon, we are sitting in a thankful home: it's Chris and Emily's home; it's Clara and Abbey's home; and it is Carter's home. He is remembered through words, through family stories and memories, and within family pictures where he is represented by "Carter Bear," the teddy chosen for him that first Christmas in 2007. Emily proudly maintains that her daughters know their brother. "Neither Clara or Abbey met him yet in their hearts he is just as much their brother as they are each other's sisters." A grateful family of five, Carter's loved ones embrace how the spirit and presence of their first born continues to shape them. "This is Carter's story," Emily affirms strongly. "Carter made Chris and I parents, and prepared us to love Clara and Abbey to the fullest. Losing him has certainly shaped our family into what it is today; we love deeply and treasure our time together. He will always be our son and for that we are thankful."

(*He made us parents and prepared us to love*: Carter's story)

Pat and her adult daughter, Kirsten, find that a time of waiting, a difficult but merciful *Now*, grows in understanding and a special kind of peace, moving them each into loving transitions and paving the way for Grace-filled transformation.

As the years go by Pat realizes her daughter will be remaining in Wisconsin. In 2011, she buys a small house in the area and sets it up so her independent daughter can afford to rent it

*and settle in. "I'm so glad I bought that house,"
Pat smiles. "It made the last few years of her life
so much better." Over the next two years she
visits Chris, learning to know and work with her
daughter anew . . . and building – not only a new
deck the two women constructed together for the
house – but also a wonderful, fresh relationship
they could celebrate. They forgave each other all
those difficult things people who care for each
other do in the name of love.*

*In the summer of 2013, Chris goes to the
local emergency room with a bloody cough and
chest pain. Not long after, Pat receives one of
those calls every parent fears – her child has been
diagnosed with a life threatening disease. By the
end of July, Pat has moved into Chris' home as
her daughter's caregiver where she will remain
for the next ten months, until Kirsten's death
from lung cancer on May 10, 2014. Together
they set up a household, mother and daughter,
and begin their side-by-side walk toward the
inevitable. The time of care-giving held so much
for these two who were traveling their individual
grieving journeys. Pat remembers the two of
them fixing things - working on completing
projects, checking each one of them off the lists
with smiles and some wonder, and beginning the
next. Chris helps as long as she is able and enjoys
taking pictures of their shared work, occasionally
looking at her mom with pride and appreciation.
The hardest time of their individual lives becomes
a time of courage for each, individually – a time*

of learning, of love and understanding for the two, together.

And from these tender transitions come healing in the form of strength for their new, individual journeys into the graciousness of transformation:

> *Pat remembers that, in time, she and Chris begin planning her memorial service. Chris records music for her own service and even starts good-bye letters to some special people. Pat creates her daughter's obituary and shares it with her; it is a reflection – a testament to the important person she has become over her short life. "I watched her fade," Pat remembers wistfully. Having talked with others who have also lost children, Pat is aware that in time the pain is supposed to get "softer." But now she is surrounded by the sharp edges of ever-present grief. "It feels like I shouldn't ever get better. If I really, really loved her and missed her, I would never get better." But then, Pat smiles through tears and continues: "And she would say, 'Mom! No! That's not what I want you to do.'" It's as if Chris is reminding her mother that reclaiming hope in life is not about getting over, but staying open - to the aliveness beyond the next thought, the next question, the next doorway, the next smile and extended hand. Out of the wreckage that is profound loss, something surprising will rise if we open to it.*
>
> (*A journey for two*: Kirsten's story)

It's an old saw, but a true one: life is a journey, not a destination. *Now* are our most authentic moments of that journey. As always we have choices: we can make the story of our lives a series of the *Now*, collections of authentic times when we're wholly available to our present; we can dwell in the pain of losing what will never return to us in its familiar shape; or we can spend time trying to control the complexities of a future time. How much time acute grief takes, how we welcome its less intense stages to propel us into surrender and, how profound grief, once accepted, gives way to transformational healing depends on each individual griever. Our transitions, sometimes small, sometimes seismic and always significant, position us for those transformations. We only need be awake to them to accept their gifts. In <u>Grieving Mindfully</u>, Kumar speaks of the impact of transitioning from the unhealthy, strict time construct toward transformation; he explains that when we, through awareness, intentionally use our own suffering as a transformative event, it has the power to shift our focus from why me? and what if? to our present, our *Now*. What relief – finding we are fully capable to free ourselves and open into the dynamic hope and forgiveness of personal transformation. No necessary timetables, no worrying schedules, there is simply surrendering into our truth, and the reality that Grace waits for us *Now*.

"The most authentic thing about us
is our capacity to create,
to overcome, to endure, to transform, to love
and to be greater than our suffering."
Ben Okri

standing by: becoming Grace in stillness

*Matt, I swear if one more person tells me that "life
goes on" or "God needed another angel" or
that your death was "meant to be," I won't
be responsible for my bad behavior.*
(*Letters for Grace:* Matt's story)

We've all been there: stunned by news, by life, and in
that place where we simply have no words – no words to
comfort, to analyze or understand, to heal or just make
it all go away. Those are the times we need to let our
stillness speak: to send a blessing to convey our love
quietly across space into someone else's heart. I knew my
friend was feeling too tired and depressed, too angry, too
confused to find the energy to put one foot in front of the
other, let alone reach out to others. The loss was still fresh.
We sit across from one another. It's uncomfortable at first
for both of us. I had to remind myself that in the midst
of profound loss commonplace communication shifts
and distorts, and even though we're friends, neither of
us knows quite what to expect in this situation. She sits
quietly, tears beginning to shimmer in her eyes, waiting
for me to do or say what she expects I've come to say or
do, and then leave her in quiet. I've already thought about
how I might begin this tender conversation, and so I start.

67

Our time together that day is private, but I can share what I didn't say. I think that's the message I'm meant to give.

Irreconcilable change, loss and their accompanying grief leave us in places that are so situational and uniquely personal that they defy conventional description. If you are a bereaved parent, this special space takes on added cultural implications. It is rare enough when someone knows just the right way to share space with another who has lost a loved one; even more unusual is finding someone in our death-avoidant culture who can comfortably be in sacred company with a parent who has lost their child. Those with whom I've had difficult conversations talk of having more experiences with others who feel the need to somehow fill any uncomfortable silences, than with those who are able to sit calmly, perhaps hold their hand (with permission), and gently be with them in their pain. But, those quiet spaces are where the most compassionate, unassuming whispers of Grace are found – in us – when we humbly stand by, unafraid of the silence, simply being an expression of care for another.

When those we care about face unbelievable loss, most of us want to be available, to somehow help, to let him/her know how much their pain touches us. Generally, we try interacting with them in the same ways we always have – after all, we know them. We've watched them respond to a variety of changes; we've been around when they've addressed very tough problems; we've shared laughter and tears with them in situations throughout the years. Is now so different? Yes, it is. And if we actually tune into and immerse ourselves within their verbal and body language, we will sense the difference; it's raw, tenuous and uncomfortable – a bit like navigating a tightrope, barefooted and in the dark. So we question ourselves: What should I do? Walk away and try again later when she's bound to feel less sad? Jump in with those same words I know others have said to him? I feel guilty; I know I should call but then what. Silence is so awkward; it's probably best if I stay from away from them until . . . I don't know, sometime later.

> **"Wisdom comes with the ability to be still. Just look and just listen. No more is needed."**
> Eckhart Tolle: <u>Stillness Speaks</u>

What many of us don't understand as we walk into the space of that person we've come to know and care about, the one we are about to hug or talk with, is that he or she is no longer the same person each was the minute before they entered into the chaos of profound loss. Life has shifted irrevocably for our friend, our neighbor, our loved one, our colleague; old messages simply no longer fit. Just lately, a lovely woman dropped by to return something borrowed. She told me she had just finished reading my book, <u>Letters for Grace</u>. She looked closely at me, touched my arm and said, "Well, honey, have you gotten over it yet?" I smiled slightly and gently replied that "getting over it" never really applies to some situations. We get through chaotic experiences and emotional upheaval; we try moving beyond the darkness; we focus life in a new direction; we relearn what it means to open to happiness, to welcome forgiveness, to recognize Grace, and even to fully let love in again. But we don't *get over* . . . we never fully *leave behind* the connection to those loved ones who have enduringly shaped our life. In one way or another we discover that some types of grief are inextricably woven into the fabric of the words we hear and speak, the faces and pictures we see, the thoughts we think, the emotions we feel – they forever color the stuff, the substance, of whom we've become.

Choosing to interact with those who are now in or have experienced heart-achingly, bottomless grief is a commitment to walking into their sacred space. If we are to move into the tender, tenuous, damaged lives of others, we must leave clichés, platitudes and easy answers behind. It requires us to stop and think, to prepare to enter the space of the one we care about on his or her terms because what we say and do in this space is elemental, significant, and often remembered.

"When we are motivated by compassion and wisdom, the results of our actions benefit everyone, not just our individual selves or some immediate convenience."
Dalai Lama X

Erin and Patrick reflect on some of their feelings and certainties regarding the loss of their cherished boy, Isaac James. They have been both witnesses and receivers of insensitive and careless encounters with those who would have brought them graciousness by simply and courageously standing by in patient, benevolent stillness.

They have learned that it seems more comfortable for others to pretend that a baby's death never happened, to simply not acknowledge it out loud. Erin believes some might feel guilty for bringing it up because such a loss seems so unnatural. She goes on to show she understands:

"It's not natural to be pregnant and have to decide what funeral home you're going to use." Still, these parents want to talk about Isaac; they want others to understand and accept the truth that they have four children – even though one cannot be seen. Erin continues, "People who have lost children all get it . . . they don't think it's weird that we talk about him." Unfortunately, they still get careless questions and hear hurtful messages from well-meaning people. Sometimes consistently insensitive encounters mean that old friendships must fall away so new ones can be forged with those who understand the realities of life after the death of a child: there is no timetable for grief.

The couple's best piece of advice is: "You can give encouragement and offer comfort, but don't try to give advice unless you've gone through it – whether you have good intentions or not."

(Our child in heaven: Isaac's story)

Lindsay and Scott decided to risk, to openly give their hearts in their quest toward parenthood . . . and they have suffered much. Lindsay journals about daughter, Lauren's, death and how the thoughts and opinions of others so easily and carelessly leave their mark.

"Everyone, at some point . . . will lose a loved one. Each person also has an opinion on the severity of injury and length of time for grieving. Each person also will want to share their opinions with you when you lose someone. You will hear every story imaginable as if in

71

*some way to make you feel better by suggesting
that you are not as bad off as someone else (but) it
does not help a grieving parent to be told that . . .
their child died for a reason or it was meant to
be. Other well-meant comments like this can be
exhausting and leave grieving parents in despair
and self-doubt."*

*With a wry laugh, Lindsay maintains that
others may think they are comforting you when
you're told, "if God wanted you to have children,
you would have children," but such a statement
only wounds. She continues, "Sometimes what
others say can make you feel as if your baby's
death is your fault."*

(The power of tiny miracles: Lauren's story)

Greg lost his beautiful baby girl, Marie, to medical
complications he neither fully understands nor can totally
reconcile as part of his reality. All he can grasp is that
his baby was unexpectedly taken from him. The support
he needs as well as any assistance he is able to accept
or appreciate become part of the grieving journey he
navigates. He talks about the first year following Marie's
loss with a kind of frustrated wonderment.

*He and his wife heard all the messages of the
"right things to do" when one suffers deeply-
felt, unexpected loss and they tried things they
thought might help. They attended a support
group for bereaved parents for a short time and
found some comfort. Talking about your story
and hearing theirs is helpful, he shares; "You
figure out 'I'm not alone.'" As I listen, I also hear*

a bitterness that bites through Greg's voice each time he remembers how friends and religious acquaintances tried to comfort him during this time. He recalls the phrases as if they were given yesterday and his anger is palpable. "God needed her," and other such platitudes meant to make him feel better by assuring him his daughter is now in "a better place," only makes things worse.
(Her sweetest gift: Marie's story*)*

In November of 2000, Hunter, a sweetly-beautiful infant, is born. Brain injured due to medical negligence, this determined little soul eventually loses his fight for life in March of 2002. The unexpected loss of Hunter's baby brother, Joshua, stillborn only two months before Hunter's death, doubles his parents' distress and suffering. The time between the early winter of 2000 and the coming spring of 2002 is a pressure cooker of anger, exhaustion, tenderness and bitter anguish for the boys' parents, Shelbie and Vic. Shelbie was working as the general manager of a local hospice when we first talked. Extremely aware of the messages many bring into conversation with those in mourning, she expresses why it is vital that we all learn what we should, and should not do and say when visiting with those living in grief.

Shelbie feels as if she was not able to start the process of grieving for years after Hunter's death. There were no support groups in her Wyoming town and many friends and family members who did talk with her told her to "just move on." The statement, "it gets better with time," she calls "fingernails on a chalkboard" because "for me it does not. People just say the dumbest things." And with a sad smile she repeats one of the most difficult things said to her as Hunter's parent: "it must have been easier for you because you knew he was going to die." It is pronouncements like that one which prompt her to continue educating her own Hospice staff. "You can do fifty things right but the one thing that's done wrong or that one thing that's said – that's the thing people remember. We teach people (that) it doesn't matter . . . I don't care if they have six kids and they lose one; it is no different . . . ."

Shelbie located and now participates with a support group for bereaved parents, 3 Hopeful Hearts. In 3HH, she can talk openly about her children's lives and deaths with others who truly understand and who don't expect her to "just move on." She now mentors other parents who have lost their children, making certain that they know someone who understands their grief and pain wants to help. "I've been there," Shelbie assures them; "You can tell me things and I'll understand."

(*Missing pieces of my heart:* Hunter and Joshua's story)

"Even within the seemingly most unacceptable and painful situation is concealed a deeper good and within every disaster is contained the seed of grace."
Eckhart Tolle: <u>Stillness Speaks</u>

Someone in grief may long to be alone, but each, in time, needs the Grace-filled, unconditionally loving and patient company of others. The parent of a disabled child once shared with me that there is peace in the presence of others even in the absence of answers. Actually therein lies the truth: there is no one, final, right, best answer for grieving. But, standing by, ready to listen without the compelling need to advise and solve the painful aching of another's grief, is one of the most gracious ways to bring comfort. Grace lives in those tender moments. If we're prepared to rest, unafraid, with the bereaved in those intimate spaces, we – in all our hopeful, imperfect humanness – have the opportunity to bring love, peace and mercy to another. We become Grace.

In time, after Ashleigh and Parshad lose their treasured Scarlett, they are opened to some valuable ideas for any who hope to make a positive difference in their own lives . . . as well as for others traveling down grief's pathways. Among them is this wisdom, the seed of Grace:

> . . . *you can just sit with people in their grief; be present and available to quietly travel through the darkness with them. And a lesson for everyone – find a bigger and wider perspective: don't be so hard on yourself and others because no one really realizes, from the outside looking in, who might be living a really tough story of their own.*

(Scarlet's story)

Knowing what not to say to assist someone in grief is as important as understanding what to say and do. Thankfully, whether through reading material, a key stroke or a phone call, good information is readily available. Face-to-face and online grief organizations, as well as specifically-designated support entities stand ready with lists of how to most healthily participate in the grief process, whether we are the grievers or one of those who has committed to support another on their journey.

Gained through years of professional, kindhearted and responsive experiences, comes a compilation of the collective wisdom of different support organizations for the grief stricken and despairing. In this collection of best hopes are also the grieving voices who shared with me what they needed from others who "meant well" but were often uninformed and hurtful. You'll note that the following list is written from the perspective of the griever . . . actually it is from the viewpoint of all of us because no one is without an example of irreplaceable loss. Think about this guide as you might the Golden Rule of your childhood . . . giving to another the unconditional loving kindness that we, each one, would want given to us.

- Don't be afraid to speak my loved one's name. If I cry, please know it is not because you have hurt me. Thank you for letting me hear his/her name and for openly sharing my grief with me.
- Please keep in touch: ask how you might help me today; let me know you are available.
- Understand that, at this moment, every part of my life has been shattered. I am no longer who I was before someone I never wanted to outlive, died. I will have good times and bad but I will never expect you to say the perfect thing to make me all better.

- Please don't rely on clichés, platitudes or easy answers. "He had a good, long life" or "At least she's out of pain" or "Aren't you lucky that . . ." are phrases that minimize a life and its loss.
- Sometimes things around me move too quickly; sometimes there is too much expected of me. If I walk away, don't take it personally. I just need some quiet moments alone.
- Please never presume that your grief is just like mine; I will do the same for you. Though we have loss in common, our situations will always be very personal and individually unique to each of us.
- Please don't give advice unless I ask for it.
- I resent it when you tell me how you think I must be feeling. I'm not you, so how can you know? To say "I know just how you feel" or "You must be relieved" hurts me. Please ask instead of tell me.
- I am touched when you remember important anniversary dates in my grief life.
- I hope that some day you will be comfortable sitting without expectation by my side, simply listening.

For one traveling on grief's byways, each hour, day, month and year is peppered with rides on the fickle roller coaster of emotion. To be most helpful, keep close some phrases and questions you know will not hurt another. Consider these: "How are you feeling *today*?" "May I call you *today*?" "How may I help you *right now*?" "I have a note/card for you. Is *now* a good time to give it to you?" Stay in the present with your comments and never presume a timeline for someone else's suffering. Grief has no schedule. As you consider these lists, visualize yourself as a listening, supporting presence who:

- can accept silence;
- will stay in touch while not probing for details;
- won't presume to understand, but will ask gentle questions; and
- will allow grief's emotions into the conversation without intellectualizing the pain.

Though we've all lived as grievers, these delicate, powerful encounters with others are not about us. This time we have chosen to act in service to others. Every grief situation is unique and though we can never always have just the right language for each, we can let our stillness speak for us; we can watch and listen for cues; we can be a gentle presence of Grace – always standing by.

recognizing Grace in community

*"I'm just there because I know how they're suffering and they
had to have something to hold on to because it's so easy to
go down a rabbit hole and not get out. I'm here to walk with
others . . . and help them understand that they can survive."*
(Remembering through the whisper of wings: Grant's story)

I want to tell you a story. Actually it's a bit of my
story – one that affirms that each of us is a part of the
human family, never really without a community who
share our reality. It goes like this: "The Mustard Seed," a
famous parable found in one of Buddhism's foundational
texts weaves a tale of despair and acceptance. The mother
in this narrative grieves uncontrollably over the death
of her beloved son and carries his corpse everywhere
in search of a remedy to Death's visit. Unable to accept
that her loss is irreversible, she searches for an antidote
to administer to the son she continues to carry in her
arms. She meets the Buddha and begs for help. Instead
of providing a healing, he instructs her to go from house
to house in search of a few grains of mustard seed, part
of the necessary antidote. The catch is that she may not
take a mustard seed from any household where Death has
entered. In time, this mother comes to understand and
accept that death visits us all, changes us all. Finally, she
surrenders and lays her son's body down.

When my son died, surrender was not in my vocabulary. Though some suggested I investigate a support fellowship of other bereaved parents and attend a group meeting, the very thought of such a session with others filled me with a different kind of pain – the despair of a stoic, an introvert who would be expected to share details of a very personal, wretched experience. It didn't matter to me what any other sufferers had in common with me; what mattered is that I, like the mother in the parable, felt I needed to bear the weight of carrying Matt everywhere with me . . . hopefully and hopelessly. At my most logical, I knew I wasn't alone; somewhere inside I grasped that others would be in community with me, could help me carry my pain. But, then, my heart was shattered and logic didn't have a chance.

I started down my own rabbit hole – one littered with misery and fear – and it lead me into dark places. I used lots of energy resisting my newest reality. I was busy demanding my own breaking heart to sew together all of its fractured places as quickly and tightly as possible so I could recognize myself again. I lived in that frantic, barren space for quite a while before it became clear that all my stitching was only making my heart space smaller. I felt puckered inside, as if my heart had drawn in on itself. It wasn't that Grace had disappeared during this time, but that my heart had less and less room for it.

> **"The wider the community of your heart,
> the wider the community around you."**
> Henri Nouwen: "Love Deeply"

Gratefully, I've come to know that the steady, unconditional support and caring of fellowship is Grace made visual. Available to all, community is a fundamental pathway toward healing. Parker Palmer, teacher and author explains community as a place of sacred connections. In Servant Leadership, he asserts that we carry alliances with others in our hearts, bringing those connections alive through the bonds we forge with those we let most fully into our lives. And in such trusting relationships we allow the "tuggings and pullings" of others to remind us to loosen the threads . . . to unpucker our hearts so grief can move through, leaving room for love to again fill the emptied, damaged spaces. Though I never did choose to join an organized community of the bereaved, I now realize I was always being held up by companions who knew, well before I, that I needed them. Looking back, I realize I was in the care of a collection of friends and family who were doing their best to be in fellowship with me as I traveled my own grieving pathways. Though I might have thought I was the creator of my own travel plans for that indescribable journey, my community was also present . . . a loosely connected network of tuggers and pullers, quietly standing by. Now I get it.

Being in fellowship with others is not a tidy reality. Any who have lived within profound grief can tell you: just as no loss situation is like any other, not every griever will have his or her needs met by the same form of community. The community of the mother in "The Mustard Seed" became every person in every home she visited – everyone who answered her knock, knew the inevitability and weigh of loss, and acknowledged her pain. Just as that community was specific to one in distress, there are as many unique types of supportive groups as there are varieties of those in need. Communities move and morph; their flexibility is their strength.

- Community creates flexible boundaries, expanding and contracting to include those who need, seek and accept its gifts.
- Community is a collection of supportive strangers who are in the right place, with important messages at the perfect time.
- Community organizes when necessary to stay together for moments . . . or years.
- Community has no perfect number, forming when two or more come together for a common, shared, stated commitment, hope or need.
- Community operates within formal or informal structures and expectations.
- Community is a place of safety; no one is there with the expressed intention of fixing another.
- Community is love in action.

These groups are the arms to hold us; they have the many languages to help us understand ourselves, to gentle us into truly believing we are not alone in a despairing panorama of loss. A caring fellowship in all its many iterations, is power. It is the struggling, generous, hopeful, crucial, moveable feast of the human community surrounding and caring for each other with love at its core.

Hearts broken wide open are first raw, lonely and hopeless, but with trust and courage, each can become grateful and accepting containers with enough room to hold some marvelous stuff . . . like new hope, surrender, heartfelt love, and gracious, healing memories. Henri

Nouwen, Dutch theologian and author, writes in "Love Deeply" of the rich possibilities of a very special kind of mystical community when grieving hearts open wide: ". . . those whom you love will not leave your heart even when they depart from you. They will become part of your *self* and thus gradually build a community within you. Those you have loved deeply become a part of you."

"Community is an outward and visible sign of an inward and invisible grace, the flowing of personal identity and integrity into the world of relationships."
Parker Palmer

My interviews with the bereaved taught me that community really does come in every make and model, form and size, and that love rather than specific organization molds them into just the right shapes. Emily and Chris are gratified to discover surprising gifts of support surrounding them at the perfect time.

> *Emily asserts that for months after Carter's death she had "never felt so uncomfortable in my own house or in my own skin." She felt lost. Each of the parents talks with gratitude about their bosses and different co-workers who handled the communication of their loss to their respective clients and colleagues. "We definitely had the right people in our lives at that time, just what we needed to try to somehow manage."*
> *Summer turns toward Fall, one of Emily's favorite seasons. She shares that . . . moving forward seems impossible. Good friends, realizing her mood and also knowing how much*

she enjoys decorating for the Fall season, come to the rescue. Their surprise intervention helps remind Emily of what she still finds lovely and lovable. They stay with her, decorating her home, reminding her of the beauty of the present. This time helps her realize she can do more than "just go through the motions of being alive."

And later, they find the sustaining fellowship of organized community. Their pay-it-forward message of strength and hope continues to spread in ever-widening circles of compassionate care.

In 2007 when Carter died, there was no dedicated support organization for bereaved parents in the area. "We felt like we were the only ones in the world that had ever lost a baby like this. We felt so alone," Emily recalls. For a time, the couple lives within that lonely reality. By 2009, Emily and Chris are involved with others who have also lost children. They discover a Candlelight Vigil is being held for bereaved parents to honor the lives of their children. After helping to publicize the event, they attend and commemorate Carter in a new and public way with others. They find comfort and healing in the company of parents like themselves, within a community of true understanding and mutual support.

Over time, the couple pays forward the love, comfort and wisdom they've received by being a part of an organized community. They champion this organization, 3 Hopeful Hearts, through board membership, mentoring other parents, speaking at support group meetings, attending and organizing events and co-facilitating groups. Emily pauses and then gently shares that in these last few years she has been able to finally accept the past with a more grateful heart.

(*He made us parents and prepared us to love*: Carter's story)

When acute grief morphs into less intense, subtle grief, survivors find the mind and heart space to reflect on how they've been surviving. In the midst of being a community of strength for someone else, Melinda and Trey discover there is more to learn, more to understand about their own grieving. They recognize and welcome the healing tears that signal a new and important awareness. And in the gifting of another they are able to discover and explore their own ongoing comfort in another grace-filled community.

Derek's parents go into survival mode over the next years. They carry their sadness as best they can by putting one foot in front of the other. They begin to experience more of what they can call normal days, but admit that they weren't actually dealing with their grief. "We put it (our grief) in a box and stuck it in the closet," says a tearful Melinda. Still, she and Trey steadily work to rebuild. Finally, the couple comes to grips with a truth: "we thought we were healed," Trey shares, a catch in his voice; "we thought we were passed it." But when Melinda's friend loses a son, the couple's grief rushes to the surface. With a short laugh and more tears, Melinda admits in a kind of awe, "It ripped our scab open and let us know we weren't alone." ". . . it's been three years and it (the grief) is the same as it was when we first put it out of sight." Trey goes on "It made it all fresh . . . I was right there at the beginning again. We'd never healed; we'd never moved on." Melinda thoughtfully refers to her feelings as a kind of "pseudo grief." She tearfully continues, "I was devastated for her, but it's my pain I'm feeling! If she hadn't lost her baby I don't know where we would be. We wouldn't have taken care of ourselves."

Melinda begins to explore possible resources to help her friend through the devastating loss they now have in common. It is during this time that Melinda and Trey discover 3 Hopeful Hearts. What began as a gifting opportunity to another is now an ongoing, very real gift for each of them. "It's been a real blessing to be able to relax and take off the masks we wear to hide, to lessen, our grief," Melinda explains. Attending the support group to share and hear others' stories is difficult but it's through those stories that they finally begin to realize they aren't alone. Trey calls their time in the group wonderful and enlightening: "when you have something that's all sharp edges and cuts you every time you touch it . . . the more familiar you get with it, the less you cut yourself . . . the less you bleed."

(*For everything a time*: Derek's story)

Kristin and Larry lost the light of their lives when two-year-old Zach died unexpectedly. In time, his loss focused the energy of his parents into actions of loving reclamation, not only for themselves but also for others. Zach is honored through organized community . . . bringing vulnerable and fractured hearts together to experience compassion and healing within the company of each other. And through their efforts, Kristin and Larry go on to become gracious comfort in the lives of many – friends and strangers alike.

> *Not too long after their son's death, Larry and Kristin sought out a support group offered by community, Compassionate Friends, and with that choice came some hope and relief. They found comfort telling their story and building friendships with others who understood an enduring, shared pain; eventually they became leaders within the group. It was then that the experience of Candlelight Vigils, where a family pauses to remember with tenderness a life lost and honoring the child who profoundly touched and changed their lives, became a touchstone for both Larry and Kristin.*

> *As a way to continue reclaiming hope in the midst of old memories and a growing, busy family life, the couple maintains involvement with Compassionate Friends as well as remains a helping presence in the organization of local Candlelight Vigils. "It's like giving back," Larry comments. The support they first felt over 20 years ago is offered today through this loving*

tradition, a tangible gift of fellowship Larry and Kristin humbly and happily provide to parents who like themselves, have lost a child.

Grief and grace continued to reveal themselves by fueling Kristin to answer a call – acting on opportunities to offer her own natural gifts of understanding, intuition and loving service to others. In 2008, with two other women, she was instrumental in the creation of a local support group for bereaved parents named 3 Hopeful Hearts. She labels it incredible work and finds herself consistently touched by parents who courageously transform their own grief through authentically sharing their understanding of life and death with one another, forming mentoring partnerships, and allowing themselves to welcome moments of real joy.

(*Zach's lasting legacy*: Zach's story)

"When we seek for connection, we restore the world to wholeness. Our seemingly separate lives become meaningful as we discover how truly necessary we are to each other."
Margaret Wheatley: <u>Turning to One Another</u>

Veronica's community develops as a network of kind and competent strangers who combine with her family to do what is necessary to provide strength and assistance. She and Guillermo need help bringing their daughter's body back from Mexico. Thankfully, a few days after Angela's death, this new community, formed at the most opportune of times, works compassionately to bring a cherished daughter home to be buried, encircled by her family.

Veronica's father in Colorado gives his daughter the name and number of someone to call who he believes can help them. Veronica, who has been trying unsuccessfully to get the funeral home to honor their business promise of providing air transport for the deceased to the states, returns to the funeral home. This time she makes a call to her father's contact. She reaches a man who is aware of her name and some details of the situation. Veronica begins to believe that the closing door might stay open just long enough for them to send her little girl home. As details unfold for the transport, more problems surface. The legalese and growing red tape wind tightly around the situation and the parents now wonder not only how they will get Angela, but also the rest of the family, out of Mexico.

Their contact from the American Embassy makes another call to see how things are going. An anxious Veronica details the latest unreasonable expectations and again he asks to speak to the funeral home representative. His words work and the family finally watches the door open fully. Angela's casket is put on a flight to Denver, two days after her death; it lands just hours later. After making certain Angela is on her way to Colorado, a relieved Veronica calls her father to let him know that his granddaughter is on her way to him.

Angela's body is met at DIA by a mortuary located in Denver as well as by the Embassy representative who promised to help them bring their little girl home. She is held in Denver as her body is re-examined and re-autopsied. After another embalming procedure and all medical considerations are met, a funeral home from the parent's hometown collects their daughter's body, bringing her the final way home. The Colorado family is now all together.

(*Love one another like it's your last day:* Angela's story)

How death enters a life triggers which pathways we choose to travel, which different kinds of communities we choose to embrace. Lisa, in her desire to honor her lost son, discovers that it may even be possible to create yet another group. Community has the potential to grow into an endowment, something grace-filled for others that might never have materialized if Death had not clarified its need.

After Brian's death, Lisa sought and found some comfort in grief groups sponsored by her local Hospice and the 3 Hopeful Hearts organization. She was able to share her grief and voice her truth with others who listened compassionately. In time, her son's death prompts her to take a journey of discovery. The many and complex revelations of her son's life and death lead Lisa down a path toward honoring Brian. Lisa looks up and in a strong voice declares, "Brian was born on Equality Day, in the

*Equality State." These facts prompt her dream of
giving her son a gift. Lisa's pathway directs her
to vision a new community, to write a proposal
to bring women together in Equality – to take
counsel with one another to identify healthier
ways to live peacefully, each with another. "My
dream (is) . . . to honor Brian," his mother states.*
(*He was my best pal:* Brian's story)

Supportive communities abide near and far. Dan
and Ginny tragically lose their young son, Kelby, and
use what they learn within community to grow toward
making some peace with their own suffering. Grace
speaks through them in the process as they take steps to
advance the cause of lessening the chances that another
family will have to endure their same fate.

*Kelby's cause of death was SUDC, Sudden
Unexplained Death in Childhood. Ginny was
introduced to this diagnosis, inadvertently, from
a bereaved SUDC mother's Facebook post she
just happened upon six months before Kelby's
death. After her own son's death diagnosis,
Ginny contacted this parent and learned that the
SUDC Program, established in 2001 to provide
information and support to parents like her and
Dan, had become its own non-profit foundation
in 2014. The proactive couple wanted to somehow
become involved. Ginny moved quickly, and,
after securing Kelby's DNA from the medical
examiner, both she and Dan submitted their own
and now all three are part of a study, committed
to helping researchers provide much-needed*

answers to the many agonizing questions that accompany an SUDC death. Ginny joined an SUDC mom's support group, an online presence she now shares with "soul sisters" located all over the world. The couple acknowledges that there is both comfort and strength in joining with others who have suffered the identical type of loss they have, those who are traveling their same road.

Together, Dan and Ginny have found that sharing within a support system of others who have also lost a child helps lead to healing. About the same time they discovered the SUDC Foundation, a local bereaved parents' support group, 3 Hopeful Hearts, also came into their lives. Since finding 3HH, mentoring other parents, as well as sharing her own loss experiences through panel presentations and participating in training sessions for police services and nurses, Ginny has noticed that her grief is morphing – some of the sharper edges have blunted.

When Dan and she share similar pain with other grieving parents, the feeling of being alone lessens; recognizing and confronting the different faces, shapes and demands of profound grief helps them acknowledge its weight and its place in their lives. According to the couple, in time you learn to fit all the various, changing pieces of grief into something you can manage, like a backpack, and then it becomes easier to carry around.

(*Love beyond loss*: Kelby's story)

The fellowship of grace-filled connections formed in community are transformational; they are the willing, the loving who commit to helping us back out of our own rabbit holes. Community, fellowship, support group, tribe – all exist because of the warmhearted blessings of the pullers and the tuggers. The pullers grab our hands and bring us with them into circles of support; the tuggers gently draw open the seams of our hearts, giving them the breathing space to remember and accept the warmth and visions of forgotten light and lapsed connections. Their gracious actions remind us that we can reclaim the wholeness of something beyond a splintered heart. And as it all unfolds within the communities of those who bring unqualified love, we are warmed by the mercy of something beautiful, by the merciful Grace of the possible.

finding Grace through ritual and legacy

*Elizabeth remembers the Halloween wake the family held on
October 31st. Friends and family alike were invited to show up
in costume to celebrate the life of an amazing person who had
dearly loved Halloween. Elizabeth smiles through tears and
calls it the "happiest, funnest, saddest day you can imagine."
(Her saint who walked in light: Hollis' story)*

I expect you've heard these sentiments as well: "Wasn't
that inspirational?" "What a lovely tribute." "I'm glad to
have a place to donate; it's a such an important way to
honor his life." "What a gift that the whole family could
be here with us." "I didn't think I'd be able to laugh, but
what she said was so priceless." "This is the perfect setting
to honor her." With each statement like these we show our
appreciation for the ritual we're witnessing created to
honor a life beyond death. And the face of Grace, seen in
the shared compassion and love of all joined in fellowship,
is beautifully visible. These are the times – funerals and
memorial services, lovingly crafted by the grieving –
that provide us the space to gather, to gently rest in the
company of one another and remember, nodding and
smiling as we wipe away tears. Coming to closure with
the loss of a life once connected with our own is a tender,
important time – a time when ritual allows us to look

back in acceptance and move ahead with hope. Whether small or elaborate, public or private, the sacred rituals we plan give us, the grievers, important personal information about ourselves – what we believe at our core about living and dying. They illuminate what we've suffered and make clear who and what we cherish. Fundamentally, finding Grace through ritual and legacy is about gifts . . . those we give to ourselves and by extension, offer to others.

Inevitably, grief after profound loss descends. Our reality is forced into a different shape. We long for balance, a quiet mind, some peace. Early ritualized observances, purposefully and tenderly formed to celebrate and honor another, are meant to help us begin processing our present as we prepare to walk into the imminent turmoil of grief. They are the first steps into our newest reality – the unfolding pathway into the next part of life's journey. Our spirits, hearts, minds and souls work as one while we create such sacred observances. Moving through the process of designing, organizing and participating in gracious, meaningful rituals meant expressly for a beloved have the power to bring a profound solace – both to ourselves and to communities of others who share our need for grace-filled remembrances. Borne of our grief, they represent the seeds of future traditions – of other structured rituals or potential legacies – organized to symbolize something greater than our solitary selves. Therein lie the ongoing gifts of ritual.

"This is what rituals are for. We do spiritual ceremonies as human beings in order to create a safe resting place for our most complicated feelings of joy or trauma, so that we don't have to haul those feelings around with us forever, weighing us down."
Elizabeth Gilbert: <u>Eat, Pray, Love</u>

Most of us, in our minds and hearts, understand that the chaos of grief will not simply disappear with a closing ritual. Still, we long for ways of saying good bye before too much time passes. In our culture there are few rituals specifically designed for the grieving aside from funerals and memorial services. Generally, as timing would have it, these ceremonies are held before the intense, long-term processes of acute grief are in full force. We prepare, participate in and endure them because we need to find ways to give voice to our sadness while also fulfilling a desire to honor what is lost. According to bereavement literature, using a ritualized service to memorialize and physically lay to rest a loved one helps us begin the long-term processes of grieving. The following list contains some of the critical ways that planning a closure ritual serve to help us move forward. They:

- create some order out of a current existence full of confused disorder;
- acknowledge the reality of loss and help move us toward its inevitable pain;
- actively remember and honor the life and death of a loved one;
- provide a safe place to express the desire to maintain an intimate connection with the dead;
- intentionally design a physical expression of an ending; and
- mark a new beginning . . . without a beloved.

I can attest to the importance, wisdom and truth of each of these activities. After two separate services to memorialize my son, Matthew, and two more ritualized opportunities with just family, I was on track to be immersed to some degree within each of the six on this list. Through ritual first, Matt's family marked both his physical end while beginning a way to stay connected to his spirit. We decided to participate in annual Arthritis Foundation events using his name. Grace, in the form of unconditional love and compassion, radiated through the unselfish actions of all who shared those miles with us during those December Arthritis Foundation 5K mornings. That physical ritual, first created to keep him alive in us, continues to also serve others who suffer from the same disease whose complications took Matt's life. First designed as an activity to honor him and bring his community together, now survives as my son's legacy to others who receive funding in his name.

Rituals and legacies were important realities in the grieving lives of most of the parents I interviewed. A variety of different memorial and funeral services were created and held to celebrate the lives of their children. Some new family traditions grew from the desire to remain connected during favorite holidays or birthdays. Other established practices, like mine, took shape to financially or otherwise actively support causes associated with a beloved's death. Interestingly, often traditions beyond early funerals or memorial services surfaced spontaneously; for personal reasons, it simply felt right for those grieving to design unique ways to fill their need for continued connection with one who had died.

Rituals are important to Dion and Taia, especially when they are created in the midst of natural beauty and attended by loving friends and family. Each year the life force of their stillborn daughter, Lyla, is recognized

through various observances. And with Taia's growing
understanding of Lyla's wisdom, comes an expansion of
her daughter's legacy in helping others.

> *One family tradition is to travel into the vast
> beauty of the mountains to Zimmerman Lake
> and scatter a few of her ashes to acknowledge and
> honor her delivery date. Tears shimmer in Taia's
> eyes as she recounts this ritual that continues
> to keep her first daughter alive in their hearts.
> "We love being in nature. We thought . . . that
> we wanted part of her there because we knew
> that would be how we would raise her; she would
> always be there when we would go there. She
> will always be in nature with us."*
>
> *The parents also establish a time to hold a
> celebration for friends and their children that
> centers around laughter, sharing, ice cream and
> birthday cake. "We created this little ritual where
> we have friends come over and their kids (say)
> 'Oh . . . we get to celebrate Lyla's birthday.' And
> they know who she is." Taia continues that these
> observances are also teaching moments – because
> as children and adults grow in awareness about
> the inherent nature of loss, they can pass their
> understanding on to others: "You can talk about
> it (death/loss). It's OK to ask questions; people
> want you to; people don't want you to ignore the
> fact that you have a child nobody can see."*
>
> *All the opportunities created to keep Lyla a
> very real presence continue to help her parents
> teach their own family and friends what it means*

to support them as well as others who live within the transformational time of profound loss. "I think creating those rituals we have around who she is in our family, and how she completes our family, will continue to help let her siblings know about her."

Taia surveys the wisdom she's received from living with Lyla's still-present energy. Lyla taught them to be more than parents who make the best of their individual lives, but to be parents who "cherish life and everything it throws at you." "And," Taia continues with another smile, "she teaches us patience." As a bereaved parent in a teacher role, Taia is able to share a unique understanding with children who have suffered losses. "Lyla gave me words I needed to help those students, especially those who have loss, helping them to know those they've lost are always with them."

(She is always with us: Lyla's story)

**"Rituals . . . are about transformation.
. . . we associate the ritual with a major life passage, the crossing of a critical threshold, or in other words, with transformation."**
Abraham Verghese

Dan and Ginny bury their beautiful Kelby in a local cemetery, deciding to make it a space so inviting that all who walk up to, or past it can smile. Their tradition – the act of creating Kelby's special, earthly spot a space for visiting – symbolizes a resting place where love surrounds and outlives death.

Kelby's unique, interesting headstone, an actual child's chair, welcomes visitors of all ages to his resting space. Its backrest displays a picture of Kelby as well as his name, birth and death dates; the seat part is for actual sitting, and the bottom front of the chair displays messages through icons and words designed to showcase Kelby's favorite things. Centered in this area is a message dear to the hearts of his parents: "We will hold you in our hearts until we hold you in heaven."

Another playful celebration of Kelby's life sits easily in the sand of a local park, just a few blocks from Dan and Ginny's home. A delightful, grey, big-eared elephant – a replica of Kelby's beloved "Winks" – stands ready to welcome any child and give him or her a gentle, spring-loaded ride. Near Winks is a commemorative plaque remembering Kelby with love. Dan looks at Ginny as he talks of their son who "people would just come up and talk to" – a son who could just . . . "draw people in." And still, today, his parents have made certain there are places and spaces where Kelby is available: to play with; to talk to; to relive precious memories; and to remind everyone present that love endures even devastating loss.

(*Love beyond loss*: Kelby's story)

Emily and Chris love being in the natural world and find it a way to bring both beauty and healing into their common life. On the first anniversary of Carter's death, the couple decides they want to recognize his steadfast presence in their growing family's life.

> *After church the family travels into the foothills together to picnic, play and soak in the natural beauty around them. The couple knows they want to continue to celebrate their son's presence in their family and decide on a yearly balloon release. In 2009, they begin the ritual of adding one more balloon each year to match the age Carter would have been. As Chris and Emily's family grows . . . so do the balloons the family of four use to pay tribute to a son and big brother who continues to grow in their hearts. Nine balloons, released by Clara, Abbey, Emily and Chris with love and laughter, dot the 2016 July sky.*

(*He made us parents and prepared us to love*: Carter's story)

"In the space between chaos and shape
there was another chance."
Jeanette Winterson: <u>The World and Other Places</u>

Rituals begin as symbols, gifts, gracious recipes for loving traditions. Within each and every ritualized action, designed so that the memory of the dead ultimately serves the living, legacies begin to grow. A legacy is a bequest . . . a grace-filled gift passed forward, intentionally, from the family members. When our ritualized traditions transcend time and place, when their role is to benefit others, to continue beyond a single action to establish an endowment from an individual family to the larger, human family, they transition into legacies. The children represented here were catalysts, not only serving as the driving force behind a family ritual but also as the reason for positively impacting the lives of others – friends and strangers alike. These families have made real for their children what Max Lucado asserts as both possible and wonderful: "Outlive your life!" – your death is not the end.

Zach, lost before he was three, has been the ongoing catalyst for a Grace-filled legacy that touches not only his family but extends to countless others who suffer as his parents have. Kristin and Larry's desire to continue to connect to their first born goes on and on in a lasting legacy.

Grief reveals you, Kristin states, sharing a favorite thought from John Green's The Fault in our Stars*. Through his short lifespan, Zach established an indelible love-filled legacy for his parents and their eventual family. His ongoing bequest has been grief's revelation through the life choices of his parents. "I've changed in almost every way imaginable . . . and it's sad in some ways and hopeful and transformational in other ways,"*

Not too long after their son's death, Larry and Kristin sought out a support group offered by the organization, Compassionate Friends. Experiences they were exposed to during this time were so transformational for the bereaved couple that they were instrumental in establishing those same kinds of honoring traditions in Fort Collins, where they moved in the late 90's. Zach's legacy of love lives each time others in grief are unconditionally supported (by Kristin and 3HH), given the opportunity to share their pain, and helped to honor and remember their lost children.

Kristin looks at Larry as she finds the words to express a deeply-felt truth: Zach's legacy is in everything. "It's in our worry about our other children, in our intentional messages and in us always being available to our kids - his four brothers and sisters - the children who might not have been born if he had lived. With a small laugh and a large amount of pride, she points to the acceptance and kindnesses given to her by her four other children. They let me be crazy and obsessive about their safety, she says with a kind of awe. And, most importantly, they still show up! They take time out of their busy, young lives to honor the brother they never knew. I can count on Zach's brothers and sisters to join us at the Candlelight Vigil, say Zach's name, light a candle, and pay tribute to his importance in our family, Kristin shares with a proud smile. Zach's legacy lives on in the sensitivity, understanding and loving gift-giving of his family.*

(*Zach's lasting legacy:* Zach's story)

When I visit with Josh and Lindsay, they share how Ella Elizabeth's family memorial service, held not far from Colorado's stunning Flatirons, helped to establish a beautiful tradition for their family.

Actual Sugar Moon white rose bushes now grace the gardens of Ella's family as beautiful,

> *living and growing symbols honoring her forever-place in their lives. Ella's Garden is both actual and symbolic – a real place to drink in nature's bounty and a reminder of the purity and innocence of one who is now in another's care.*

And Ella remains a presence when each Christmas her memory spills over, lovingly, as a legacy to others.

> *To keep Ella a real and growing part of their family life, Lindsay and Josh begin a Christmas tradition where each of the four family members chooses a present for her. Moving from baby to toddler gifts and beyond, each passing year's gifts are bought to match the age their little girl would be if she physically lived in their world. They imagine what their daughter and sister would love, and purchase it for another little girl to enjoy. The four gifts are donated to families who have little ones the age Ella would have been. Ella's parents keep her alive and growing within their hearts while passing on loving kindness to others and demonstrating generosity for their sons.*
>
> *(Where love blooms:* Ella's story)

Grace and grief mingle throughout Johanna's story. A strong and compassionate young woman, Johanna was committed to helping the underserved. After her murder, family members used her considerable talents and accomplishments to begin traditions to reveal a legacy affecting countless others. Johanna's father, Dan, talks about his extraordinary daughter.

His exceptional daughter remains alive, connected in spirit, and through legacy bestowed freely and lovingly in the form of simple and complex gifts. An example resides in Kibera, Kenya, where a twelve-grade school and accompanying clinic have been built and staffed to serve young girls, teens and women. The health facility carries the name Johanna Justin-Jinich Community Clinic, honoring a young woman whose short but memorable life continues to influence others to work toward becoming their best selves. Though Johanna was gone by the time the school began, she was a part of its dream, a force behind its ambitious purpose. Close friends who were inspired by her dedication to service and her love for causes that had at their core the health and safety of girls and women, carried her in their hearts as they breathed life and put flesh and bone into the buildings that have become a haven for others. "It's a thriving organization," Dan declares with pride; it is an amazing dream-turned-reality, a community that is helping to transform lives by fulfilling the promise of a better future through access to education and health care.

Another of Johanna's gifts grew from a decision to spotlight her Jewish identity using her wit, maturity and intellect to serve the cause of transcending misconceptions and discrimination. Johanna wrote and illustrated a children's story highlighting ways to overcome differences and promote tolerance when she *was only fifteen. <u>Julia's Star</u>, according to her father's words in its prologue, was written to help teach others about "the injurious effect of intolerance, and how curiosity, friendship, knowledge and trust can overcome prejudice." After Johanna's death, Renate, her maternal grandmother and a Holocaust survivor, wrote an epilogue to the story including words from Johanna's 2006 college essay: ". . . we long for hope, hope that tolerance, humility, and life will surmount the despair of death, prejudice, and destruction throughout the world." Sonia, Johanna's paternal grandmother, spearheaded the actual publication of <u>Julia's Star</u> and helped it find its way into elementary classrooms in California and Connecticut, where it is still used as a teaching tool to aid understanding and combat prejudice.*

Tears shimmering in his eyes, Dan remembers during that dark time in Middletown, as he endured the trial (of his daughter's killer), he was able to visit a classroom where <u>Julia's Star</u> was being used. Listening as fourth graders reenacted the story and talked through what they were learning, he was able to witness first-hand the impact Johanna's loving and courageous spirit had on others. Dan still receives thank you notes from young children who read and learn from her book. He gently unwraps to reveal one set of colorful notes written by youngsters, all shaped like open hands whose fingers, palms and backs are full of messages of hope and good will; Dan

*spreads them out, a riot of bright joy, and what is
possible in a world filled with tolerance, openness
and love is laid out before us.*
(An exceptional loving force: Johanna's story*)*

Beginning as ways to honor, move forward, fulfill a longing for connection and share our beloved as a gift to others, rituals develop into gracious legacies. Death's grieving chaos is not meant to be the last word in any life. The enduring light of those we have lost need not be extinguished – a flame, snuffed out, never to warm us again. Grace continues to whisper through them, weaving its intimate language of tenderness and peace into our rituals, and paving the way for transforming love through the legacies built in their names. One light, once keeping us company in our human life, is traded for another – a gracious, eternal flame, always close to illuminate our way. A new day opens . . . what was lost continues to be found.

beyond grief: moving through the paradox

"The promise of paradox is . . . the promise
that if we replace either-or with both-and,
our lives will become larger and
more filled with light."
Parker Palmer: <u>The Promise of Paradox</u>

Paradox is generally understood as a statement that seems contrary to common sense and yet could perhaps be true. It seems the main intent of a paradox is to point out a truism, even when its elements contradict each other. Nobel Prize-winning physicist, Neils Bohr, goes a step further by stating that though the opposite of a correct statement is a false one, the opposite of a profound truth may actually be another profound truth. (Hans Bohr: "My Father") What interesting, hopeful news: there may be a separate, positive, even profound reality – perhaps only hidden in the creases of our own grief. Discerning the opportunities in a paradox is neither simple, nor readily obvious. When you're a griever, it requires an open, accepting heart – one courageous enough to expand into new territory, to actually welcome some truthful and fearless travel into the unfamiliar. It is challenging, but moving intentionally and thoughtfully into and through a paradox can also be exciting, even uplifting, because by its very nature this action invites us to dynamically participate within our own transformation.

A paradox does suggest that both of its contradictory ideas could be true, but it never promises those truths will exist at the same time. Welcome to the paradox gap – the distance in between. According to Palmer (<u>The Promise of Paradox</u>), the gap is a space that lies "between reality and possibility, between what is and what could and should be." I've lived in that place. On one side of my paradox gap was my once-held truth: *experiencing overwhelming loss promises a life lived in some form of ongoing shadows and suffering.* It was my familiar place, accepted and recognized as reality. On the other side was another truth, waiting to show itself: *profound loss is an intelligent, merciful teacher.* Put another way: *My greatest despair is also grace-filled wisdom.* For years, such an alternate idea was nonexistent, far beyond my ability to consider seriously. It only materialized after I was able to let go of one side of the gap – and slide fully into its center – surrendering my hold on an old truth and accepting the whispers of a Grace call to examine an optional reality.

> *"When you are traveling toward your destiny*
> *in the belly of a paradox, as we all are,*
> *there are no certainties. But the creative*
> *opportunities are boundless.*
> Parker Palmer: <u>The Promise of Paradox</u>

Wholeness has been on my mind since the beginning of my foray into reading, writing, thinking and talking about the interconnections of grief and Grace. It's such a big concept, a bit intimidating with its richness of both opportunity and uncertainty. Like Grace, wholeness has no easy definition; it reflects the layers of complexity abundant within the human experience. During my time wrestling within the contradictions of paradox living, wholeness came to the fore because of the dynamic place it holds in the gap. Wholeness, I learned, begins with vulnerability – with surrendering to the fact that we feel damaged. It is not about existing within the fictitious ideal of perfection; instead it involves accepting, indeed authentically embracing our brokenness. Wholeness demands that we open to the *whole truth* of our lives – its tragedy and comedy, its ugliness and beauty, its drawbacks and possibilities – if we expect to travel our own restorative journey into the fullness of a *whole life, into wholeness*.

When my life was in pieces, fractured by loss and buckled tightly onto grief's roller coaster, I had no concept of the fullness of a whole life. I felt irretrievably injured, incomplete, broken and fully vested in the grief side of a paradox. And then, as it will, subtle grief began to displace the more intense, acute grief. I took some deeper breaths, unclenched the tight, resisting hold on my heart, let my mind wander and explore different choices and new boundaries.

In time, wholeness became a very real goal for my own healing – aiming for a peace-filled space of self-acceptance, where I could compassionately welcome and lovingly hold myself, even in all my messiness. It was in such surrender that I began easing toward the place of *both-and* thinking where wholeness dwells. Embracing it meant advancing past one living truth and toward another – shifting into the gap. The contradictions existing within that space challenged me to look beyond my confirmed, intellectual reality. They directed me to become more transparent to myself, admit to my own longings and then believe I possessed the courage and the power to inhabit the mysterious divide between my present reality and another, equally-profound truth, held in waiting for me.

To access and then delve into life's important paradoxes require we stand purposefully in their gaps, to patiently dwell in the irritating, disquieting impossibilities for a while and then try using some *both-and* reflection. Palmer talks about this space as where we hold "creative tension." That special kind of unease nourishes our ability to first confront old ideas and then entertain and actually create opportunities to challenge our own contradictory truths. The gap is the heart space where Grace encounters grief, where transformation confronts misery. For me, it became a place of decision: which would I use to fuel myself forward – the grief of my present or the compassionate Grace of another reality? They both lived in my heartfelt contradictions. Each was ready to participate with me in the creative authoring of my next reality. The choice was mine.

In <u>Real Magic</u>, Wayne Dyer tells his readers that each of us makes choices about interacting within our created reality, based on how we *feel* about what we *think*. Take a moment and read that line again; it's critical to gap thinking. Once we sink those chosen emotions deeply into our inner most selves, our minds direct our next thoughts and actions to reflect them. In essence, either intentionally or unwittingly, our choices – which have moved from our thinking, to our feeling, to our behaving – translate into our reality, one we accept and live out as our truth. The size and design of our world depends on those truths we consent to call our real world. And, for each of those established truths there is a paradox waiting. The flames of our struggles with our own reality and the flashes of light directing us toward the unfamiliar fires of other possibilities, smolder and flicker as choices within us. When we are ready, they promise to illuminate the darkness of our *either-or* thinking, and light our way into the *both-and* – the deliberations of the gap.

> *"It is truly a great cosmic paradox that*
> *one of the best teachers in all of life*
> *turns out to be death. No person or situation*
> *could ever teach you as much as*
> *death has to teach you."*
> Michael Singer, The Untethered Soul

Grief is born in the seeds of profound life changes, difficult losses . . . the disappearance of who and what we love. It occurs to me that one's relationship with death reflects, in large part, an established relationship with grief. Denial and anger toward one dictates a path of suffering and fear within the other; acceptance of one sets a course for surrendering to the other. Unpacking the role we allow grief to play in situations of irrevocable change, loss and death sets our course for future choices. In Death Be Not Proud by John Gunther, Frances, the author's wife, gives interesting relationship advice concerning dealing with the figure who took their son: "Look Death in the face; . . . it's a kindly face, sad, reluctant, knowing it is not welcome but having to play its part when its line is called, perhaps trying to say 'Come, . . . I understand how you feel, but come – there may be other miracles!'" How do we portray the worst outcome we can conceive for our lives?

Is that outcome a figure named Death – a dark apparition who comes alive clothed in our own fears, armed with the ultimate power over how we will chart the pathways and relationships for our life? Gunther's reflections ask us to think about death differently: to look it in the face, to give ourselves the power to create an authentic relationship with it, and intentionally look for the miracles, the Grace, always available.

Singer, in The Untethered Soul, also puts a different face on death. He names it a friend; an inflexible natural law, without human qualities, who evenhandedly touches our lives while teaching us undeniable lessons. Neither good nor evil, death serves to remind us of our common lot in life: we are all temporary because nothing on this planet we share lasts forever. Kindly, death's dependable assurances that all things will pass help us bear in mind that we have choices and we shouldn't tarry to employ some good ones. How will we live our lives to honor those we love – not only those who are now with us, but also those who have died before us? *Live wholly in the here and now, and be present for it all* is death's powerful message.

And with those words, death hands us another paradox to ponder: an end is a beginning. Death's cosmic finality provides sharply clear and sweetly tender meaning to life. It wrests away our complacencies and hands us another chance to live fully by forcing us to pay close attention to the moment – all those moments where our choice is to either immerse ourselves in being present in the *Now*, or to remain mired in the worry of death's inevitability. Without saying a word, death inexorably provides us, over and over, the opportunity to choose a life – in fear and pain, or in wholeness and Grace. Eckhart

Tolle (Stillness Speaks), shares an idea I have come to understand as one of my gentle and fearless truths: "When you see and accept the impermanent nature of all life forms, a strange sense of peace comes upon you." I believe in that promise of peace. I keep reminding myself to deeply breathe and fully surrender and immerse myself within it as I travel forward, knowing that uncomfortable changes, unexpected losses, and death will all come when they may.

> *"The beauty of embracing deep truths is that you don't have to change your life; you just change how you live your life."*
> Michael Singer: The Untethered Soul

I had been sitting with her for two hours; she, crying while recalling her nightmare, and I, listening and wondering how I might be able to help. Then Veronica said, "When my daughter died, my son used to say we're cursed . . . . Everybody around us dies and it's kind of feeling like that to me now." Though Angela's story, told by her mother, Veronica, is filled with passion and the still-present pain of a suffering parent, it ends with thankfulness, and a family, finally at home and able to honor their beloved child with loving dignity. Still, this story leaves me with unspoken questions: Does Veronica feel cursed because death lingers around her? Because many she has loved so dearly are gone? Because she has survived when her own daughter did not? I didn't ask these questions during our interview because I was concerned they weren't appropriate during her narrative. But this mother's words made me consider how we who've lived through irreversible loss have had to deal with one more layer of grief – the pain of surviving our children. Surely that truth can feel like a curse.

Survivor guilt, I've come to believe, is a very real condition: a tension, distress, even horror one lives when he or she believes each has done something very wrong by surviving a traumatic event. Every parent I interviewed displayed unutterable sadness and dismay surrounding their child's death: some described over and over, in various detail, their immediate disbelief and shock accompanying their child's loss; some shared lingering feelings of guilt or contrition, some tenderly articulated their inability to still comprehend what exactly happened to them, and some felt cursed by the event. Each survivor had heard and felt deeply the words of the well-used statement: it's unnatural to outlive your child. Did we do something wrong? How could our babies, no matter their age, find death before we, their parents? Surely there is something amiss in life's order when parents need to bury their children.

Laurence Gonzales in his work, Surviving Survival, shares a series of profound stories highlighting men and women who faced incredible, personally-challenging situations filled with trauma, grief, sadness, fear and pain – and survived. Bereaved parents hold a very specific place in survival stories. Those of us who remain alive are left to grapple continually with our unanswerable questions, bitter recriminations and uncomfortable interactions with others; they cycle on and on. And grief blossoms – to hijack our hearts, our thoughts and behaviors, and to mire us deeply into living whatever despairing truths we create to describe our reality. Our choice for either wholeness or long-term grief begins here. The decisions we intentionally make, the Grace whispers we either by-pass, deny or answer with ready acceptance, will begin the creation of our future. We are this undeniable paradox: in our weakness is our strength. Within our surrender to the fact that we have no control, no power to turn back time and keep alive what we've lost, lies our courage. And it is within such bravery that the endurance, desire and power to do more than simply survive, rests, ready to flourish.

> *"Wanderer, your footsteps are the*
> *path, and nothing else ..."*
> Antonio Machado: <u>Campos de Castilla</u>

There are countless pathways within any gap between its paradoxical truths. So many choices to go forward, to find yourself in distracting or destructive loops promising comfort and diversions, or to retrace your steps back to the still-familiar truth. It's uncomfortable sitting in our own messes, holding tightly to all the accepted thoughts, emotions and interactions awash in suffering. I remember all too vividly believing that if I disturbed the tender and intricate balance of my own mixture of pain, guilt and hopelessness, I would lose any ability to navigate and balance my way through a life I had acknowledged as my full reality – and if I couldn't do that – well, I would cease to exist. That was my certainty. Though I'd love to say I had visions of brilliantly-lit signs directing me to "Turn here for the Gap" or "This way to Wholeness," I can't. But what I can tell you is that it was only after I stopped relentlessly clinging to my old truth, heralding the darkness and suffering of loss, that I was finally able to dream about my Matthew, the treasured son I lost too soon. There he was, smiling and standing without pain.

It was that gracious dream that softened and opened my heart to the possibility of something more than pain. I began to hear the faint call of another truth, and my own reclamation process bumped and jolted forward in earnest, finding its way into a gap.

Both-and pathways provide a wide and dynamic view; alternate routes and branching arterials give options for travel and lots of opportunities for surprising adventures. It was in Spring when I was able to commit to a radically different kind of path – this time in pilgrimage. I felt called to leap into reinvention, to travel an unfamiliar pathway toward the fullness of a whole life. I said yes to walking *The Way*.

On the Portuguese Camino I met Simon, a Frenchman whose old-soul wisdom helped to remind me of the ultimate responsibility we each carry in directing our lives beyond the darkness of chaos toward the light of harmony. As we talk, I also listen and learn. He turns out to be a true pilgrim; he's made spiritual quests often and tells me that this *Way*, The Camino, is a university of life. He shared his truth, the paradox of our common journey: for the seeking pilgrim, there really is no set Way to travel. What we look for – the absolute and right path we expect for traveling forward – really doesn't exist. For any life traveler, any survivor, lying ahead of us are only the best trails we somehow decide to blaze as we pilgrim on, day by day.

I discover Simon has more books in his backpack than he does clothing. One book he shares over lunch is a volume of verse by the Spanish poet, Machado. The words I find there characterize my own traveling . . . and not only during this trip: looking backwards is a futile and painful exercise; the journey forward is all we have; our own footsteps carve out the channels, the trajectories of those trails into the future of our imagining. Soon, Simon walks on and so do I – going at different paces toward the same destination. In his wake he has left me a little stronger, clearer and more at peace. These words by Antonio Machado are the gift my new friend left with me:

> *"Wanderer, your footsteps are the path, and nothing more;*
> *Wanderer, there is no path, the path is made by walking.*
> *By walking one makes the path, and upon glancing behind*
> *One sees the path that never will be trod again.*
> *Wanderer, there is no path –*
> *Only wakes upon the sea."*

"Proverbs and Songs 29" in <u>Campos de Castilla</u> (1912)

When intense grief stands squarely in the midst of our sadness, directing the moments of a life steeped in the suffering of profound loss, it is sacred time. And there will come another time, equally sanctified, when we realize we need to be at peace with ourselves, to surrender into the unacceptable, and to believe that Grace really does call through our own heartbeats. Then we must begin moving beyond, entering into Machado's world: *Wanderer, your footsteps are the path, and nothing else . . .*

Ways to mend our lives into one of recovery exist within the paradox gaps we are brave enough to recognize, enter and confront. They hover in those *both-and* spaces where the grief of the known encounters the Grace of the possible. They are the wisdom that call us to wholeness, that remind us to be truthful, gentle and fearless as we enter fully into our own healing. They are the whispers of Grace.

- Remember that you have the power to influence your own life. You do not live in either grief or grace because of the whims of life; you have the power to choose and then create your own reality.
- Believe without reservation that acute grief is not forever; when time and love have done their work, intense suffering will change and morph, helping you find light for the journey forward.
- Accept that the pain you feel cannot be circumvented. Grief, in its many iterations, must be experienced. We must go down to be able to push off the bottom and rise again.
- Be open to a loving support community, a safe place with one or many, where you can be fully authentic. Share without reservation your outrage and anxieties, your fears, hopes and joys.
- Hold on to the beauty of the possible even at the blackest end of despair. There will be better times; you will genuinely laugh again without guilt, trust in love, and build on the hope of a different future.
- Have courage. Seek out the places that lie between what is and what can be. Immerse yourself gently and fearlessly into that gap – and know without question that a new, profound truth is possible.
- Establish a daily practice of inviting Grace to be present in and around you. Find a mantra, use prayer, meditation, talking to the angels – whatever brings you healthy, loving, deep comfort.

- Stop trying to organize and plan for a life of the familiar. You are now in the land of the new and different. Open to the *new*; Give *different* a chance to lovingly surprise you.
- Look for mystery and miracles all around you: immerse yourself in the natural world, in ideas, people, art, music – all things that uplift you, that bring love, harmony, surrender and joy into your life.
- Be in gratitude: celebrate the love in your life; tenderly honor those you've lost, and extravagantly cherish whomever and whatever is still present with you.

"Whatever your life situation is, how would you feel if you completely accepted it as it is – right Now?"
Eckhart Tolle: <u>Stillness Speaks</u>

Addendum

Parents tell their Stories

The following stories recount journeys of the courageous. Grief expects to be at the core of the following stories and, indeed, that is how each begins to unfold. The fearful chaos of grief, represented through anger, despair, guilt and deep pain abounds here. But more importantly, what I also encountered, displayed in the words that almost always followed parents' most profound grief statements, were their expressions of love, their descriptions of grace moments. Each child I took in as my own, every story narrated by their heartbroken parents helped to shape and eventually deepen my own understanding of the beauty, mercy, peace and forgiveness that embodies grace. I am honored, humbled and grateful to have shared sacred space and time with these children and their families, and am forever changed because of what each brought to my life.

Marie: Her sweetest gift

We have a quiet room, one with a door that closes out the hushed murmurings of others who also want to quietly talk, study something, or maybe, like me, discover what's in the heart and mind of the person I'm with. This area I've staked out for us has a table, four chairs and two windows - enough space for us to spread out comfortably if we wanted. But we don't . . . spread out. Instead we stay relatively close to face each other across the table. I wonder what he's thinking about his decision to meet me here today. I take a second to speculate how I can make him comfortable. How do I help him know my heart is open to his? We are friends, Greg and I. But there is a kind of cautious air between us because this time we're together so he can share a story that is deeply personal – one I've never heard because he's held it very close to his heart. I decide to turn toward one of the general questions he's agreed to answer but before I can pose one to break the ice, he stops me with a comment that lets me know he has thought about what he wants to say today, and he expects to deliver it his way. So we begin.

Greg's story starts in September of 1986. He is in his second marriage; he has fathered one daughter who is presently living with her mom. Greg is building his life with another and they are happily pregnant with their first child together. He recounts that the pregnancy had some difficulties early on, but those health issues seemed to have smoothed out over time and he was excitedly awaiting the birth of his child. But trouble resurfaced during his wait, and Marie, the new love of Greg's life, was born prematurely. She weighed in at only 3 ½ pounds and was immediately put in the hospital's Intensive Care Unit. Happily the baby's situation improved both rapidly, and seemingly, easily. Marie rallied; she grew stronger and developed well and, after only three weeks in the hospital, was released to go home with her new parents. She was a beloved miracle.

It is a joy to watch Greg's face light up as he describes Marie. She was "pretty incredible," he declares with wide eyes and a happy grin. She smiled early, even rolled over on her own before her amazed parents knew what was happening. Here she was, a premature baby, already mastering so many milestones. Greg's face is full of wonder as he recalls how his tiny baby girl worked so hard to communicate back to him, how earnestly she tried to mimic and answer him with her own special language. It's easy to hear the special, loving bond this dad feels for his child as he speaks softly of her sweet personality: "She wasn't fussy at all; she was very content, very quiet." It is clear he believes his Marie was someone remarkable.

And then, with a subtle shake of his head, Greg shares the beginning of the darkness to follow. He noticed Marie began having difficulties holding down her feedings. Something was not quite right. Not long after the parents had identified this concern, their worst nightmare began to unfold. Greg was heading home early from work and as he drove closer to home, he noticed an emergency vehicle parked close to his house. An earlier 911 call had summoned help; Marie had stopped breathing. At home, Greg found emergency personnel working to save his daughter's life. One of his last memories of Marie is seeing her intubated and placed in an ambulance that would race her to the hospital. Within the hour a doctor joined the anxious parents to tell them Marie was dead. An autopsy followed quickly and the devastated parents, who knew only a little baby who "externally . . . was perfect," were given SIDS as the cause of death. An additional report of chromosome irregularities left bewildered parents to walk away from their daughter holding only the many questions and the chaotic confusion unexpected death leaves in its wake – their dream of a life raising and loving their little girl, lost. How could this be? In September, the gift of a sweet life was given and only 7 ½ weeks later that gift was gone. Profound grief with its companions, guilt, anger and fear, settled deeply in and around Greg.

Greg talks about the following year with a kind of frustrated wonderment. He and his wife heard all the messages of the "right things to do" when one suffers deeply-felt, unexpected loss and they tried things they thought might help. They attended a support group for bereaved parents for a short time and found some comfort. Talking about your story and hearing theirs is helpful, he shares; "You figure out 'I'm not alone.'" As I listen, I also hear a bitterness that bites through Greg's voice each time he remembers how friends and religious acquaintances tried to comfort him during this time. He recalls the phrases as if they were given yesterday and his anger is palpable. "God needed her," and other such platitudes meant to make him feel better by assuring him his beloved daughter was now in "a better place," only made things worse.

But there is no time to sort out and deal with all of grief's colliding emotions because Greg discovers even more strength will be required of him very quickly. Only months after Marie's death the couple discovers they are pregnant again. It is during this usually happy and expectant period in a couple's life that Greg finds himself living in the unbelievably vulnerable and confusing time of deep grief. My baby is dead! Now I'm supposed to make room for another? The medical professionals tell the couple that all the tests and signs are positive for a healthy baby boy; "This will be so much better," they smile. Greg only hears his baby girl being disrespected; it sounds to him as if others are saying his remarkable daughter was somehow not good enough. And it is in this busy, planning time, with no space for mourning or healing, he awaits the birth of his son.

In October, 1987, a healthy baby boy is born into the family. It was a difficult birth and there was a time Greg feared he would also lose his wife, but she survived. And life, as it will do when left to its own, settled into a rhythm for the family. I asked Greg about his life during this time of shaping a new family while still reeling from overwhelming loss. Greg honestly professes his pain, his confusing concern over the resentment of another child brought into his life too soon, his lack of time or energy to fully grieve the daughter he lost, and his anger at religion, and for a God who failed miserably at being the "Father" to whom he once prayed. The beauty of this newest gift, another child, at this time in his life was a hidden treasure – one he couldn't fully appreciate until later. He survives the following years, working hard to be a strong enough father, husband and bread winner to keep his newest family unit together. He admits to me that he never took more than "moments at a time" to grieve, but always remembered his Marie on her birth date with painful tears of loss. As time passed, Greg's marriage disintegrated and, as he has always operated throughout his life, he persevered and began to build again.

My friend has now created a new life with a woman he loves; he tells me he has found peace and recounts with a big smile that he is now happier than ever. I ask him to look in retrospect and share what he has learned about grieving and healing. Greg takes a few moments to think and finally relates that what he believes about his grieving process matches his best hopes for sharing his story with others – the understanding that grief is easier when it is a shared experience. He says losing someone you love is "terrible," and then continues, "but you're not alone. It's not your fault." He adds, with a short laugh, "You'll have bad days and that's OK. You'll have a lot of great days too." Telling and hearing stories aloud makes them real and helps people know that they are not in this awful situation by themselves. Greg's belief, "It hurts to go forward but you have to go forward" describes how he has lived his life since his Marie died over 29 years ago. His wide-eyed smile punctuates his next, loving line. "This is the first year I have not cried on her birthday." Greg's clear message about moving ahead gives hope that all is possible when we take the time to share both our pain and our happiness with others.

As our interview winds down, some personal anecdotes Greg shared earlier lead me to steer our conversation more deeply into situations he has used to learn and grow through his grief. Two very personal accounts indicate that he realizes he has been touched by a power beyond the world we know. "Flashes" of a spiritual presence and irrefutable happenings lead him to know "something's out there." His first description is of a time when his son amazed him with a tender revelation. Greg remembers his son of four or five telling his parents that when he was up in heaven, he saw them. The boy confidently shared that he knew he was meant to come and be with them because they seemed so sad. Greg shares this simple, moving story with tears shimmering in his eyes. How wonderful that the second gift, his son, given to him at a time when grief filled his life, always knew he was meant for Greg.

His next, equally powerful story surrounds his mother's death. Loved ones had been called in anticipation of Greg's mother's passing. They gathered together, spending time with her and each other, as they waited. Hours before her death, he remembers her excitedly calling out to the family – she was seeing someone or something she wanted them to witness with her. As they surrounded her, asking what she wanted them to look at, she indicated a space where no one stood. Looking at each other, they questioned her more. What were they supposed to be seeing? Who was there? Happy and alert, she smiled and joyously declared she was looking at Marie. Greg is quick to note that his mom had no trouble knowing who was physically present in the room; she recognized all the names and faces of her loved ones. Marie, as an unseen presence, neither frightened nor confused his mother. Instead it seemed to give her both joy and peace. Again tears fill Greg's eyes as he recalls the beautiful memory of his mother finally coming face to face with the grandchild she never had the opportunity to meet on earth. And, how amazing it is that this first meeting takes place when Marie's father is in the room with them both. It has been said that when one is in the presence of real healing, there is a grace that hangs in that moment. Greg's story holds such healing grace.

As we close the interview, I ask Greg to tell about something he would like to reclaim. From that space of grief that he inhabited for so long, what would he like to take back? He waits just a moment and then leans back in his chair. Quietly he lifts his hands and places them together near his heart. "Just hold her again," he murmurs. "That's what I know of her. That she would snuggle up to sleep right here," he continues, gently moving the flat of one hand on his chest. We sit for another moment in silence, and I ask Greg what one last thing he might like to say about his daughter. He answers with loving assurance that his son would not have been born without Marie's life. It is on this lovely idea of Marie's sweetest gift that we end.

Zach: Zach's lasting legacy

I pull up to Kristin and Larry's home and break into a grin. I don't have to look at the house number; I know I am in the right place: a sparkly reindeer positioned close to the small glittering replica of a rooftop chimney, a wooden bench and festive, green wreaths decorating the front of the house all call out a welcome to family and visitors alike. A smiling Kristin opens the door to bring me inside where I meet Larry and am ushered into rooms that are thoroughly and intimately lived in. Graciously, Kristin and Larry give me permission to spend a little time to soak in an environment crafted with the needs and hopes of children at its core. This is a home created for a family – its walls awash in family memories; a dining table whose complete top is the collection of well-loved, preserved photos; and various wood pieces lovingly-fashioned by Kristin's father are all reminders of the adage that home is where the heart lives. A wood-burning fireplace merrily warms the room in which we three finally land. As we begin, the couple settles side by side, close enough to hold hands, and Kristin starts with a wish.

"I want, after 22 years, for there to be a little bit more about the lessons we've learned rather than the trauma of the story." The agonizing grief surrounding her son's death event, which once was all anyone could really concentrate on, has softened and, according to his parents, no longer defines their memory of Zach. "That wouldn't be reclaiming hope for people – to think that after 22 years you're still focused on that day," Kristin continues. Her family lives a different reality now, one that was definitely created with the impacts of Zach's life and death in its mix, but not one that is consumed with the overwhelming pain of his death.

Zach was born on July 18, 1990, to a pair of kind, smart overachievers who were also "young and clueless," according to a nostalgic Kristin. An upwardly mobile couple, Larry and Kristin were both studying for different degrees at Colorado State University as well as working full time. After Zach's birth they realized they were going to need support to tame the incredibly busy lifestyle they found themselves living. They sought help and found it in two family members who happily took on the co-raising responsibilities of a much-loved baby boy. Family life was full and joyful. Kristin recounts that Zach was a remarkable child who taught them every day. A calm, gorgeous baby with piercing blue eyes and blonde curly hair, he was "dang cute!" Larry quietly recalls that his son had a kind of special sense about him. He and Kristin share situations to punctuate the gentle and surprising instincts of a son who didn't demand much from anyone, but just seemed to intuit the needs of all around him. "One size didn't fit all" Kristin states, relating how Zach adapted himself to those who cared for and loved him. Most everyone who spent quality time with this remarkable toddler commented about how well he read situations, understanding what others needed from him and then giving them those needs as gifts. Kristin grins through her tears, sharing how Zach gleefully gave his dad the gift of "finding everything he did hysterical." Joyful belly laughs often rang through the house – whether it was when Larry bounced Zach higher and faster, tossing him in the air, or during those times he belted out some favorite rock songs just for his son's delight. Loving parents paint the picture of a happy, spirited little boy as if he were still only a room away.

Zach was the first grandchild on both sides of the family. "He was so deeply loved . . . so treasured," Kristin says wistfully. Kristin's grandmother, Dorothea, was one of Zach's caregivers. "Grandma Dorothy" and Zach share a birth date and Kristin calls their relationship "mystical." Grandma set up her kitchen just for him and the toddler loved the freedom to play, create and discover to his heart's content everything available in the lower cabinets, cheerios and all. When his grandma had a terrible fall, requiring her to wear an apparatus to hold her bones in place with pins and bolts, eighteen-month-old Zach demonstrated his innate gift of reading people and situations by behaving so gently and perceptively around his grandmother that she was able to continue to care for him even as she healed from the break. Zach's second extra caregiver was Larry's sister, Lori, who turned 21 only one day after Zach was born. Though still young, she was amazingly loving and responsible in her care of her nephew. Throughout his short time in this world, Zach brought out the best in every adult around him. Intuitive, sensitive and unselfish are not the qualities generally ascribed to a toddler, but it is clear to any who knew him, Zach was anything but ordinary. He touched the lives of his parents in very special ways, leaving them with a lasting legacy – the continuing, very real memories of their son's extraordinary gift of freely-given unconditional love. "Me love you," Zach reminds, even today, all who love him.

Kristin and Larry's lifestyle has transformed since the traumatic death of their first born. Zach was welcomed into the hearts and home of bright, young parents in the midst of building their future. They kept an open-door policy into their home for their many friends and family; they were carefree, seeking time to play as well as develop their own deepening relationship; they were hard workers, enjoying all the opportunities and possibilities that education and economic stability could provide; they were safely and lovingly raising their son together with affectionate, responsible, family helpers. They were happily positioned for success, professionally and personally. And even though everything was perfectly in place, July 14, 1993, happened, and Zach died.

Grief reveals you, Kristin states, sharing a favorite thought from John Green's *The Fault in our Stars*. Through his short lifespan, Zach established an indelible love-filled legacy for his parents and their eventual family. His ongoing bequest has been grief's revelation through the life choices of his parents. "I've changed in almost every way imaginable . . . and it's sad in some ways and hopeful and transformational in other ways," Kristin clears her throat and wipes at tears as the next chapter in this couple's story begins to unfold, rich with hope, transformation and worry – all those changes she and Larry have forged and embraced since Zach's death.

Not too long after their son's death, Larry and Kristin sought out a support group offered by the organization, Compassionate Friends, and with that choice came some hope and relief. They found comfort telling their story and building friendships with others who understood an enduring, shared pain; eventually they became leaders within the group. It was during that time the experience of Candlelight Vigils – where a family pauses to remember with tenderness a life lost, and honor the child who profoundly touched and changed their lives – became a touchstone for both Larry and Kristin. Those yearly vigils were so transformational for the bereaved couple that they were instrumental in establishing similar memorializing traditions in Fort Collins, where they moved in the late 90's.

Before Zach's death there was no thought of having more children; he was enough and life was wonderfully full. But his loss immediately collided with deeply felt emotions: "must quit job; must have babies – lots of them; there was this huge need to be needed," Kristin remembers. So, against all counselor recommendations, the couple quickly became pregnant. Within the first year of Zach's passing, Kali is born, July 2, 1994, and the family begins to take on its new shape. In a grief-revealing decision, Kristin leaves the corporate world behind, moving to a career where she could work nights. We became the sole caretakers of our kids, Larry reports as one of the couple's first major life shifts; he takes the nights while Kristin stays the totally-available parent each day. And their family continues to grow. In 1996, Josh joins his sister, followed by Cooper in 1998, and eventually Zoe rounds out their family with her birth in July of 2005.

As a way to continue reclaiming hope in the midst of old memories and a growing, busy family life, the couple maintains involvement with Compassionate Friends as well as remains a helping presence in the organization of local Candlelight Vigils. "It's like giving back," Larry comments. The support they first felt over 20 years ago is offered today through this loving tradition, a tangible gift Larry and Kristin humbly and happily provide to parents, who like themselves, have lost a child. Grief continued to reveal itself by fueling Kristin to answer a call – acting on opportunities to offer her own natural gifts of understanding, intuition and loving service to others. In 2008, with two other women, she was instrumental in the organization of a local support group, a kind of loving community, for bereaved parents named 3 Hopeful Hearts. She labels it incredible work and finds herself consistently touched by parents who courageously transform their own grief through authentically sharing their understanding of life and death with one another, forming mentoring partnerships, and allowing themselves to welcome moments of real joy.

Always in awe of a person's ability to survive the loss of a child, Kristen remains acutely aware of the reality that children die even though they have caring, responsible parents. "Amazing people lose children," she firmly states; "you can be the best parent possible and tragedy can still find you." And it is that belief which propels her to continue the tender and heart-wrenching work of unreservedly supporting others who lose their children. Zach's legacy of love lives again, hopeful and transformative, each time others in grief are unconditionally supported, given the opportunity to share their pain, and helped to honor and remember their lost children.

Kristin looks at Larry as she finds the words to express a deeply-felt truth: Zach's legacy is in everything. "It's in our worry about our other children, in our intentional messages to our children, in our fears for our children, and in us always being available to our kids – his four brothers and sisters – the children who might not have been born if he had lived. Kids always come first; I'm never going to miss another memory," Kristin asserts. "The kids' schedules, needs, desires should always trump our needs or whatever . . . ." And because they no longer pursue friendships in the same ways they once did, sometimes it's lonely to watch the kids grow up and make their way outside of the home. "The loss of Zach is such an unfillable void that I've tried to fill it in ways that are completely unrealistic," Kristin says softly as she brushes at the tears that continue to gather. Looking around, gazing at the walls filled to overflowing with family memorabilia, she describes herself and Larry as the home; "that has been our choice" over the past 22 years. "We are open to all the needs of our children . . . they are always more important than ours." Zach's short time with them left Kristin and Larry with an unshakeable understanding: they have to live in the present with their children, to enjoy life together in the here and now, no matter what.

Shrugging her shoulders Kristin admits with some sadness, "I miss the carefree person I once was. My level of fear is completely unreasonable." We bump into unhealthy times, Larry responds, but he also believes they don't overdo it and ride there all the time. It's just that in an instant life can change. It's the not knowing . . . the consistent worry that something bad is bound to happen that plagues her. But Larry chooses another path and they laugh about their differences. His more hopeful self believes that most likely things will be alright and it is this delicate balance between hope and dread that keeps the couple centered as they continue their own journey through their most profound loss.

Kristin thoughtfully ponders how Zach's death and resulting legacy have affected their other children. With a small laugh and a large amount of pride, she points to the acceptance and kindnesses given to her by her other children. They let me be crazy and obsessive about their safety, she says with a kind of awe. They may roll their eyes or tell her she's being unreasonable – that her issues are not their deal – but "they don't resent Zach for my craziness." She confesses an amazement that they don't blame him for her actions, for all those demands and boundaries that she instigates. And, most importantly, they still show up. They take time out of their busy, young lives to honor the brother they never knew. I can count on Zach's brothers and sisters to join us at the Candlelight Vigil, say Zach's name, light a candle, and pay tribute to his importance in our family, Kristin shares with a proud smile. Zach's legacy lives on in the sensitivity, understanding and loving gift-giving of his family.

I'm reminded of another John Green line from *The Fault in our Stars*: "That's the thing about pain; it demands to be felt." Grief calls forth its pain to make demands from those who live it, and the gracious transformation of that same grief is revealed through their life choices. Its demands can buckle a fence beyond redemption, or its reclaiming, revealed decisions can brace that same fence so strongly that no matter the wind velocity, grief can only leave scars. Kristin points out the kitchen's sliding glass door toward a fence that is braced with a series of 2x4's and makes the comparison that she and Larry are like that fence; we're not pretty but we're still standing. The neighbors don't see this side of the fence; people don't know what it's like – what we've been through, she continues. Even though she can't be a new fence, Kristin recognizes, without a doubt, she is standing because of her own supportive communities: her kids, loving friends, special work colleagues and Larry – "Larry braces me," she affirms. She and Larry look out at the scarred and supported fence that shields and separates their home from others, then turn slightly and smile knowingly at each other.

Derek: For everything a time – to grieve, to wait, to heal

The sun shines radiantly around the area I've secured for our meeting. Two of the room's four sides have clear windows, filling three quarters of their wall space. I'm treated to a gorgeous, unobstructed view of a cloudless, deeply blue sky and crystalline snow that brightly clings to tree trunks, winking decoratively from their branches. The recent snowfall still covers the playground equipment located just outside the west facing window – its playhouse barely visible, swing seats leaden with white mounds and a slide that is streaked with white fingers of snow. I've decided that Trey and Melinda should have the opportunity to witness beauty around them as we talk, so I take a seat with my back to the window. The dazzling scene they will face as we talk may help to gentle the pain of the story they have come to tell. I take a gamble that having the playground in their site line, reminding them that their son, Derek Earl, will never play there, won't somehow distract them. Washed in sunlight's warmth I settle in. Soon a smiling Melinda, with husband Trey, enters and they sit next to each other, across the table from me. Anticipating a need, Melinda discovers she has no Kleenex and I go on a successful search. And, finally, we face that moment of awkwardness when the storytellers have to begin the account of their worst nightmare while deciding if and how much they can trust their listener to truly understand. In <u>When the Heart Waits,</u> Sue Monk Kidd writes that each of us needs to find our own unique ways of expressing the despairing pain and chaos inside, and knowing the truth of that statement I decide to simply wait.

Melinda begins by sharing her intention of talking about time and its importance in their story. "The biggest thing is the amount of time," Melinda reports. "We spent . . . probably more time preparing and trying . . . than we did actually being pregnant." Though Melinda brought her daughter, Jammie, born in 1997, into her marriage to Trey, the couple was looking forward to having more children together. Eighteen long months after they first begin, they become pregnant. "Those were a long eighteen months," Melinda reports. "When you're trying to make a baby, it doesn't just go month by month; it's week by week, and sometimes even day by day. Once you start trying to time things . . . it makes for a long, constant process." The summer of 2011 finds them pregnant and waiting again – this time, happily.

The couple joyfully includes friends and family in their hopes and dreams for their new baby. But much too soon, it's over. After only 3 ½ weeks, she miscarried. Though there was great sadness, Melinda and Trey felt the comfort of sharing their sorrow with those same others who had helped them celebrate their earlier joy. "It was devastating." Melinda asserts. "But we didn't really let that derail us. We kept on going right down the fertility treatments . . . and planning." She nods toward her husband and remarks that, in time, Trey was able to label the miscarriage as "progress." Now the doctor was able to assure them that they could be pregnant – all they had to do was keep Melinda pregnant. A few months later they discover they are again pregnant. But this time, they decide to wait before giving others their news. Together, they begin preparing for their baby, knowing they want to go slowly. The timing to include others just isn't right yet.

Throughout the first trimester they wait, keeping their news hidden, protected – until a safe number of weeks have passed. Holiday and special family times have them putting off telling others throughout the rest of that year. They recall how difficult the sharp curves of the emotional and physical ups and downs of 2011 were to navigate. The year held both family and professional times of deep sadness; it was also still full of the memory of their unexpected miscarriage, an awareness resting just below the surface of this new, happy, but anxious time of their latest, secret pregnancy. They hold their unborn close to their hearts, joyously loving it while also quietly keeping the fact of another pregnancy to themselves. It seemed wise and somehow safer to wait. Melinda talks more about their decision: if they had known, their family and friends could have grown with them in the excitement, but then "they would also have felt the heartache we felt – why would I want that?" Then, in February of 2012, all the latest lab results and ultrasound were positive and confirming; Melinda and Trey feel confident in celebrating their happy news with family and friends. The time was finally right. "We thought we were safe," Melinda softly states with tears in her eyes. We were in the midst of "planning our forever" and then reality shifted, Trey quietly adds. Only 2 ½ weeks later, on February 22, 2012, Derek Earl, their beloved son, is stillborn.

The parents were stunned; their dreams, so closely held to their hearts, lost. Derek Earl was neither a full-term baby, nor was he a miscarriage; "it's like he didn't count!" Melinda announces emotionally. The couple felt incredibly isolated in their grief. Trey describes how he and Melinda just tried to keep breathing. "You can only take so much . . . and then you go on auto pilot." Though the couple remembers the many sweet times they planned and celebrated together during those twenty-two weeks with their growing baby, they never observed it outwardly, never included others into their joy. Since they hadn't shared their excited anticipation with others, they found themselves alone in their grief. "It wasn't real for anyone else," Trey states. "It never became real for them," he speaks of their family and friends, "and he's really not real to them now."

They each recall times when words and facial expressions of loved ones and strangers alike let them know their grief wasn't understood. There was the hospital chaplain who thoughtlessly assures them that "at least you don't have to spend four months in a NICU;" a father who declares, "Are you not over that yet;" and the various reactions of others around them who so clearly show they think the couple is still "wallowing in their grief." So much misunderstanding, so many hurtful responses only serve to remind the couple that they are truly alone in their suffering. "We carry this every day and we're going to carry him every day for the rest of our lives." Four years later, there are still moments in the midst of family and friends where they feel the same raw isolation they experienced when they first lost Derek Earl. "If they were more vested, they would be more understanding," the couple shares with sadness.

The profound grief of losing a child carries with it a whole host of guilt-ridden, angry and helpless "what ifs," no matter when, where or how that loss occurs. Melinda and Trey sometimes find themselves being swept along the currents of that emotional tidal wave. Calling herself *"what if* by nature," Melinda, a nurse, continues to question what might have happened during that February day to have brought about a different outcome. *What if* she had called the doctor earlier in the day; *what if* the hospital's health professionals felt the same sense of urgency about the pregnancy as Derek's parents; *what if* her cervix had been checked earlier; *what if* she had been welcomed immediately into the hospital's ER for triage; *what if* they hadn't had to spend those twenty extra minutes in OB admissions; *what if* her water hadn't broken; *what if* the Wyoming wind hadn't been so brutally fierce, shutting down the interstate to Denver? *What if* the timing of all these things surrounding Derek Earl's birth day had unfolded differently? The ghosts of *what ifs* are covered in sharp edges, often keeping those who most need balance and healing from moving around and beyond them. It is years later, when searching for ideas to support another, that Melinda and Trey finally discover a way to begin quieting the whispers of their own ghosts and find a new path toward healing.

The couple goes into survival mode over those next years. They carry their sadness as best they can by putting one foot in front of the other. They begin to experience more of what they can call normal days, but admit that they weren't actually dealing with their grief. "We put it (our grief) in a box and stuck it in the closet," says a tearful Melinda. Still, she and Trey steadily work to rebuild, adding to their lives by continuing to prepare for and have more children. They have their second son, Liam, in October of 2013, and then their daughter, Kennedy, in June, 2015. Then, in 2014, the couple comes to grips with a truth: "we thought we were healed," Trey shares, a catch in his voice; "we thought we were passed it." But when Melinda's friend loses a son, the couple's grief rushes to the surface. With a short laugh and more tears, Melinda admits in a kind of awe, "It ripped our scab open and let us know we weren't alone. . . . it's been three years and it (the grief) is the same as it was when we first put it out of sight." Trey goes on to talk about what they discovered as they were living through their friend's loss. "It made it all fresh . . . I was right there at the beginning again. We'd never healed; we'd never moved on." Melinda thoughtfully refers to her feelings as a kind of "pseudo grief." She tearfully continues, "I was devastated for her, but it's my pain I'm feeling! If she hadn't lost her baby I don't know where we would be. . . . We wouldn't have taken care of ourselves."

The time was right. Melinda begins to explore possible resources to help her friend through the devastating loss they now have in common. It is during this time in September of 2014 that Melinda and Trey discover 3

Hopeful Hearts. What began as a gifting opportunity to another is now an ongoing, very real gift for each of them. They both acknowledge how helpful this supportive community has been in their walk toward healing. This last year has been their best; they have been around people who are traveling similar paths. "It's been a real blessing to be able to relax and take off the masks we wear to hide, to lessen, our grief," Melinda explains. Attending the support group to share and hear others' stories is difficult but it's through those stories that they finally begin to realize they aren't alone. Trey calls their time in the group wonderful and enlightening: "when you have something that's all sharp edges and cuts you every time you touch it . . . the more familiar you get with it, the less you cut yourself . . . the less you bleed."

The couple continues to change and grow in positive ways, but it isn't always easy. Real anger and pain surrounding Derek Earl's death still survive. Once devout, Melinda talks about her anger toward the God she sent prayers to daily, the God she believed was benevolent and loving, the God she thought had the power to change the outcome; "I felt I was doing everything that needed to be done," she says of her prayer life. Even though Melinda wants her kids to have the "childlike" faith she once had, she says Derek Earl's death has taken that kind of faith from her. "I can't unknow what I know," Melinda reflects. Derek still died, they still grieve, and all the ugly *what if* and *why* questions remain. She recalls continuing to go to church after both the miscarriage and Derek Earl's death in an attempt to feel the spirit move within her again. She describes the picture of her leaving her car far back in the parking lot so that during her walk toward the front doors of the church she could intentionally, like Ironman, put on pieces of armor, one by one, to protect her before she enters the service. About fourteen months ago she decided to no longer attend a church. She's afraid she won't ever experience that deep faith she once loved, but Melinda is hopeful that when she and Trey move to Alabama, what she calls the "bible belt," she might again regain her belief.

Now Melinda talks about her decision to no longer live in a fear-based world. She's come to realize that she isn't able to control everything; she wants to let go of fear and put the *what ifs* behind her. "I am more detached on what I have no control over and more attentive on our here and now," she confirms. Mother of three living children, she wants to live life in a loving today. No one who is arguing can leave the house; loved ones are always kissed and told "I love you." Seat belts are double and triple checked and attention is paid to each and every member of the family. Melinda acknowledges there are many things out of her control – "It is what it is" – but she also believes that if she takes the time to be supportive and nurturing, no matter what happens, those she loves will always know they are cherished.

Trey and Melinda treasure their time, experiences, and relationships with others in their grief support group. "An unexpected part of our grief journey is to be able to give back and help and be a support to others. I would not have ever known that supporting others would benefit us had it not be for 3 Hopeful Hearts," Trey asserts. The couple talks about some of the important things they have learned through the help and counsel of others: Acknowledge those who are gone; talk about them; say their names. Your life will be changed fundamentally and forever. Be genuine. You don't have to fix anyone or anything, just be in the trenches with them. Find something to honor your child that will also help you heal, and don't be afraid to share your pain with others. Trey gently describes his understanding of sharing grief, "You're taking everybody else's weight . . . and it's probably not as heavy to you as it is to them, but you know, they're taking some of your weight too." The weight of a parent's grief is something you can move – not away from – but on from.

On Derek's first year's death date, Melinda decided that "this day has to be different." She posted her heart-felt story of loss on Facebook; she needed people to acknowledge his presence in their world. The responses she received were beyond her expectations. "They gave me exactly what I needed," she says smiling through more tears. "We have four children," the couple reminds me. Derek Earl will forever be honored as a very real and ongoing presence in their lives. The time will always be right to speak his name, to graciously share grief's weight . . . and to move forward.

Kirsten: A journey for two

We are in a corner room, Pat and I, with windows taking up the majority of two walls. The day, once sunny, is growing cloudy, more windy and colder, but I want to keep the shades up to let in at least some manner of natural brightness. I feel as if we will need light around us as we talk about the profound loss that brings Pat into my life. She surprises me by telling me she has just finished my memoir, <u>Letters for Grace</u>, and follows with a statement of sympathy for my loss. Her choice to begin our time together with such genuine kindness reminds me of something I hold as true: when bereaved parents are together there is a bond, both implicit and appreciated, that connects them. Authentic listening, generous words, gentle smiles and warm hugs are natural expressions of understanding that happen without plan or expectation. Because Pat and I have walked some common steps on our individual grief journeys, I sense her trust in my desire to listen, discern and accept the tender story she is ready to share. I am grateful. So on this raw day, where clouds begin to threaten snow through patches of weakening sunlight, Pat settles in to begin the tale she does not easily tell.

At the core of Pat's story is an intelligent, generous, headstrong tomboy – her daughter, Kirsten. Kirsten's life and death was a series of transitions – of starts and stops, of hopes and disappointments, and ultimately of courage and love. Born in the late 60's, Kirsten begins early to assert her independence. In elementary school she starts what will become her practice of initiating changes – one of the first is deciding others should now call her by her middle name, Lee. Defining who she thinks she might be – who she wants to be – on her own terms, becomes a hallmark of a growing and changing Kirstin Lee. "She was more interested in GI Joe than Barbie; she loved cowboy things," Pat shares with a smile. As she enters her teen years, she grows more and more difficult; Pat affectionately calls her beloved daughter the "teenager from hell." Extremely bright and capable, Kirstin "never liked being told what to do," and often uses her considerable creative nature to find ways to "land . . . in trouble." In time the path Kirstin chooses to follow is worrisome enough for Pat to arrange what grows into long-term therapy for the rebellious teen.

In her late teens Kirstin plunges headlong into more change. Her behavior continues to land her in more and deeper trouble. Eventually she begins drinking, and before she grows into her twenties she takes on a new name – Chris. Though even as an adult she never legally changes her name, Kirstin becomes Chris for the rest of her life. Pat acknowledges that she became aware of her daughter's identity issues when Chris is still a teenager. Chris finally comes out to everyone in her mid-twenties. Pat is reflective: "I was not surprised. We (the family) accepted her as she was. I would not have chosen it for her because it made her life a lot more difficult. And it's too bad it couldn't have been these days instead of twenty some years ago." Then she adds hopefully, "But that had to have been a relief for her, I think, to finally resolve that dilemma and stop struggling with it."

Times continue to be turbulent for Chris. Her drinking persists as does her frustration, expressed through poor decision making and defiant behaviors. Unable to find peace, she stays on a path to eventual alcoholism. With little money and no evident plan, Chris initiates another change, a major one: she packs up and moves on her own to a small town in northern Wisconsin. Perhaps she is hoping to leave her troubles behind; maybe she no longer wants to depend on the ongoing help, as well as the advice and censures of loved ones; it might be that traveling to the unfamiliar for a new beginning seems the best way to try again to define the person she wants to be. Pat indicates that she isn't totally certain of Chris' reasoning for that big change and her sadness for her daughter's troubled life is palpable.

"Most of her jobs were atypical," Pat says as she remembers how Chris chooses to make a living once she gets to Wisconsin. She lands work at a dairy farm and finds the job a good fit. Chris lives on the property, milks the cows and masters all the other chores necessary to be a good farmhand. When the farm is sold, Pat recalls how sad Chris is, not only because she must find another job but because she felt a real belonging there – "she loved it." Chris chooses more businesses where she is often the only young woman. Over the years she finds work at oil change shops, auto parts stores and finally at a place where large rigs are refurbished. She establishes herself competently in each position, and is eventually given her own work space where she can proudly lay out and use her own tools.

With no small pride, Pat tells of her daughter's fight out of alcoholism. Realizing she can't be the person she wants to be if she remains caught in addiction, Chris signs herself into a treatment center when she is thirty-four. Ninety days later she emerges clean – and stays that way for the rest of her life. Free of her disease, Chris more easily extends herself to others and a loving friendship unfolds with her mother. Pat recalls her daughter's desire: "she really wanted to be a drug and alcohol counselor," to take advantage of all of her own counseling experiences and turn them into ways of helping others. Pat lovingly asserts that after spending time with her sober, adult daughter and her Wisconsin friends, she comes to understand Kirsten/Lee/Chris in her wholeness. Not only is Chris still some of the old behaviors, her mother recounts with light laughter, she is also an intelligent person with a great sense of humor, a generous nature, an ability to authentically listen and unselfishly empathize with others, and a woman of enormous courage. Having "been there and done that" in her own life, Chris could have been able to put all those skills to very good use. But, even though she tries to make her dream a reality, it wasn't to be.

As the years go by Pat realizes her daughter will be remaining in Wisconsin. In 2011, she buys a small house in the area and sets it up so her independent daughter can afford to rent it and settle in. Making certain she has a safe place to live is important to Pat and she is happy to find that Chris takes pride in having, repairing, and caring for her own home. "I'm so glad I bought that house," Pat smiles. "It made the last few years of her life so much better." Over the next two years she visits Chris, learning to know and work with her daughter anew . . . and building, not only a new deck the two women constructed together for the house, but also a wonderful, fresh relationship they could celebrate. "I've always loved her. I'm so glad that she was able to quit drinking and we became best friends," Pat shares; they forgave each other all those difficult things people who care for each other do in the name of love. All the while, Chris continues to create a life, building friendships and finding some peace as a capable person who has much to give.

In the summer of 2013, Chris goes to the local emergency room with a bloody cough and chest pain. Not long after, Pat receives one of those calls every parent fears – her child has been diagnosed with a life-threatening disease. By the end of July Pat has moved into Chris' home as her daughter's caregiver where she will remain for the next ten months, until Kirsten's death from lung cancer on May 10, 2014. Together they set up a household, mother and daughter, and begin their side-by-side walk toward the inevitable. Pat tearfully recalls the two suicide attempts Chris made while she was still drinking to point out the drastic reversal in the younger woman's life. *Chris: "There were so many times I wanted to die and now I want to live and I'm going to die."* In a tight voice, Pat finishes, "It wasn't fair." The time of care giving held so much for these two who were traveling their individual grieving journeys. Chris makes lists – one after another – of those many things she wants to get done around her beloved home, and her mother relishes being up to all the tasks. Pat remembers the two of them fixing things – working on completing projects, checking each one of them off the lists with smiles and some wonder, and beginning the next. Chris helps as long as she is able and enjoys taking pictures of their shared work, occasionally looking at her mom with pride and appreciation, saying, *"I didn't know you knew how to. . . ."*

The hardest time of their individual lives becomes a time of courage for each, individually – a time of learning, of love and understanding for the two, together. Northern Wisconsin's winter of 2013/14 was one for the record books. Pat and Chris hunker down in their home as the Polar Vortex sweeps across the terrain. Cold, dark times surround them. Chris suffers her treatments, six rounds of Chemo in all. "I would have loved for her to come back here (Fort Collins), and done everything back here, but that wasn't her home. . . . She wanted to die at home." And though in our kindest moments we know they do more harm than good, the unending list of what if's that plague any caregiver, also haunt Pat: "Should I have done things differently? Would a different doctor have been better?" There are no answers. Pat does the best she can; she continues the journey with love. Finally, she talks Chris into coming back to Colorado while she can still travel; they settle on a holiday visit. Pat thinks of it as closure – the last family Christmas. Though they don't stay long, Pat is able to visit her own home and help give the Colorado family and friends who love Chris the time to say good-bye.

They return to the frigid and drear Midwest, and life picks up where it left off before the holiday. Pat remembers that, in time, she and Chris begin planning her daughter's memorial service. Chris records music for her own service and even starts good-bye letters to some special people. Pat creates her daughter's obituary and shares it with her; it is a reflection – a testament to the important person she has become over her short life. Finally, Chris loses the use of her legs. Her cancer has metastasized to her brain and spinal column and though radiation treatments relieve some of the pain and give her minimal use of her legs again, relief doesn't last long. She ends up in a wheelchair. Much of this time as she watches her daughter grow more and more frail, Pat is creating a special gift for her beloved girl. Chris has always been a Harley Davidson fan. She owns and enjoys wearing her Harley t-shirts. Pat earlier asked Chris if she'd like a quilt made of some of those shirts to keep her warm during the Wisconsin winter. Though it took her a while to decide which shirts to give to the project, Chris finally turns some over to Pat and before the spring, a lovingly-crafted gift, the Harley t-shirt quilt, is ready to spread across Chris' shoulders. Ultimately, in the spring of the year, a few months before her death, Pat brings Hospice in to help. "Hospice is remarkable," Pat says with a gentle smile, her voice catching. The vital human resources they supply provide the needed support for Pat to walk through the final months of her daughter's life.

Kirsten Lee was cremated in the Spring of 2014. The family held a service for her in the mountains. Her ashes, the remains of this vital, forty-six year old woman, reside in various places and with different people who love her. Pat will always keep some with her, but also knows that when the time is right she will place the rest in a well-loved spot where Chris' father's ashes were originally spread; "that's what she wanted," she acknowledges. Life since her daughter's death has been lonely. So often "people don't understand what the loss of a child is like," Pat articulates. "It's the way it is . . . they just don't get it . . . I'm lonely. I miss the life I used to have. It's never coming back."

"I watched her fade," Pat remembers wistfully. Her grief is still raw; she misses the closeness she and Chris shared not that long ago. "I don't want people to forget her – she mattered!" Pat states, pain in her voice. She has memorialized Chris' Facebook page so that people can still post, still "talk" to the Chris they remember. She also discovered a way to hear from her daughter, through FB, for a year after her death. The first year anniversary of Chris' death fell on Mother's Day and because she had checked the right FB box, a surprised and grateful Pat received a Mother's Day greeting from Chris, sent before her death. Having talked with others who have also lost children, Pat is aware that in time the pain is supposed to get "softer." But now she is surrounded by the sharp edges of ever-present grief. "It feels like I shouldn't ever get better. If I really, really loved her and missed her, I would never get better." But then, Pat smiles through tears and continues: "And she would say, *'Mom! No! That's not what I want you to do.'*" It's as if Chris is reminding her mother that reclaiming hope in life is not about getting over, but staying open - to the aliveness beyond the next thought, the next question, the next doorway, the next smile and extended hand. Out of the wreckage that is profound loss, something surprising will rise when we open to it.

There are ancient religions, belief systems, whose premise is that our humanness is not simply our form or body, but something much more divine, guided by forces beyond our understanding, but always at work within the universe. As I recall Pat quietly talking about Chris fading from her life, I think of the connections between that concept and her story. While Chris' human body was failing, a vital, sacred relationship was growing. Mother and daughter created, laughed and cried together; they had courageous and forgiving conversations; they built tangible and transformative connections where beauty and love still thrive. Though Pat might not have gotten one of her daughter's special good-bye letters, through those months when they walked that fading, human path together, she was able to hear the two most important messages this mother could want. "I know she loved me . . . and thought I was a wonderful mom." Writer Anne Lamott calls hope a conversation. The conversations between Pat and her beloved daughter are surely the loving truths, the gifts, of which hope and grace are made.

James: I know some day I'll see him again

It's Valentine's Day. The sky is cloudy and there are bursts of a brisk February wind blowing tree branches as I make my way into where I'm to meet Cathy and Jeff for our interview. I'm struck by parallels between the meaning of today's annual celebration and the meaning of the story I'm meant to hear on this day, told by a mother who tragically lost this son, more than once. Valentine's Day is synonymous with love - of believing in love's possibilities, and of gifting others in the name of love. Legend has it that this February holiday originated to honor Saint Valentinus, a priest of Rome, imprisoned for performing acts against Roman law. During his confinement, it is written that he displayed an unselfish act of love for another before his death. Cathy's story is of a son, also imprisoned for a crime against the law. Once a troubled, confused, impressionable and angry teen, James eventually also uses his time in prison productively – to learn and grow into a more creative, gracious, and unselfish man. On this day known for its historical place in all the many forms of love, I listen to a love-filled story about a son, James LeRoy.

Cathy begins this first story in 1997: Michael, her oldest son, has moved out and is living with his grandparents, while James, seventeen, is still at home with his mother. Life is far from easy. "He was hanging with the wrong kids!" Cathy asserts strongly. And her story of a summer gone very wrong begins to unfold: Its early summer and James is the driver, his car filled with three other boys. They make the decision to stop for and pick up an adult who has alcohol and is willing to share not only it, but also his pain pills with the teens. The story turns even more ugly. Before the night ends, the man is stabbed to death by the oldest boy, nineteen, and to show solidarity with his friend, James, who has a gun, shoots at the already-dead man. The four boys leave the body and in his haste to get away, James inadvertently drives over it. During the following few months, Cathy grows more and more confused about the drastic changes in her son's behavior. He isolates even more and begins drinking and using drugs heavily. Then, in August, James is arrested. Cathy is called to the county jail where she finally discovers the reason for her son's disturbing behavior.

A young, single mom with limited resources, Cathy is overwhelmed by the fear and confusion of what might lie ahead; she finds herself totally immersed in denial, the disbelief that her son could be involved in any kind of serious crime. When she reaches the police station, she finds a silent James – unwilling to talk to her or to the police. He tells his mother he won't talk without a lawyer. Cathy explains with a mixture of sadness and pain that in those moments she just couldn't fathom the seriousness of their situation. What could the police be talking about? Murder? What? My son? How can that be? There had to be a mistake and she is convinced that an explanation by James can clear it up for everyone. It takes time, but ultimately he tells the account without a lawyer present, and with that his fate is sealed. A still-confused and distraught mother watches as her youngest son is charged with murder.

Cathy, unable to pay for anything more, settles for a public defender to fight for James. The other boys have more resources, and expensive, experienced lawyers are retained for them. Cathy notes with real anger the discrepancies in how the other teens with more money are treated both during the trials as well as at the sentencing hearings. In the end, James is found guilty of 2nd degree murder. He remains in the county jail for two years before he is sentenced to up to twenty-eight years in prison with a five-year mandatory parole time. In August of 1999, James is transferred to a medium-security prison.

Jeff, James' stepfather, enters the family in 1998 and meets James for the first time when he is in jail. After months of visits, Jeff begins to know and understand the different sides of his soon-to-be stepson. Over many card games and lots of ice cream, the two form a lasting bond. Within James' fifteen years of prison incarceration, he is moved six times – each of those times to another of Colorado's minimum security facilities. But, regardless of where he is placed, Cathy and Jeff faithfully visit her son. "No matter where he was, every six to eight weeks we would go visit him," Jeff remembers. "It made for a long weekend; they were all really far away," both parents share. James is becoming a grown up in prison. He makes decisions first as a teenager and then as a developing adult, but all of those decisions are shaped by his environment and are sometimes shocking to his family. Cathy recalls the time she visits a son who has shaved his head; the time he surprises her with his tattooed sleeve of an arm; the time he shocks her with the news of a "marriage" to his "wife by proxy." Undeterred by actions she doesn't understand or condone, Cathy continues to search for ways to support the child she loves.

Jeff and Cathy nod at each other, "He was a model prisoner." James took advantage of many of the educational and creative opportunities available to him. He learns how to work with dogs over his time in prison. James takes in and trains several different dogs, each over a six to eight-week period, as he continues to serve out his sentence. He had a dog by his side the whole time; he was training each of them, Cathy remembers. She continues that dogs can bring you comfort and joy no matter how bad a day you can be having. "It was a good thing for him; . . . he was pretty good at it," she chuckles. James also develops a real passion for art. He creates charcoal and colored pencil drawings which he shares with Cathy. He moves into beading and crocheting as his creative side grows and flourishes. Cathy talks with pride about the beaded medicine bag, the original painted, designer mirrors, and the beautiful crocheted afghan she treasures – all created by her son while he is incarcerated. In time tattoos become a way he uses to express himself. James learns the artistic side of tattoo creation and soon he becomes his own canvas. Jeff recalls with a gentle smile how James' tattoos began to be a reflection of his story – the "light and dark" of his time in prison.

The complexity that is James LeRoy continues to unfold as, in 2012, he is finally able to shift from a prison environment to a halfway house in Northern Colorado.

Incarcerated as an impressionable teenager, James exits prison life in a thirty-two-year-old man's body. Though he is now closer to the parents who unconditionally love and support him, he is also an adult who is expected to understand, reenter and begin building a very different kind of life beyond the prison confines he has survived for fifteen years. He finds work quickly and continues to seek even better opportunities. Eventually he is able to take advantage of his training in prison and becomes a welder for a local company; he loves the work and the opportunity. Equally important to his new-found, limited independence is the freedom to not only work with others, but to also form adult relationships. Two relationships, one begun before James leaves prison and the other after his release, shape and influence his actions over the last years of his life.

Though there are questions about the legality of his 2008 "marriage by proxy" to a girl he first met during his arrest in 1997, he takes their connection seriously. They have corresponded during his years in prison and he asks Cathy and Jeff for help to bring her into the area now that he is actually able to be in closer contact with her. They support his decision though both worry that he is being taken advantage of. Cathy recalls her son's words: "Mom, what you do for her, you're doing for me." Even though this young woman surprises everyone by arriving in town with her two children, James' parents help secure an apartment as well as provide safe and reliable transportation for them. James continues to live in the halfway house the entire time they are in the area. "They had never lived together . . . never spent a full 24 hours together" the parents share. In December of 2013, after many disappointing months, she and her children leave the area for good. During 2014, the last year James spends in the halfway house, the young mother appears to be out of his life. *And though she appears briefly right before and soon after his death, she no longer has any connections with his family.* James continues to work hard at a job he enjoys and begins to think about life in the long term. Because independent living looms in his future, Cathy and Jeff offer to again help him plan his next steps and encourage him to move toward divorce. In January, 2015, James exits the halfway house and moves in with his mother and stepfather.

His second major relationship begins while his divorce is in process. James meets another woman in February, 2015. "She had a lot of problems, but you know what, she was like my daughter at the time. She had a good side. . . . She walked right in like she belonged here," Cathy reports. The parents appreciate that she is willing to fit in as part of their family. And, most importantly to them, "she treated James well." Things seem to finally be working out for her son, and Cathy begins to have real hope for his chances at happiness. All things change on April 22, 2015. The two women in James' life unexpectedly discover each other's presence through a text on his phone. They argue and one's outrage over the previous "other woman" ultimately spills over onto James; he drinks during their argument and finally leaves the house, angry and under the influence. And in a matter of hours, James' promise of an easier life ends.

A series of texts begin the tale of the tragedy. After James leaves home, she texts Cathy, concerned about James. "Would you text your son and see if he is OK . . . . He left here mad . . . he's drunk." Cathy texts James three times searching for word that he is safe, but she never receives an answer. "After the third text I knew something was wrong because he always texted me back. . . . He didn't want to worry me," Cathy explains in a shaky voice. And in the background, close to Cathy's home, the sirens begin. Within the hour Cathy is told that James has been in an accident and taken to the hospital. Jeff receives a similar message and the two worried parents get to James as soon as they can. At the hospital they are told that James was in a single car accident – that he rolled his vehicle and was ejected. He has several serious injuries, including brain damage, and the next 72 hours will be critical.

As soon as Cathy walks into her son's hospital room, she is immediately transported back to a time when her own brother had suffered a terrible accident. Her voice calm, resigned to the tragedy she is describing, Cathy remembers aloud: "Walking into this room was like walking into my brother's room that was identical with almost identical injuries and we finally had to take him off life support after about five days. So here we are again with my son and I'm just sitting here going – Why! I've already lost one . . . and now . . . him." She goes on, her voice shaking with the painful memory, "Of course, I go in there thinking he's going to be OK . . . he's not going to die. He can't die because I've told him he can't leave me. I've told God He can't take him."

Members of the family and work colleagues join them at the hospital. Cathy is supported by an outpouring of kindnesses. The 72 hour times passes and there is no response from James throughout the tests. The doctors' messages are grave; the damage to the brain stem is massive; chances of survival are slim and James is on life support. Cathy is faced with a horrific decision. She listens to information from medical professionals, and soon members of James' family also weigh in with their thoughts and questions. An already-difficult decision for Cathy becomes even more heartbreaking and confusing. She never leaves the hospital and four days after the accident, during the night, James seems in such distress Cathy is overwhelmed by his pain. And that night she finds clarity about what she must do – her son deserves peace. The decision she has been agonizing over is made; she authorizes taking him off life support. The next evening, April 27th, all family and friends who wish to say goodbye to James surround him and Cathy. Loving wishes and farewells are said and life support is removed. The morning of April 28, 2015, James' girlfriend visits his room and Cathy urges her to talk with him, to tell him what is in her heart. The young woman spends quiet, private time with James. Soon after, James grows calm and dies.

And it is that remembrance of a son she loves and misses that forces Cathy to once-again face the pain that continues to surround her. During those last months when James was living with them, she was called for jury duty. As she thinks back to the instructions of the District Attorney, those familiar words take on new and terrible significance. You (jury members) must find him "guilty beyond a shadow of a doubt . . . have an open heart and know that it is up to me (the DA) to prove him guilty." Tears fill Cathy's eyes as she bravely faces her guilt: As I heard the

DA, I knew that "everything I told him [James] in the jailhouse was wrong. I went home feeling so guilty." She follows with the conversation she had soon after with James: "I looked in his eyes and said, 'I'm so sorry. If it wouldn't have been for me you probably wouldn't have been in prison most of your life.'" But her son affectionately replies, "It's OK Mom. It turned me around. I was going the wrong direction. It helped me. You don't have anything to be sorry for." Cathy's voice is gentle and filled with awe, "He was so gracious to forgive me."

Our room grows quiet and we each think about the young man, gone too soon. Cathy and Jeff are reminded that James had consented to being a tissue donor upon his death. Cathy and Jeff both brighten at the memory of his decision. They share that the donation of this son's bones, tendons, retinas and skin helped to give more life to ninety-eight others. Though no one would declare James a saint, like St. Valentinus, his final acts were to graciously forgive and unselfishly donate himself to others. Tears shimmering in her eyes, Cathy smiles tenderly. "He was a good man." And now, "he's in a better place. He's with Michael."

Michael: I know some day I'll see him again

Cathy and I meet again. In this same room just a few weeks ago, she told me the story of the death of her youngest son, James. And here we are a second time – this time to record the death of her oldest, Michael. Outside, it is a glorious day, sun-filled with the soft feel of a coming springtime. Children and their parents laugh and play in the small park just beyond our window while squirrels scamper from roof to tree to ground and back again. The lively energy outside this room speaks of promise and joy. But the atmosphere inside, where we face each other, is heavy with the sadness of a mother who feels the responsibility to talk about another unspeakable loss. Where the last story seemed to pour out of her, demanding to be told, this one holds back. The heaviness of it hangs in the room. But I am moved to begin because I want to understand the differences between the story of one son that so strongly needed to be told, and the story of the other that may still be too sorrowful, too confusing, and too painful to even be totally understood by the mother who lived it. I sense there will be fewer details shared about her oldest boy; that the events surrounding the last half of his life and his heartbreaking death are being protectively cradled within his mother's heart, still too tender to be trusted to a stranger. Gently, we begin the story of Michael, another cherished son.

"I don't have as much to talk about as I did with James. I don't have as many years." Cathy reveals. The first fifteen years of her oldest son's life are marked by deep affection and hope. The picture she paints of a young Michael is one of a joy-filled son, a boy who is both loving and close to his mom and stepdad, Zeke, and an intelligent student who always earns excellent reports from his teachers. "Michael was my good kid." Cathy says gently. A sweet smile and great sense of humor also describe her first born. He was a "funny kid that always had me laughing," she smiles. She talks about the joy she got from Michael wanting to spend time with her; the two of them would take walks and Cathy remembers some of their conversations. She especially recalls warning him about the dangers of smoking and doing drugs. It made her happy when Michael replied, "Mom, I'll never do that stuff." With both pride and sadness Cathy shares, "He had so much potential."

When Michael was fifteen, everything shifted in their lives. Though Cathy doesn't know exactly what happened to stifle her oldest son's potential, she recalls that things changed drastically in both boys' lives when they were teenagers. Zeke, Michael and James' stepfather, died on April 15, 1993, and it wasn't long after his death that Cathy noticed changes in not only Michael but also his brother: "They weren't my same boys anymore." She goes on to explain that when her husband died she was in such mourning that she didn't realize the kind of pain Michael was feeling. Zeke's death and the resulting grief of that event pinpoint when Cathy believes Michael began walking down the dangerous path to drinking and drugs.

She continues, "I felt like I lost both of my kids at the same time. . . . I lost them to drugs; I lost them to their peers." Her relationship with Michael was never the same again.

The following years are tough ones. Cathy and the boys move to Northern Colorado and work to create both their individual and family lives within new communities. In his junior year of high school Michael declares he's had enough of school; he wants to quit. Cathy has watched her smart, motivated and affectionate son change into a dangerously unhappy teen. She tries some tough love conversations with him about how dropping out will change both his present and future life opportunities and how she cannot support his decision. But the seventeen-year-old continues on his path and eventually goes behind her back to contact his grandparents who offer him a place to stay. Michael moves out of Cathy's house and into their home, where expectations are different and Cathy believes other choices are available to the troubled teen.

Her voice sad and resigned, Cathy refers to Michael's time from 1995, when he is turning eighteen, until his death in 1999 as really hard years. She remembers, "I didn't know what to do to help him. . . . Every time I talked to him he was either drunk or high." She tries to reach out to him, to talk with him about the dangerous road he is traveling and her worries for his future. But he moves farther and farther away from her influence, and their estrangement deepens. Within this same time period, James, her youngest, has been charged with 2nd degree murder and is awaiting sentencing in the local jail. Michael watches the family he has loved continue to unravel as his own struggles intensify. In 1998, a year

175

before his death, he moves out of his grandparent's house and into a home of his own.

Cathy's life story is also moving into a new chapter: she works; worries and prays on a daily basis as she provides a home for James while also dealing with his risky, and eventually tragic, decisions; she meets her future husband, Jeff; and Cathy begins the steps of refashioning her life. As a strong Christian, her prayers from the time of Zeke's death throughout all those difficult years are for her sons. "I prayed for my boys – after Zeke died it was like constant prayer for protection over them because they were teenagers. When teenagers lose one parent or the other (it seems like) they go wrong." So Cathy repeatedly asks for help from God. "Please just protect them til they get their brains back." And then adds softly, "but He didn't."

In late March, 1999, Cathy receives an unexpected call from Michael. He is sober and sounds happy. He tells his mother that he is planning on getting professional assistance; he will be seeing a counselor and asking for help with his depression. A surprised but elated Cathy feels hopeful for the first time in a very long time. Maybe he will have a chance at happiness after all. But only a few days later at 3:30 am on April 1, 1999, she receives the call from Michael's aunt telling her that her beloved son is dead. For reasons Cathy doesn't know, Michael has spiraled from the hope-filled phone call to his mother, down into a place of utter hopelessness. She discovers that he chose to heavily drug himself, and after an argument with a girlfriend, go into his garage, close the door and start his car. He also finds a rope, creates a noose and uses it to hang himself as the car's engine continues to run. He dies of asphyxiation. Cathy suspects that her son was trying to stop his emotional and physical pain once and for all. "If one didn't do it, the other would," she says, her voice filled with sorrow.

Springtime in 1999 is filled with heartbreak and chaos. Cathy is not only burying her oldest son, but also steeling herself for the sentencing hearing of her youngest, who is soon to be transferred from the local jail to a medium-security prison. Cathy, realizing it is impossible for her to say good-bye to both of her boys at the same time, uses some of her last strength as a grieving mother to advocate for herself and her sons. She is able to get James' sentencing moved forward to August. Then she secures permission for him to be released for a few hours so he can come to the mortuary to be with his family and say his own final good bye to his brother. She remembers thinking: "This is the last time I'll be with my boys, together, on earth."

Losing Michael was a devastating blow – one from which Cathy is still trying to recover. "Michael's death was one of the hardest because of the lost years. . . ." She still feels the ache of being estranged from her first born during the last five years of his life. Cathy holds onto the comfort of knowing from her niece, Casta, who was closer to Michael during their estrangement, that her son "thought she was a good mom and he loved her." But questions about what she might have done differently still hang in the air when she recounts those lost years. Cathy wonders aloud about the relationships of other parents with their children. "What do they do differently, that I didn't do – those parents who have 'perfect' children?" Then she goes on to share that watching other parents' experiences have finally taught her that "even good people can lose their children to really bad things." And though this understanding – that all kinds of parents can have things go very wrong and feel deep pain – does not make her feel good, it does help her realize she is not alone.

She describes the decade following Michael's suicide as a time of terrible, debilitating grief. She self-medicated, had suicidal thoughts, spent times hospitalized, and lived almost constantly with guilt, anger, depression and intense physical and emotional pain. If it weren't for the fact that her husband, Jeff, helped her understand she still had another son who needed her, Cathy is certain she could not have found the will to move beyond Michael's loss. She recalls, "I didn't want him [James] to get out [of prison] and not have me here. . . . I put my life into James." With James' death, her grief spiral began anew. Now, still within the first year of grieving the death of her youngest son, Cathy continues to fight through the daily physical and emotional pain of loss. She is once again, with the help of others who love her, trying to gather the strength to rebuild her life.

Cathy now visits the two different gravesites of her sons. For years, she was unable to go to Michael's. It was just "too hard and too real to see his name on that stone," she relates. Michael and James were buried in different towns, but after James' death, Jeff and Cathy decide that somehow, symbolically, the two brothers need to rest side by side. Jeff dug up some ground from around Michael's grave and brought it to be poured into the vault with James; "we have a piece of Michael with him," Jeff explains.

There is a plaque naming both sons, as well as something tangible – earth – from their individual gravesites now located in the same place. When she wishes to, Cathy can finally visit her sons together.

Cathy's loss stories highlight the fact that acute grief and the chaos that surrounds it can make healing seem impossible. People in profound grief often lose themselves. She talks openly about losing her purpose after each of the boys' deaths, and the downward, pain-filled spiral she experienced. Cathy came to realize that somehow she had to learn how to climb out of its grip. It was finding an intentional reason to continue to live that saves her today. "I always felt like I messed up," Cathy admits. But she goes on to say that her faith is returning, even stronger, because she believes she's starting to understand God's purpose for her. "I didn't lose God at all . . . though I got really angry with Him. . . . He's the only reason I survived." Cathy's niece, her identified "guardian angel," believes Cathy's purpose is to help others who have had losses. And the still-grieving mother of two agrees. She feels more at peace when she is able to give to others; her faith shines stronger when she feels needed. With both awe and calm acceptance, Cathy says of her struggle: "I lost my purpose . . . and then one day God just gave me peace."

Finally, Cathy takes a moment to think about how her experiences with profound loss might be helpful to others. She says, with all seriousness, that if she can live through such losses, anyone can. She continues with the reminder that even though it never goes away, all those feelings attached to losing a child do get softer over time. "Remember the good stuff," she advises, and find people who are like minded to share your experiences. Most importantly, according to Cathy, "trust God." Cathy states with concern, "I don't know how people lose their children without the hope that they're going to see them some day." She goes on to talk about her sons by saying that sometimes she still can't comprehend that they are really gone. Then she says with assurance that there are other times when she can see them, up there in heaven, running around on streets of gold, happy and at peace, seeing her mom and dad, her brothers and cousins – all those she has loved and already lost. "They're happy. . . . I know some day I'll see them again."

Hollis: Her saint who walked in light

On an absolutely glorious Sunday afternoon, a smiling Elizabeth welcomes me into her home. After a mutual, warm greeting, a casual glance to the left immediately draws my attention into her front room – a musical garden of plenty. She leaves me time to wander and look around, to get a feel for the parent who will soon unfold for me an account of her worst nightmare. And, in no time, I discover I will be talking with a woman who has deep passions and a love for expressing them through the art of music making. Though I soon understand there are sixty-six instruments in all, inhabiting parts of her home, my focus is on this area where furniture, plants, friends and family share space with an array of musical instruments: a piano; at least two guitars; several recorders; a pennywhistle; an interesting variety of percussion instruments including an udu, a djembe, a tambourine and at least one handheld shaker; a lovely Celtic harp; and even music stands, a microphone and a small sound set up. We eventually settle in at the adjacent dining-room table for our interview session where it becomes quickly apparent that Elizabeth is not only a sensitive, passionate and spiritual person, but also a very proud mother of three who is still walking a deeply personal grief journey for her middle child, Hollis Elijah. As if worried there could never be enough time for her to tell about her amazing son, his mother begins quickly. And, to clarify the many pieces of this life richly lived, Elizabeth gathers and shares pictures, CD's and collections of drawings and poems to help her paint the beautiful collage that was her son.

"I clasp a small bird in my hands.

I seal my fingers so tightly and softly as I hold it. I carry it close to my heart and whisper soothing reassurances.

It chirps to me small scared questions. It has been sick for some time, and we have done all we can.

Tears arrive as I give it carefully to her.

She does her best to make a young boy not worry, but I know what will happen next.

My father's large hand pats my shoulder as we turn to leave.

One last sweet tweet makes the tears well, and we are gone.

How do you say goodbye when neither can understand the other?"

Unspoken Loss found in Hollis' personal 2011 journal

Elizabeth's story really starts before the birth of her middle son. She has traveled with her husband, John, and nine-month old son, Previn, to meet John's family for the first time. The event is a sad one: Raymond, John's younger brother, has died and they are attending his funeral. Elizabeth talks of her condition during that time: "I didn't know I was pregnant; I had just had surgery – four hours of surgery. I had a lot of drugs: pre-op drugs, post-op drugs, (and) x-rays." On the heels of the surgery, she discovers the pregnancy and asks her doctor how all of the earlier procedures and medications might affect her unborn child. After a long list of possibilities he ends by stating, ". . . or your child could get Cancer at three, ten or thirty." She follows with a question about what the doctor suggests she could do, and hears him say: "I suggest an abortion."

Shaken, she and John discuss her options, eventually agreeing they will have the child and deal with whatever happens. Then, when they are three months pregnant, John wakes her in the middle of the night to excitedly tell her: "Elizabeth, I just had a dream and Raymond came to me. And he said, 'Johnny, Johnny, I'm coming back. I'm going to *get it right* this time . . . I'm the child inside of Elizabeth!'" She goes on to share the compelling similarities of these two – Raymond and her son, Hollis. They both were thirty-one when they died; they each were the second son of their mothers; they both were in the military; they both became Buddhists near the end of their lives; and they each died on the 24th of the month. Hollis, a middle son who well may have been the incarnation of another second son, is born on October 3, 1980.

Elizabeth believes in prayer; she also embraces the idea that life holds inexplicable mysteries: some beautiful and grace-filled, some confusing, some ephemeral, some unfathomable, and some profoundly painful. "I'm open to whatever is going on," Elizabeth says, her hands expressively opening into the air around her. She shares that she intentionally prayed for the type of children she wanted to bring into the world; in the case of Hollis, "I prayed for a saint." His middle name, Elijah, is chosen from a book she is reading of the same name. She continues with the story of the Old Testament's Elijah, who is said not to have died, but instead to have ascended directly to heaven. His mother gently reports, "There was no grand plan on my part but I have to say in retrospect that Hollis had a profound influence on a lot of people around him and brought his own positive energy and light to the people who knew him." Hollis Elijah *"got it right"* before his ascendance from this place; he rose to heights of talent, compassion, generosity, humor and success throughout his short life. Elizabeth's intention-filled prayers were answered.

An affectionate "homebody," called the "cuddly one" by his mom, Hollis lived and loved "as big as he could." He was beloved by family and friends alike; Previn, his older brother, writes in his tribute to Hollis: "It's still impossible to imagine this world without his smile or his laugh, or absent of his fantastic sense of humor, his fine mind, or his genuine compassion." His incredible musical talent is undeniable. Hollis mastered the piano, as well as played both the trumpet and drums. As an eighth grader he composed a piano work, "The Passing," and then as a high school student, performed it in a recital hall at the local university. He learned to accompany himself and perform with ease. He enjoyed singing those songs that somehow spoke to his heart. Whether it is in listening to him play an original composition or in watching him perform Jason Mraz's "Mr. Curiosity" or Kermit's "It's Not Easy Being Green," audience members can't help but feel the freedom, playfulness and passion of a young man who clearly loves making music for others to enjoy. In additional to his musical gifts, Hollis possessed a "fine mind." A numbers wizard and problem solver with a keen intelligence and generous nature, Hollis was also a natural and talented communicator. He dedicated himself to work that he loved and was successful both in military and civilian positions. Previn remembers a brother who ". . . was beautifully original and unique, and there will never be anyone quite like him again."

Hollis graduates from high school in 1999 and begins a series of governmentally-aligned positions. He joins the Marines right out of high school, ultimately achieving the rank of Sergeant and earning an award for exemplary service while helping his unit to be acknowledged as the "Control Center of the year." Before he leaves military service in 2006, Hollis has been promoted, given an exclusive security clearance, and is operating as a head of communications. Though other smaller and equally successful positions intervene, another job shift in 2009 sends him home to Colorado and NORAD. While he is working in this position his skills as a communicator shine. He appears with a small speaking part in a dramatization of the 2000 terrorist attack on the US Cole which is aired on the History Channel. It is also during this time that life presents Hollis with love – as well as with one of his greatest challenges.

At age twenty-nine, Hollis enters into a ten-month exhaustive fight against a rare, aggressive and unrelenting disease – Burkitt's Non-Hodgkin Lymphoma. He eventually leaves NORAD in order to manage treatment. Crystal, a woman he meets, falls in love with, and eventually proposes to, remains close and helps to support him as he carries on this first cancer battle. In 2010, Hollis is released from treatment, declared "cured" by his doctors, and accepts a civilian position as an encryption specialist. His multi-tasking skills and exceptional problem-solving and numbers abilities garner him both respect and success in this, his last job. On April 1, 2011, "Cancer 2.0" appears; Hollis is diagnosed with Leukemia.

Elizabeth pauses to explain about the significance of the first day of April to her family. Hollis' younger sister, Aria, was born on April 1st and his mother and father's wedding anniversary was also celebrated on that date so, unselfishly, Hollis shows his compassionate nature and waits until April 2nd to tell his family of this latest diagnosis. This time his battle takes a different path, and in June of 2011 Hollis moves from treatment in Colorado to a center in Texas. During the next six months, Hollis and those who love him ride the second, frightening, chaotic roller coaster that accompanies this newest cancer diagnosis.

By August, Hollis' body has been ravaged by both the disease and the treatments he undergoes and he suffers the first of two comas. A still-bewildered and angry Elizabeth speaks of medications and treatment trials her son endured during the times he spent fighting for his life; she clearly still feels as if Hollis deserved better throughout his time on this journey. When he comes out of the coma in August, she notes her surprise at finding him clear, without the "chemo-brain" everyone expects. He shares with the family some sharply-detailed memories of his time in the coma and his descriptions eventually become an illustrative, artistically-designed rendering by his brother, Previn. Previn creates a depiction of this intimate and vulnerable time as a tribute to Hollis; it is a testimonial to a fighting spirit – a beloved child, brother, loved one, and friend. Ultimately, medical professionals tell the family that Hollis is not a candidate for a stem cell transplant and, according to his mother, "sent him home to die." Those who have been with him off and on over the last months in Texas help find Hollis an apartment in Houston.

Elizabeth turns her attention to those months in Houston when Hollis is in the care of his family. Smiling gently, she talks of the time she and her son went shopping for a ring crafted specifically for the young woman he's come to love. The memories of his experiences in coma, where Hollis believes Crystal's love has had a hand in bringing him safely out, lead him to propose to her. There are tender moments of hope and happiness as the family celebrates the loving relationship of the two in their midst.

At this same time, Elizabeth has found a mission: she will do everything she can to help her son gain quality in whatever life remains. With the help of a cousin, a nutrition specialist living in the Houston area, she begins providing healthy organic and vegan foods for her son and insists he follow specific dietary restrictions. Over time he begins to feel better and gather strength. By September, 2011, Hollis is declared strong enough to be able to have the stem cell transplant surgery. Aria, Hollis' sister, is to be the stem cell donor. Again, hope tentatively weaves among those who love Hollis. He emerges from the transplant surgery, clear-headed and with his fighting spirit intact. But just a few weeks later, Hollis succumbs to pneumonia. He is put on a ventilator and induced into his second coma. His doctors tell the family there is no hope for life beyond artificial support and that fact, plus Elizabeth's belief that Hollis has found peace, lead her and the family to withdraw life support. Hollis dies on October 24, 2011.

Throughout Elizabeth's storytelling, she pauses to share with a kind of wonder, various circumstances that have unexpectedly tied people and events together; on one level, a surface level, they seem to be random occurrences. However, when she considers the coincidences in more depth, they feel ethereal – as if a life force beyond our knowing has stepped in to create connections for her at just the right moment, for just the right reasons. Her first, earlier example detailed the dream her husband, John, had before his son's birth, identifying Hollis as a possible reincarnation of John's dead younger brother, Raymond. She stops to consider their similarities, their undeniable connections and calls it one illustration of how she feels touched by circumstances beyond her full understanding, leading her to acknowledge that life unfolds beyond simple coincidences.

Another example happens at the end of his life, when Hollis is on life support. Elizabeth wrestles with the decision about keeping her son alive artificially; what is best for Hollis, she wonders. She remembers his words to her – "Don't give up on me; just don't give up on me" – and she weighs her choices with those words ringing in her ears. Hollis remains in the coma and family stays close. One way they pass the inevitable waiting time is to play a word game called Bananagrams. During her turn, the lettered tiles Elizabeth randomly draws spell out the phrase *"HALT AID."* Another random draw provides letters that form the connected words *"O IM RICH."* Elizabeth takes these two statements as a message from her son – he is at peace and ready to move on.

Elizabeth's third life-altering account comes after her son's death. Three days after Hollis' passing, Elizabeth and John, having just completed some packing up of their time in Texas, are driving back to Colorado for his burial. As they travel through Austin, Elizabeth notices a very little house on the side of the road with what appears to be a statue of a Buddhist Monk on its porch. Next to the house is a long, blue building with only one word on it – *Moonlight*. Elizabeth, who shares that Hollis had become a Buddhist near the end of his life, feels strongly that she is meant to stop the car, turn around and return to the place where she first glimpsed the house. The statue turns out to be an actual monk and she and John take the opportunity to meet him and the others who live in their small monastery. After hearing Elizabeth's story about Hollis and his interest in Buddhism, the monks graciously perform the Buddhist ceremony of thirty-one, using incense, water and fire. It becomes the first of four services of remembrance dedicated to a very special and beloved son. It is here in her story when Elizabeth refers to a poem, written for Crystal, she's found in Hollis' effects. The recovered poem remains one of the reasons she stopped and turned the car around on that day in Austin. *Moonlight* not only names the building next to the monastery, it also sustains a dear memory for her of Hollis' words. She pauses in her story to softly and expressively recite them by heart.

"For her, I will be the moon. I will bring soft light where once there was darkness. And she will be my stars.

For every look, every action every perfect movement she makes sets a small fire within me.

Together, our love will bathe over this world, And illuminate the night for lovers.

And her immeasurable twinkling kindnesses will remind all others of the goodness within their souls, and the possibilities that exist for them.

I am her moon. She is my stars. And our love will forever be framed in the night sky for all to see."

The Night Sky found in Hollis' personal 2011 journal

Hollis is celebrated in three more special services of remembrance. With a lift in her voice and a smile, Elizabeth remembers first the Halloween wake the family held on October 31, 2011. Friends and family alike were invited to show up in costume to pay tribute to, and celebrate the life of an amazing person who had dearly loved Halloween. Elizabeth smiles through tears and calls it the "happiest, funnest, saddest day you can imagine." On November 1, 2011, at 1 pm, Hollis is memorialized and buried in an historical cemetery in his Northern Colorado home town. The last memorial, held on November 11, 2011, at 11 am, is in Chicago, where old colleagues, friends and extended family gather. Elizabeth goes on to share that her other two children, Previn and Aria, planned the headstone for his gravesite. Called "the best headstone ever," the playful message Hollis wanted to leave first began when his wonderful sense of humor bubbled up during a conversation with Elizabeth. After his death, his siblings use his unique idea to create the final sentence that has become a wonderful reminder of their brother's sense of humor. It continues an ongoing conversation starter for the many visitors who tour the cemetery: "Claims he died while saving 37 orphans in a fire." (from Previn's tribute to Hollis)

"He gave me a song," Elizabeth declares with assurance. In 2012, the two, mother and son, collaborated during one of those ethereal opportunities on a song she composed called *Walk in Light*. Hope and belief unite in remembrance of a life, not lost, but very much alive in the hearts of those who will always love him.

Elizabeth begins with her questions:

"Sayin' a prayer to you; you fill up my head. Just the thought of you dissipates the dread. Struggling every day, I miss you so. Is there something you wanna say? Something I should know? I feel you watching over me, from all around. You're puttin' a smile on my face; you make me proud. Show me something new almost every day - good and the bad. But if I can hold onto hope, how can I feel sad?"

And each time an answer comes:

"Walk in light – Walk in light is what you said. Walk in light – Do it every day. Don't walk in dark instead."

The Bridge replies:

"And aren't we all   –   And aren't we one
Asleep in our blindness   –   Til this dream is done
Ascending as morning   –   Descending as night
Turn from the darkness   –   Turn into the light"

"Walk in light – Walk in light is what you said . . ."

"He makes me laugh still," Elizabeth affirms as she talks about her son. She feels healing every time she senses his presence. "I'm still trying to figure out this whole existence thing we get to share here." She continues, "I just think we're supposed to learn how to get through it all with love." And it is the love she feels for and from her son that sustains her through her ongoing walk in grief. Elizabeth realizes that her original intention to bear and nurture a saint was a lofty one, but one she believes came true. If we trust that our worldly saints walk compassionately and generously in light while bestowing blessings on others, then Elizabeth can surely call the lifetime and legacy of Hollis Elijah, saintly. He absolutely *got it right* this time.

Kelby: Love beyond loss

Its early spring and the weather can't quite decide if it should bless us with a gentle shower and then blow away the gathering clouds to make way for sun or simply remind us that cold winds still have a place in our Colorado springtime. Hoping for sun to win the day, I make my way toward Dan and Ginny's, stopping to study the front of their house. The porch is full of color: yellow and teal abounds in a seating area of pillows, footrests, a bench and chairs, and a bright banner telling us all to enjoy life. To the right of the steps going up to the front door is a cross designed of small rocks, all held in place by wrapped wire. The cross stands as a welcome to all and is joined by polished stones, an oval plaque and triangular rock, each sharing messages of love, faith and hope. And then that yellow door jumps out at me! The couple's front door is painted a bright, sunny yellow and seeing it makes me smile because though I know this is a home where grief arrived, it has not been allowed to consume the lives inside.

The couple greets me at the door. A smiling, pregnant Ginny sporting a jaunty grey hat over her short, brown hair swings wide the door for me to enter. We've met before and I'm treated to an easy hug. Dan, whose warm eyes appraise and then welcome this stranger, shakes my hand and draws me farther into their home. I meet their son, Kelby, immediately; his infectious grin, downy, adorable and oh, so touchable hair, and electric personality jump from the many photos placed to greet any who enter the house. We make our way to the kitchen. The images in every room I can see paint a picture of a home of traditions, of abundant laughter and of family. I find myself looking forward to hearing how Kelby continues to enrich the lives of the parents who join me at the kitchen table. I quiet my questions to let them prepare to share the story of a beloved child and unimaginable loss.

Kelby *William Alan* carries a weighty name. Ginny grins, "I thought it was the coolest thing to have two middle names." Her younger brother, *William*, had two middle names and Ginny shares she was always just a wee bit jealous. *Alan* is a family name from Dan's side. Always a middle name, it is given to the oldest boy and Kelby became the fifth generation Alan. It soon becomes clear that Kelby could handle an extra name . . . or two . . . or more. Intelligent, loving, imaginative, animated, fun-loving and strong-willed all describe Dan and Ginny's first child. "He was definitely something different," Ginny says of her son. For the sixteen months of his life, from September 13, 2012 until February 2, 2014, Kelby brought brilliant sunshine, awe-filled days, joyful challenges and new adventures into the lives of his parents: "He was like the coolest kid ever!"

Kelby was part old soul enjoying his young life and part lightening in a bottle: he understood so many things early, almost as if he had already experienced them and, at the same time, his energy and personality were electric. Dan recalls his son as "a really easy child." A great sleeper, he knew his own bed-time. "He would grab his Winks (his beloved stuffed elephant) and his binks (his pacifier) and he was ready to go upstairs." He and Ginny smile at each other, recalling how their son, armed with Winks and binks, would shake the baby gate to the stairs as if to say "OK, I'm ready!" Eating, however, was not Kelby's thing beyond using the time to fuel up for his next adventure. He never took a bottle but went directly from nursing to drinking from a straw and cup. His parents taught him some sign language; they laugh at how the "all done" sign morphed into very busy hands that often entirely cleared not only his plate but the table around him. A "live wire" in perpetual motion, Kelby rarely sat still. However, on football afternoons when his dad went to the recliner to enjoy a game, Kelby loved to join him. He would bring stuffed animals, one by one to encircle his dad and then climb up on Dan's lap to sit, sometimes for as much as thirty minutes. Whether a whirlwind in forward motion or a gentle, wise-beyond his experiences toddler, Kelby William Alan was extraordinary.

As it is with those, regardless of age, who know what they want and need at any one time, Kelby declared his desires. He had no problem saying no to things and people with confidence. Their son went almost everywhere with Ginny and Dan. "Kelby would draw people in," Dan shares. Even random people would want to talk and be with him. But as early as four months he communicated clearly that he didn't need anyone except his parents. Very few others were in Kelby's circle of trust. Even loving, extended family members were not immune to being told no when they wanted to be close to him. However,

Miss Laura, who first met Kelby as a child care employee at Ginny's gym, was an exception; after much time and gentle trust building, Laura was able to earn a valued place in Kelby's small circle. Their friendship grew from baby sitter to breakfast buddy to great friend. He would even leave Ginny's arms to be with his Miss Laura. And though he is gone, relationship between her and Kelby's family continues. Laura and her twin sister still spend a lot of time in Dan and Ginny's home. "She has a connection to him (Kelby); she has memories she can share," Ginny says of Laura's continued place in Kelby's family. Shared memories rather than just repeated stories are part of the cherished moments that keep love alive beyond Kelby's loss.

"Being a stay-at-home mom was the best gift," Ginny shares softly, tears clouding her voice. "I don't have any regrets. I am so thankful," she continues. "I never spent a night away from Kelby . . . I unplugged. It was like I had some knowledge that I wasn't going to have him long. . . . I knew how precious that time was. I knew to cherish any time he was awake." Visiting and playing at the library, chasing and catching each other around their established path, and eating red velvet cupcakes were some of Ginny and Kelby's favorite things to do together; they marked their days with lots and lots of love, adventure and laughter. And it was toward the beginning of one of those busy, normal weeks, just as January was turning into February, when Ginny took Kelby to the doctor.

He was diagnosed with a cold and she was directed to use standard remedies to treat it. By Wednesday he was sick enough to keep Ginny up all night, holding and keeping a close eye on her son. She called her doctor again the next day, Thursday, and was assured that she should just hold the course for another few days. Kelby, having had more sleep than his mom, found the energy to play on his own with his Legos and by the time Ginny noticed, he had cleverly separated them, organizing all the blues into a row. Ginny remembers with wonder the quick intelligence of her son, so sick just hours earlier. On Saturday Kelby was eating again, feeling well enough to have a "dance party" with his mom, and delighting his parents by mastering his first solo chair climbing experience with ease – even with Winks and binks in tow. By Saturday night Ginny and Dan began to again relax into the lovely normal of family life.

The next morning, Sunday, February 2, 2014, Dan went into his son's room at the usual time to collect him. It was a Broncos Super Bowl Sunday; a fun family day lay ahead. "I'll never forget the way he said my name. . . I knew something was wrong," Ginny reports as she begins the story of that day's next horrific hours. Dan discovered that Kelby wasn't breathing; he rushed his son into their bedroom, Ginny called 911 for help and Dan began CPR. The police arrived within minutes and immediately raced to the bedroom to take over Kelby's care. The EMT's and firemen were close behind. "We had the best of the worst experiences of our life; we had the best treatment," the couple says of their encounters with those first responders. The rescue team members sent them downstairs and continued to work on Kelby. "They tried so hard. They did so much upstairs," both Ginny and Dan share about those who joined them in the battle to save their son that snowy, cold morning. The fight moved to the hospital and the first responders stay with the parents until Kelby is officially declared dead. Ginny and Dan look at each other as they recall the compassion of a nurse, their champion, who, though it was unclear if she had the authority to do so, unhooked Kelby from all the emergency lines and devices, placed him in their arms and assured them they could have as much time as they needed to hold their son and say good bye one last time.

In every case during that February 2nd morning, Ginny reports with a kind of awe the care and compassion shown by each individual, each team who "did everything they could. They were amazing." When the couple returns to their home, it is afternoon. The police have gone and a rare stillness claims the house. Gently, as if in explanation of a dear memory, Ginny describes the indelible, physical sign that still remains as a marker of that frantic, frigid and unforgettable morning. "We have a little spot on our carpet where they got one of the lines in" (to Kelby). "It looks," she halts slightly, ". . . just a little blood spot. I don't want to ever get rid of it. I don't know; I just want to keep it there." Dan quietly interjects, "We stole him for sixteen months." Born a week overdue with the umbilical cord wrapped twice around his neck, Kelby easily could have been lost to them. But he lived – loudly, sweetly and fully – staying with his parents for sixteen more months, making certain to leave them with enough love to last well beyond his loss.

Kelby's cause of death was SUDC, Sudden Unexplained Death in Childhood. Such a diagnosis follows when the unforeseen and unexpected death of a child over twelve months remains unexplained after a thorough investigation, including a complete autopsy. The parents learn that an SUDC diagnosis is only given when all known and possible causes of death have been ruled out. Even though SUDC has been formally recognized as a credible cause of death from as early as 2001, to date there has not been enough research done to identify risk factors, common characteristics or prevention strategies for this acknowledged killer.

Ginny was introduced to this diagnosis, inadvertently, from a bereaved SUDC mother's Facebook post she just happened upon six months before Kelby's death. After her own son's death diagnosis, Ginny contacted this parent and learned that the SUDC Program, established in 2001 to provide information and support to parents like her and Dan, had become its own non-profit foundation in 2014. The proactive couple wanted to somehow become involved. Ginny moved quickly, and, after securing Kelby's DNA from the medical examiner, both she and Dan submitted their own and now all three are part of a five-year study, committed to helping researchers provide much-needed answers to the many agonizing questions that accompany an SUDC death. Ginny joined an SUDC mom's support group, an online presence she now shares with "soul sisters" located all over the world. The couple acknowledges that there is both comfort and strength in joining with others who have suffered the identical kind of loss they have, who are traveling their same road.

Kelby is buried in Grandview Cemetery. His unique and beautiful headstone, an actual child's chair, welcomes visitors of all ages to his resting space. Its backrest displays a picture of Kelby as well as his name, birth and death dates; the seat part is for actual sitting, and the bottom front of the chair displays messages through icons and words designed to showcase Kelby's favorite things. On its left is a Superman logo sporting a capital K instead of an S, and on the right, a set of Mickey Mouse ears atop a small face with wide eyes. Centered in this area is a message dear to the hearts of his parents: "We will hold you in our hearts until we hold you in heaven." Surrounding are more examples of Kelby treasures, placed (and replaced) by family: his Legos; a Mickey Mouse balloon; a red velvet cupcake; and a colorful array of interchangeable brightly painted rocks sent from his grandma, Dan's mom, made for viewing, reading and even for playing.

This area of the cemetery pays tribute to a child, ever-present in the hearts and thoughts of those he profoundly touched. Another playful celebration of Kelby's life sits easily in the sand of a local park, just a few blocks from Dan and Ginny's home. A delightful, grey, big-eared Winks stands ready to welcome any child and give him or her a gentle, spring-loaded ride. Near Winks is a commemorative plaque remembering Kelby with love. Dan looks at Ginny as he talks of their son who people would just come up and talk to, a son who could just draw people in. And still, today, his parents have made certain there are places and spaces where Kelby is available: to play with; to talk to; to relive precious memories; and to remind everyone present that love endures even devastating loss.

Due on 8-8-16, the couple is happily and gratefully pregnant with their next child. Ginny wistfully recalls, "I didn't have a lot of hope and this baby is hope; I didn't know how to live on this earth without being a mother to another child." She looks at Dan who nods as she continues, "We have so much love for Kelby, and another baby deserves that love and to know about Kelby." Ginny gives voice to an ongoing sadness: "It's hard not having his light here." With tears in her eyes and a catch in her voice she shares, "We're very hopeful and happier for this new baby but it's not our Kelby. I miss him a lot." In the midst of this genuine mix of new joy and unfinished heartache, the couple reflects their own understanding of how love and loss, birth and death, the past and the future can inextricably connect. Light comes back into her eyes and Ginny affirms, "This baby is part of Kelby."

Both parents acknowledge that grief is a lonely place to dwell, a very heavy weight to carry, and they talk about what they have found helpful as they continue to face its presence in their individual and common life together. For Ginny, personally, "I needed to change everything about my outward appearance. I didn't want to be who I was . . . I couldn't be that person." Besides hair color, new friendships, different activities and personal style changes, Ginny re-welcomed tattoos into her lifestyle. She calls her tattoos healing; they move the pain that lives inside her into the light. Her body art might show up as a mantra, like the simple and profound, *"breathe,"* she carries on one finger, or as a more elaborate message like the one that accompanies the angel wings on her back: *"I will hold you in my heart until I hold you in heaven."* Bringing the inside, out, and bearing visibly her heart's deepest feelings give Ginny comfort and a sense of clarity.

Together, Dan and Ginny have found that sharing within a support system of others who have also lost a child helps lead to healing. About the same time they discovered the SUDC Foundation, a local bereaved parents' support group, 3 Hopeful Hearts, also came into their lives. Since Ginny has been mentoring other parents in 3HH, as well as sharing her own loss experiences through panel presentations and participating in training sessions for police services and nurses, she has noticed that her grief is morphing – some of the sharper edges have blunted. She sometimes catches herself talking about grief experiences in the past tense instead of the here and now; she smiles and names that change as real progress. When Dan and she share similar pain with other grieving parents, the feeling of being alone lessens; recognizing and confronting the different faces, shapes and demands of profound grief helps them acknowledge its weight and its place in their lives. According to the couple, in time you learn to fit all the various, changing pieces of grief into something you can manage, like a backpack, and then it becomes easier to carry around.

Life has transformed. A family has become a couple who now only seek deeper, authentic relationships with others. Dan shares that now "the petty stuff goes away." No high drama allowed, the little things really mean nothing any more. "Our faith is so much stronger," Dan continues. He and Ginny have a God-centered marriage where prayer, surrendering problems into God's hands, and knowing that you will see your child again are unfailing, living truths. They acknowledge the natural and very real struggles a couple faces when their child dies. They know their own tragedy severely tested their strength as a couple but with time and work, they found themselves again. Ginny smiles, "I've always been so proud of us . . . of who we are. I have so much confidence in my marriage again. We both just said, 'This is us' and we made it to the other side. We didn't give up on each other. Thank goodness!" This "warrior mamma" talks about every day being a new battle that she will win. "And every day is one day closer to my son who I will spend eternity with." She looks over at Dan who gives her a small smile: "We both will."

Kelby is still very near. Ginny and Dan share inspirational examples of how circumstances beyond their earthly understanding continue to make them aware of Kelby's spiritual presence. Messages from Kelby, delivered through friends to his parents from a Medium neither of them has ever met; children of friends who innocently report to seeing or hearing Kelby at random times and places; a quick, passing glimpse of him just outside his room; unsolicited, unexplained events, all very real, lead Ginny and Dan to know that their son is with them and he is fine. Cherished gifts continue to be exchanged between a beloved son and the parents with whom he shared understanding, affection, laughter and life during his short, rich time on earth. They endure as the evidence that love lives on, love wins, love continues beyond heartache, beyond loss.

Lauren: The power of tiny miracles

Blue sky and the warmth of a Sunday spring afternoon sun usher me into Scott and Lindsay's neighborhood. I pull up to their home and even before I gather everything from the car, I notice it – a stately and beautiful array of white and purple iris, in full bloom – a sign that the people within care for and about lovely things. Standing at the front screen is Lindsay, her smile welcoming. Just inside, Scott waits and I'm treated to meeting them both for the first time. The couple isn't quite sure what to expect but have tried to make certain I have everything I need to comfortably write as we talk. I get to meet Tucker, their exuberant, young "fur baby" dog, and am offered something to drink as they work to settle him for our quiet time ahead. We decide to sit in the living room, surrounded by the light that streams in from both the living room and dining area windows. Scott and Lindsay sit close to each other, Tuck lying at their feet, and I'm struck by the gentleness with which these two treat each other. For our first moments together the only sounds heard come through the front door, open to the outside neighborhood. The three of us look expectantly at each other. This is a new process for them, so after hearing a few of the ways other parents have started their stories Lindsay tearfully begins the story of the devastating loss of Lauren Grace, their tiny, beloved miracle:

"Sometimes MIRACLES arrive so tiny that we cannot feel the weight of them – and yet we are still changed and we are blessed none the less . . ."

"It's been seven years of us trying to have children," Lindsay first reveals, and then further captures the couple's heartache: "I've had three pregnancies and brought none of them home." Though fertility treatments have marked Scott and Lindsay's lives throughout the years since Lauren's stillbirth, Lindsay's pregnancy with her daughter happened naturally, six months after the couple first began trying. Lindsay calls it a rough pregnancy where, though Lauren seems to be thriving, Lindsay is sick much of the time. Because doctors are watching a cyst during her pregnancy, Lindsay is monitored closely throughout. During a third ultrasound, just two weeks before their due date, on a Tuesday, the parents get the good news that their baby's heartrate and weight are fine and there is no indication of trouble.

On Saturday, Lindsay awakens to an uneasy feeling; the baby has shifted dramatically. She and Scott go their separate ways that Saturday morning, assuring each other there is probably nothing really wrong. But within hours Lindsay contacts Scott and asks him to come home in order to take her to the hospital. "I'm just worried about her." Lindsay reports. This time the ultrasound results are heartbreaking. Wiping away tears, Lindsay shares the doctor's unexpected words: "I'm sorry; I'm not finding any heartbeat; she must have died a little bit ago." The shocked parents, told just days before that their baby was doing well, are totally unprepared for this horrific blow. With hearts aching, the devastated parents can do nothing more than mark this date, January 15, 2011, as the day their tiny miracle is lost.

The next days are a nightmare. Their baby daughter is dead yet still very much a part of them; how can that be? What do they do? The couple relives those next difficult steps through the telling of events leading up to the delivery of Lauren two days later. Doctors give the parents options for her delivery. Lindsay brushes at fresh tears as she shares their choices: the couple can return home and wait for Lindsay's water to break naturally and then return to the hospital; or they can choose to have Lindsay induced now, remain in the hospital, and deliver. She and Scott decide quickly: "We want to see our daughter as soon as we can." Because the baby is breech, the doctor tries over the next many hours to shift her into the head-down position but is never successful. Eventually they decide it is best for Lindsay to deliver Lauren vaginally rather than by Cesarean, and so the long, agonizing birthing process continues. Lindsay's water is finally broken at 1:00 pm on Monday, January 17, 2011, and Lauren Grace is delivered stillborn at 2:44 pm that same day. They recall the sadness in their doctor's voice as she delivers their child and shares the ultimate cause of death – their "poor sweetheart" has the cord wrapped four times around her neck. Even though the excruciating wait is over and the parents are able to finally see their own miracle in person, the reality of what has happened is now both palpable and tragic.

The couple's family members have been in and out of the hospital during the long, laboring days. Lindsay and

Scott, however, keep their daughter's delivery private. They ask the hospital chaplain to baptize Lauren and then invite the family in to see, hold, and finally say good bye to the new baby. This tender time is recounted by Lindsay through flowing tears. She continues that when their family leaves and they are moved off the maternity floor to another area, hospital personnel tell her and Scott they are welcome to be with Lauren as long as they want. The parents stay with their baby daughter, rocking her, studying her features – her long fingers, her nose, so like Scott's, her dark hair, so like her mother's – and are amazed by the utter perfection, the beauty of the child who so clearly has been created just for them. At 9:30 pm, January 17, 2011, they turn Lauren over to one who will deliver her body to be cremated and held ready for her later funeral service. With a voice halting and tear-filled, Lindsay recounts: "The hardest thing I ever had to do was hand her over." She remembers Scott stopping them as they were walking out of the room with Lauren, saying, "Wait! I want to hold her one more time." Openly weeping, Lindsay reaches for Scott and says, "You just can't ever have enough time to fit in a lifetime of what you want to say to them. The hardest thing about this is you can love somebody you've never really met." Their ongoing grief echoes through Lindsay's next words: "We missed everything with her."

Scott and Lindsay are certain; they want to be parents. The years following Lauren's death find them committing to different rounds of fertility treatments as well as dealing with Lindsay's health challenges. Living with all the serious and difficult complications of Stage Four

Endometriosis, she has had at least eleven medical procedures, including a surgery that necessitated the removal of an ovary. And though her body keeps her from easily becoming the mother she believes she's meant to be, Lindsay persists in trying. Between Lauren's death in 2011 and now, there are two more pregnancies, Taylor and Quinn, each a miscarriage. The couple names each baby in remembrance – keeping them real and human and ever-present members of their family. Taylor, believed to be a Tubal Pregnancy, is lost at seven weeks; Quinn, diagnosed as the rare Partial Molar Pregnancy, lives to almost nine weeks. The ongoing, recurring cycles of painful loss, lived again and again through the death of three individual babies, weigh heavily on the grieving parents. "It becomes very isolating so you don't talk about it much," Lindsay reveals.

Family and friends, those who have never experienced the same reality as the grieving couple, seem unable to understand. They have not dealt with the layers of heartache, worry and helplessness that have engulfed Lindsay and Scott: the roller coaster of expensive, unsuccessful fertility treatments; the tender hope of new possibilities followed by poignant sadness when those possibilities end; and the awareness of the relentless ticking of their own biological clocks. The couple, alone, knows the pressure of hiding their own, very real pain because of the needs and misunderstanding of others. Lindsay recalls hearing an apt analogy to their situation: "It's like this bad movie that everybody else gets to go home from, but it follows you . . . it's what you live." And though they still experience moments, caught in the script of this bad movie, there are now more days of laughter and hope, and times when they seriously consider parenthood – this time through adoption.

These two have grown stronger, closer, through the last, extraordinarily difficult, five years. They openly discuss the questions that can still plague them. Lindsay wonders aloud if she had called Scott earlier to get them to the hospital, if she had not second-guessed her own feelings of concern – if she had delivered earlier – would Lauren have been alive today. But then the couple also realizes that had their baby girl lived she might be profoundly disabled because of oxygen deprivation. They agree there is no definitive or right answer for such wonderings. Still questions persist: Lindsay declares with fresh tears, "We almost bankrupted ourselves to have children and I feel bad that I didn't just say let's just stop." Scott reaches to his wife to gently comfort and support her; he quietly whispers, "No, baby." She looks at him: "If I didn't have Scott I don't know if I would have lived through it all." She continues to talk about how her husband has been with her for every surgery, every procedure, every disappointment – always present and holding her hand. Scott responds with a quick laugh, "You're my rock, baby." They know that couples have deteriorated after trying to navigate the kind of profound grief they continue to live through and they count each other as a true blessing.

Lindsay journals about what she has been learning since her daughter's death:

"Everyone, at some point . . . will lose a loved one. Each person also has an opinion on the severity of injury and length of

time for grieving. Each person also will want to share their opinions with you when you lose someone. You will hear every story imaginable as if in some way to make you feel better by suggesting that you are not as bad off as someone else . . . (but) it does not help a grieving parent to be told that their child died for a reason or it was meant to be. Other well-meant comments like this can be exhausting and leave grieving parents in despair and self doubt."

With a wry laugh, Lindsay maintains that others may think they are comforting you when you're told, "If God wanted you to have children, you would have children," but such a statement only wounds. She continues, "Sometimes what others say can make you feel as if your baby's death is your fault." Scott echoes that sentiment; when Lauren died he asked himself, "What did I do wrong that I need to be punished?" Thankfully, those toughest times are easing and they are certain good things are just ahead. Scott and Lindsay take the time to share a short list of how they want to continue treating each other as they walk into their future: Be kind; stay positive; stay nice to each other, especially on the tough days; be understanding; and stay together. "It's been a long journey and we're done with that part . . . we keep moving forward, together."

This loving couple is committed to respecting their own loss journey while working toward healing. One way they accomplish this is to be available to help others. Together, they still attend grief counseling whenever they feel the need. Also, when they felt ready to share Lauren's story with others, they sought out bereaved parents' support groups, both in person and online. Both mention that the unconditional love and uncanny understanding and support of animals have additionally been important to their healing. Lindsay and Scott acknowledge their daughter's place in their life in ongoing ways – a balloon release, support group fundraisers, various remembrance and celebration-of-life opportunities – all mark ways they continue to honor Lauren. Most of all, Lindsay is committed to sharing their experience so "other people won't get hurt like we did." She declares, "We hate to see anyone suffer because we stayed quiet." Lindsay believes that the couple's biggest gift to others is to make them aware. "If you second guess anything . . . go in and check," she tells others. She also reminds everyone that even if your concerns seem silly – pay attention; don't let anyone make you feel stupid; anytime you're worried about your pregnancy, always go into your doctor to have those worries checked out. Lindsay actively stays available for others who have questions about their pregnancies and just want to talk. Their own healing journey advances every time they help someone else realize that their family's loss story does not have to be repeated by others.

The couple considers the part the ethereal plays in their lives. "Scott is soulful," Lindsay says, and then calls herself spiritual. She goes on to voice that their three heartbreaking, unfulfilled pregnancies and all the complications attached to them "tests every belief you have to your core." Both Lindsay and Scott are open to the possibility of a power beyond their known world. Tears appear again as Lindsay shares the story of an inspired message from Lauren, delivered to her by an online friend, another bereaved mother who Lindsay discovers is also a medium. According to this messenger, Lauren was insistent that Lindsay understand that her tiny daughter knew she was loved; "she wants you to know she knows." In a voice thick with emotion, Lindsay recalls how healing that conversation was for her. She affirms, "You have a connection with your children even if they don't walk the earth." It is apparent that their daughter is a very real presence in the couple's everyday life. She has appeared vividly in her mother's dreams, and they share that "we both ask for Lauren's help on really bad days." Scott grins and states with assurance, "When I die, we're going to have a family in heaven."

But, even before heaven, these two are ready for a family. They talk of adoption; Lindsay maintains that they are ready for this next step. She states her belief that, more than a blood relationship, parenting is the essential practice of "finding a connection with a child and being able to give them love." The couple shows me to the room that was to be Lauren's, and I take my time looking at a variety of cherished items, some gathered years ago to welcome Lauren to her family, and others, given later, to celebrate her life after death. Atop a chest of drawers sit treasured remembrances of their daughter's place in their lives. Among them is a square, sweet, silver box which, like the locket that hangs around Lindsay's neck, holding Lauren's ashes, contains some of both Lauren and Quinn's cremains. And in a prominent place, close to it, sits a lovely, engraved, lighted crystal memento picturing mother, father and daughter. Five and a half years later, this room – this entire home – still holds the many hopes and dreams of a couple who were, and still are, ready to love and parent a tiny miracle. They continue learning from the many and complex lessons of grief; yet they also know, without a doubt, that all their experiences have "made us better together." When I ask what lies ahead, with a lift in his voice, Scott declares, "better days."

Lindsay and Scott are poised to move into those better days – to let their hearts grow wider and deeper, to find and connect with other children and to know, again, the power of another miracle.

Scarlett: Scarlett's Story

I travel through a lovely, older part of town in search of a yellow house. The June weather makes for an enjoyable drive and I'm early enough for our interview to meander a little, to take in the quiet neighborhood. And before long there it is, just as Ashleigh described it: a cute yellow house close to the corner. The yellow is a bright, joyful color; the front of the house sports a vivid red mailbox, its numbered address in blue and white tiles, and two planters, positioned on each side of its small front porch, with red geraniums in full bloom. Just to the left of the beautifully-crafted wooden door is a wind chime, designed with delicate dragonflies, circling gently. The picture painted by the front of this home is both charming and carefree, providing the perspective of a joy-filled place. Then, as I move from the car toward the front door, I glance up at the sky and remind myself to be careful, because perspective is a complex and capricious thing that is rarely able to see in full the pictures life paints for us. The unpredictability of today's sky, only in part a beautiful blue, mirrors the story of the family in this house who know only too well how quickly and unexpectedly dangerous clouds can gather and perspective, shift. A brief knock brings both Ashleigh and Parshad to welcome me into their beautiful home and, in time, into their story of unbelievable loss and grief.

On December 20, 2014, the couple gets 'the best Christmas present ever" when it is confirmed they are pregnant. They keep this tender secret to themselves, waiting to share their joy with family and friends until close to Ashleigh's birthday, right after the holidays. Though during their first trimester they have a scare, a Subchorionic Hemorrhage, soon the spotting clears and they are assured all is well. After that experience, no other problems surface; during the normally-scheduled ultrasounds at twelve and twenty weeks, their infant measures on track, healthy and developing normally. The couple recalls the wonderful months of their pregnancy. Ashleigh looks over at Parshad who sits close to her on the couch, "Our lives were just so great. Wouldn't you say? . . . pretty much perfect?" They spend hours with dear friends, also pregnant, together sharing month-by-month milestones while spinning hopes and dreams for their individual, soon-to-be newborns; they are able to travel to attend a friend's wedding in Grand Lake; and also celebrate their fifth anniversary making happy memories through a trip to Key West, Florida.

And as the months of pregnancy unfold, Scarlett Kathryn receives her name. Ashleigh talks about the iconic figure for which her daughter is named: Scarlett O'Hara from *Gone with the Wind*. She planned that her own daughter, Scarlett (one who wears red) Kathryn (pure in heart), would eventually embody qualities Ashleigh admires in the movie's heroine: independence and the strength and clarity of her own ideas and values. From the couple's vantage point, their perspective, they are already Scarlett's parents. They have carefully prepared themselves and their home for the last thirty-eight weeks and painstakingly followed all the important rules for nurturing new life; they feel more than ready to welcome their baby.

Ashleigh and Parshad are happily in the midst of last minute preparations when, just eleven days before Scarlett's due date, Ashleigh goes into her doctor's office on Tuesday, August 18th, for the normal "belly check." Though Parshad is usually with her, today he works from home while waiting to hear from his brother. Everything is so close now – Ashleigh only feels excitement; she knows her baby is fine and on track for the upcoming delivery. Her voice fills with emotion and tears flow as she recounts that visit. Her OBGYN, only minutes into the routine examination, asks for the ultrasound machine. She tries to allay the young mother's fears but is unable to hide her concern; the truth, though not yet stated, is close. Ashleigh recalls, "She knew all along; she just didn't know how to say it." The doctor asks the ultrasound tech to also look at what she believes she's discovered. Both professionals cry when everyone's worst fears are confirmed: "I'm so sorry Ashleigh, but your baby passed away."

Ashleigh cannot believe what she's hearing: she walked into this appointment as a mother and now, suddenly, she is a grieving parent. The panicked denial she describes is still palpable. "This is a horrible nightmare that I'm going to wake up from; . . . it didn't happen."

Her phone calls begin as soon as she's able. She first finds her husband to bring him to the doctor's office; then best friends and family are told the shocking news. Soon

Parshad arrives to be at Ashleigh's side and the anguished couple is given their birthing options. Joined now by Ashleigh's mother and grandmother, they take a break from the doctor's office to walk to a park across the street. They spend time crying and talking – processing options, searching for some sort of acceptance of their new reality, of the unbelievable information they've been given, and attempting to somehow console each other. Ashleigh takes a moment to breathe and wipe her eyes before she shares her truth. The waves of pain are overwhelming: "I just wanted in that moment to die . . ." so when she notes a car coming toward them as they are re-crossing the street to return to the doctor's office, Ashleigh considers stepping in front of it. Though she doesn't, she admits that as the darkness of pain and fear escalate and hope's light diminishes, the thoughts of taking her life continue beyond this moment. What begins as a day to celebrate, to check off as one day closer to Scarlett's homecoming, moves on as a day cloaked in endless heartache.

Parshad talks about the onslaught of decisions to come and how emotionally distraught and unprepared he and Ashleigh are to navigate all that is asked of them. Over the next hours that fill that August day, until they leave the hospital on August, 21, 2015, they are expected to deal with numerous questions whose answers could impact not only today and the next few days to come, but also the years ahead when they emotionally, mentally and spiritually revisit the decisions they make now. He takes a quiet moment to gather his thoughts and then relate his memory of how those relentless, crucial decisions swirled around them, all demanding action now. "I was thinking more like . . . trying to be a voice of reason for her so she doesn't decide something on the spur of the moment and then later regret we did that."

Back in the medical facility, the couple's decisions begin. They opt to stay at the hospital and deliver as quickly as possible. "I can't go home . . . go to sleep, knowing she's gone," Ashleigh remembers thinking. Once checked into a room, they are introduced to a new and unfamiliar doctor who is taking over their case. He presents them with the next step in their process: how to deliver. He believes her body is not yet ready so Ashleigh will be induced and then potentially labor with Scarlett for the next twenty-four hours. At first it seems this second decision is made – natural delivery is the preferred method to set the stage for an easier delivery for their next child, but Ashleigh's heart sinks even lower – twenty-four hours of waiting is unimaginable. Parshad asks for another ultrasound. "Maybe it will be a miracle; maybe she will be alive." This ultrasound, like the others, shows no heartbeat. The pall of utter hopelessness deepens. And then a bit of light appears: they discover their primary OB, whose shift had ended, has returned to check in with them. A grateful Ashleigh shares her worry about more waiting and then asks her trusted doctor for counsel on this next major decision. She understands Ashleigh's concerns, supports her and they decide that a C-Section will be performed.

Another decision made, the couple wait for the delivery preparations to proceed. By now Ashleigh's parents and grandparents are close and Parshad's family is in route – all wanting to be close, to help console the two in any ways they can. But even though the strength and love of family and friends is available, Parshad recalls this particular time as "utterly by yourself." Within the hour Ashleigh is wheeled into the delivery room. Her husband wants to be in the room with her as the epidural is administered; he is gowned and ready, but has to wait just outside the doors, alone, while the request is considered by the medical staff inside. In the quiet of that outside hallway, he waits during the longest five minutes of his life before permission is granted. "It's a very strange moment; I'll never forget. . ." Parshad continues to explain those minutes as he experiences his new, painful reality, "You've lost your child; your wife's on a surgery bed in the next room . . . and you're utterly by yourself. That's one of those weird moments . . . you look back and . . . (wonder) what am I doing? (It was) a moment in time that just stood still." At 9:07 pm on August 18, 2015, Scarlett Kathryn is stillborn.

Though the decision making, preparation and waiting are a crazy mixture of both interminable and hurried, Ashleigh calls the delivery itself "very quick." Their doctor stays into the evening to deliver Scarlett; she tells the couple, "It looks like her cord is wrapped around her neck and both of her ankles." Fresh tears fill her eyes when Ashleigh shares her memory of the birth: "It was so quiet . . . dead silent." She remembers aloud her dreams of the moment when she would hear her child's first cry. Then she recalls the family story of her own first cry: "I cried like a lamb;" she wonders if her Scarlett would have made that same sound. Though the couple earlier decided to wait until they were in the recovery room to first see their daughter, Parshad agrees to an unexpected invitation to glimpse Scarlett right after delivery, and is able to tell his wife how beautiful their baby is.

The couple then makes the decision to see their baby alone, requesting that family see, hold and say their goodbyes to Scarlett while Parshad and Ashleigh transfer into the Recovery Room. Ashleigh remarks that she was just unable to witness her loved ones' reactions as they meet their new grandchild, great grandchild and niece. She goes on to articulate another fear: earlier in her life after losing important loved ones – her brother and a cousin – she made the decision not to view either of them after death. "I didn't have to see someone dead to have closure." But now, there is no other way – she must see her daughter. "I was so scared to meet her. How am I going to see my baby dead? How can I do this?" And though she doesn't call herself brave, Ashleigh lovingly welcomes new baby Scarlett into her arms, telling her how much she is loved. "She looks so perfect . . . like she was sleeping."

The new parents take the time to study the wonder they created: Parshad's ears, Ashleigh's hair, and hands and feet, all easy to identify in their new baby. Parshad shares his discovery of a new and amazing feeling: "Even though the outcome is not what you expected and your child is not alive, you still feel like every other parent tells you you're going to. . . . You know love and then you get a totally different (feeling) . . . and then you're like – oh, this is unconditional love. You still get that feeling . . . right when I saw her for the first time." Quietly, he continues, "And then you remember . . . ." Both parents report becoming physically ill during the intensely emotional stay with their baby, and each needs to take breaks from holding her so they can gather themselves to be with her again . . . and again . . . and yet again.

The first night in the hospital passes with more decisions to make. As August 18ᵗʰ turns into the morning of the 19ᵗʰ, the couple says yes to a photographer joining them to shoot and provide an array of poignant, keepsake pictures of Scarlett, alone and with her parents. The hospital chaplain also comes by their room to offer consolation as well as a blessing for their daughter. Parshad and Ashleigh thankfully accept this opportunity as she sings an old, familiar hymn in blessing: *May the Lord, Mighty God*.

After this time together, the parents say their final good byes and the chaplain gently removes their baby to transport her to the waiting funeral director. In just a few weeks, she again provides her loving support to Ashleigh and Parshad by conducting Scarlett's memorial service at the Children's Garden. The couple takes a moment to comment on the amazing kindnesses they experienced from each of the medical professionals who acted as an incredible network of support during the most difficult time of their lives.

The couple bides their time in the hospital as Ashleigh physically heals from the Caesarian. Even though Parshad calls the hospital the "safe place" where they can delay the reality of transitioning home without Scarlett, he also voices how difficult those nights are for him and Ashleigh. Their days are filled with the busyness of communicating with family and friends, the necessary details of tending to Ashleigh's healing, and navigating the hospital routines, but "the nights in the hospital room cause you to relive it over and over." They leave on August 21st.

Ashleigh uses a moment to take a sip of water and then shares a still-vivid memory: "Instead of carrying a baby out to the car, I was carrying a gift bag and some flowers." This last decision, to go back to their home without the company of family or friends, they both admit, was wrong. The house feels so empty; there is a nursery, waiting, in a house now prepared for three. Their beautiful, quiet, and oh, so empty home is a painful reminder of what should have been. No matter how exhausted the couple is, they decide to take a ride instead of facing the utter stillness and heartache of a home without Scarlett in it. Ashleigh names this space she and Parshad inhabit as an odd space – "we're already parents but our child is not here." Their common life together has been stretched to a new dimension – from a couple to a set of parents – and there is no going back. They are forever changed.

"I was destined to be her mom," Ashleigh asserts. She continues talking about how, at first, she is so angry at God. "I have such an interesting relationship with God because . . . I choose to believe in Him and I choose to believe Scarlett is in a better place with Him. At the same time I'm so angry that this could happen because I grew up believing that if you love God and praise Him – if you're a good person, you'll be rewarded and good things will come your way." She goes on to express the tender but agonizing question to her God: "What lesson are you trying to teach me?" Thankfully, some lessons have surfaced. Since their baby daughter's death, Parshad and Ashleigh have been opened to some valuable ideas they want to practice. Parshad grabs his phone to read some of his latest thoughts: realize how precious life is because there are no guarantees; have greater compassion for others; live life more slowly and simply in order to take enjoyment in all things; take a step back and look at what we are doing with our lives in the *now*. Ashleigh adds the wisdom of knowing you can just sit with people in their grief; be present and available to quietly travel through the darkness with them. And a lesson for everyone – find a bigger and wider perspective: don't be so hard on yourself and others because no one really realizes, from the outside looking in, who might be living a really tough story of their own.

"A lifetime of memories are gone. . . We were robbed," Ashleigh says, fresh tears in her eyes, her voice strong. This young mother is still familiar with those very dark places grief so easily provides, but with her husband's help she's decided that, "I don't want Scarlett's legacy to be that her mom was angry and hateful forever. Scarlett's legacy is love and life and we need to be that for her." The couple is gratefully poised to have another daughter, Penelope, in September of 2016. They fight to stay positive, needing to believe that all will be well this time. "I need her to be born; I need her to live." And though Ashleigh realizes, "It's not her responsibility to make us happy," this new child gives her "a reason to be here." Their new baby will be introduced to her older sister in gentle, sweet and ongoing ways because Parshad and Ashleigh believe Scarlett's story should always live; "it deserves to be told." They want to share it not only at home, but also with other grieving parents, to help them know they are not alone in their loss, and to encourage them to tell their own stories. Openly crying, Ashleigh quietly articulates a heartfelt truth: "Just because she died before she was born doesn't make her life any less meaningful. She was our life . . . our child."

Listening to this story, I am struck by the ever-present concept of perspective – one's point of view, attitude, outlook, state of mind – and its ability to be life-altering. Both of the parents give examples highlighting the significance of perspective. It becomes another voice in our conversation – the voice that shares how one's existence can shift with the turn of life's kaleidoscope; where a new context, either pleasant or horrid, can instantly become a remodeled reality. The picture of a leaf cupping a drop of water is lovely and peaceful until Ashleigh discovers it stands as the indicator of a child's death, that the drop of water is most likely a teardrop, and what appears so life-giving actually signals profound loss. Parshad first smiled at the many signs picturing the happy baby, located throughout the hospital's hallways to lead prospective parents like himself from one area to another – until his child is gone. Now those same signs are endless, mocking reminders of what is lost.

The circumstances of a couple's life, once carefully planned, accepted and understood now rest on shifting sand, where sure footing is no longer an absolute. A once wonderful home, lovingly prepared for a child, now can look incomplete and unfinished; a circle of dear friends who once shared common plans, journeying together toward a familiar future, experience life differently and their perspectives route them onto separate paths. But just as often, the kaleidoscope turns toward light and grace. Ashleigh's last words to me as I leave are about love and the hope it brings. I am grateful that Ashleigh and Parshad unpacked both their hearts and some of Scarlett's treasured keepsakes for me to experience before we finished. I especially appreciated being able to read Parshad's letter to his daughter:

Dear Scarlett,

Your mom and I only got to be with you for a very short time, and while your life might not fit the traditional picture of what we are used to seeing, I know that your life was picture perfect.

Even though it hurts me that we can't spend more time together, I know that your life was a divine design by God and that he must know what is best. I know you are with God now, and that gives me comfort.

We love you so much Scarlett and we will not forget you. You are a beautiful spirit that was only meant to be with us for a short time, but it doesn't mean we won't miss you.

I love you.

Your Dad

Walking back to my car, I smile. I now understand that, even in the shadow of their own loss where they may find themselves returning to the question *Why me?* this courageous couple will continue to travel together toward something beautiful – a place of grace beyond grief. I look forward to the time they will say easily and with assurance, love always wins.

Hunter and Joshua: Missing pieces of my heart

Green lawn, lacy, green leaves, and a cozy front porch, fronted by white, picket fencing and decorated with two white, wooden rockers, all welcome me to Shelbie's home. A rabbit in the side yard wiggles a hello as I move past, heading up the walk toward her front door. I've found a family neighborhood – quiet, friendly, with smiling neighbors and yards full of color, trees and plants. And though I'm surrounded by a tranquil scene, I remind myself that I'm visiting a family who has been, and still is, living with heartache. Shelbie opens the door after my quick knock and I'm treated to her lovely smile and an invitation into her home. After we exchange greetings, she brings me further into the living room where pictures of her children rest all around the fireplace. We take seats on an L-shaped couch facing the fireplace where Shelbie grabs a light blanket and settles close to a large pillow I later learn was lovingly sewn for her son, Hunter's, bedroom. We look at each other quietly and then begin a two-hour conversation filled with the complicated and heartbreaking story of irretrievable loss.

"I had . . . and I have four children, not two," Shelbie affirms in a clear, strong voice. And though the majority of her story recounts experiences surrounding the loss of her two middle sons, she also proudly shares some of the details of her two other children. Both are bright, enterprising and determined: Jeremiah, her oldest son born on September 7, 1994, is now an engineering student on scholarship at the University of Wyoming; Shelbie's youngest, Madeline, was born June 5, 2003; her mom calls her a great kid and then says with a gentle laugh, "she's thirteen," as if that description is all anyone needs to know to understand a bit more about her daughter. In between these two well-loved children are Shelbie's lost boys: Hunter, who lived from November 9, 2000, until March 2, 2002, and Joshua, whose birth and death date is January 16, 2002. "I lost him a month and a half before Hunter," Shelbie softly states. And though these two sons did not know each other in life, they are now together; Joshua's cremains found a resting place with his older sibling in Hunter's pale blue satin casket. "It's just nice to know they were buried together," says their still-grieving mother. And, placed on that casket is the sweetly tender note – *"There's always going to be a piece of my heart missing"* – written by six-year old Jeremiah to honor his siblings, especially Hunter, the little brother he lost after sixteen months. Trained in Perinatal Loss and Bereavement, as well as working for many years as a NICU and Labor and Delivery nurse, Shelbie, now the General Manager of a local Hospice, understands at the most elemental level how profound the feelings are when a parent experiences his/her child in crisis, especially when that suffering ends in death.

On November 8, 2000, Shelbie is on her way to son, Jeremiah's, school for a conference. Having lived through thirty-seven weeks of a healthy pregnancy, she is surprised and somewhat alarmed to be feeling so ill – something feels very wrong. In pain, pale and sweating, she tries to meet with Jeremiah's teacher, but soon has to call her doctor who eventually diagnoses her with kidney stones and tells her to get to the hospital. By this time, Shelbie is in contact with her husband, Vic, and soon they are on their way to the hospital. A Urologist is also called into her case and the gathered medical team prepares to insert a stent in order to let the stones pass; the doctors label it a "five-minute procedure;" one that is neither dangerous to her or her child. *Shelbie takes a moment to reiterate that since she is thirty-seven weeks along, her son can now be safely delivered if necessary.* Before the procedure begins, a fetal heart monitor is attached to give doctors base line information on baby Hunter; he is pronounced healthy and strong. The monitor is then removed. The "five-minute procedure" lasts over two and a half hours. There are seven attempts at inserting the stent correctly before the doctors deem it successful. Late on November 8th, the surgery completed, Shelbie, now in terrible pain, notes that the fetal heart monitor is back. In retrospect, she believes she was feeling contractions, and though her baby might have been delivered safely then, mother and son remain joined together, bleeding and in distress, for the next several hours.

Though Shelbie is a trained Labor and Delivery nurse, during these many hours she is a patient in pain, a mom who wonders and worries about the health of her unborn baby, and a pregnant woman who has put her trust in the attending medical professionals to keep both her child and herself safe. In the early morning hours on November 9th, the fetal monitor is removed. The concerned mom tries to rest, trusting that Hunter must be out of danger since the medical team has chosen to no longer so closely monitor his progress. At 8:05 am they begin monitoring again, and again the strips reporting Hunter's progress are read, and again the monitor is removed. The November 9th morning turns toward midday and Shelbie, in both physical and emotional distress, begins reporting that she can no longer feel Hunter moving and she knows, intuitively, something is terribly wrong. She asks twice for her doctor. The fetal monitor is attached again and, finally, Hunter's dangerous situation is acknowledged. The medical team swings into action and eventually an ultrasound shows one beat from Hunter's heart and, as Shelbie remembers, "the screaming starts." She is rushed into the OR where Hunter is delivered by C-Section. Vic has been called and returns to the hospital to watch their pediatrician work feverishly to resuscitate their newborn. Shelbie articulates her pain, "I assumed I'd wake up and he'd be dead." But Hunter, a miraculously strong and determined little soul, lives. And now, tragically, instead of the healthy baby who checked into the hospital within his mother only hours earlier, Hunter is now a sweetly beautiful, gravely-injured infant.

Hunter diagnosis is HIE – Hypoxic Ischemic Encephalopathy, the kind of brain injury that occurs when an infant's brain and vital organs don't receive enough oxygen and blood. About 1:00 am on November 10, 2000, Hunter is rushed from his Wyoming birthplace to a Denver hospital; Shelbie, unable to travel, remains in the hospital while Vic accompanies his son to Colorado. where doctors work hours to stabilize the newborn. In time, Shelbie is healed enough to travel and with her family's help, temporarily moves to Colorado to be close to Hunter. It is not until Christmas Eve, 2000, when Hunter is finally able to leave Colorado and join his family – Shelbie, Vic, and older brother, Jeremiah.

As so often happens, the full story of an experience only unfolds with time. Shelbie realizes that some of that time leading up to her son's birth is a haze of physical and emotional pain, but declares that, without a doubt, she will never forget the events of those hours surrounding Hunter's birth. It takes some time, but Shelbie and Vic gather all the shocking details surrounding her surgery and the circumstances leading up to Hunter's eventual birth and diagnosis. Shelbie learns of the angry dismay of Hunter's Colorado medical team who felt they were not properly prepared for his arrival from Wyoming on that early November morning. She reports, "They basically said 'You need to look into this;'" which the parents do as soon as Hunter is stable enough to be brought home. Looking back, Shelbie is now certain that her uterus was ruptured during the attempts to insert the stent; through tests demanded by the Denver doctors who study Hunter's records, she and Vic learn that both mother and child were hemorrhaging before the procedure was completed.

After researching her own medical records, Shelbie is able to pinpoint times when her unborn baby was suffering more and more distress. The fetal monitor strips, read by doctors and nurses while charting Hunter's failing health, tell a despairing story. At 8:05 am on November 9th, an "ominous strip," one that identifies a Sinusoidal Pattern, an abnormal fetal heart rate pattern, appears. The "ominous" pattern requires emergency intrauterine fetal resuscitation and immediate delivery of the unborn. But mother and child weren't rushed to the OR then;

instead the monitor is removed and not re-attached until hours later when yet another reading shows Hunter in crisis. "You can watch him die on paper," Shelbie reveals with tears in her eyes. Even though there is joy in finally having their son with them, it is coupled with all the information – those horrific experiences and details – they can never un-know and un-see. They've watched their new baby fight for his life; they've uncovered details surrounding his profound injuries; they've begun to more fully understand how Hunter's diagnosis will impact their family's day-to-day living; and they now realize that the people they trusted most with their precious son's life appear unworthy of that trust.

Shelbie and Vic strive to balance the parenting needs of six-year-old Jeremiah and baby Hunter while contending with work schedules, finding and then partnering with lawyers to navigate the complexities of filing a law suit, and fashioning a different kind of lifestyle for their new family of four. Each week Physical and Occupational Therapists come in to work with the little one, and his mom happily massages and cuddles with him daily. Because of his injuries, Hunter sleeps no more than twenty minutes at a time and is prone to seizures – both issues make healing rest incredibly difficult for the parents. The couple, committed to the best for their children, perseveres through days that are full, stress-producing and exhausting.

In the midst of spending hours caring for an adored, high-risk baby and his well-loved, loving older brother, life springs another family surprise: the couple discovers they are pregnant. Her gentle voice indicating remembered disbelief, Shelbie shares, "I still think it was like the

Immaculate Conception. . . . It's hard to describe; I don't even know if I was present . . . I got pregnant with Joshua while Hunter was declining. . . ." Joshua's conception in the midst of the couple's stress-laden life is simply beyond belief. As this new miracle is accepted, Hunter's care regime becomes more assimilated into family life. But this now-fragile family of four has experienced month after month of staggering, pressure-filled events and each family member naturally feels the fallout. The experiences before, during and after Hunter's birth prove to have a profound effect on the caring, sensitive Jeremiah. Shelbie thinks back to the anxieties young Jeremiah exhibits during this time, as well as in years beyond. "But I get it," she maintains; "he was six when all this was happening . . . even seven. I know it changed me. I'm not the same person. I mean how can you be?"

As 2000 turns into 2001, Shelbie and Vic decide to speak with lawyers about what they've discovered. Eventually, using a team of lawyers, the couple files a two-part law suit against the responsible medical parties directly involved in Hunter's birth and resulting injuries. Shelbie calls their case, filed in February, 2001, a "meritorious case," meaning the factual evidence is so clear cut that "we were going to win no matter what." Before all is settled, medical experts from around the country are able to study the events and ramifications of Hunter's case. Additionally, the factual records detailing the experiences of mother and son now reside in training manuals highlighting procedural do's and don'ts of fetal monitoring. Throughout 2001 and beyond, the couple remains embroiled in the grim details and unrelenting responsibilities of their lawsuit.

2001 flows into 2002 and Hunter's health is steadily failing. The family continues to live life in a pressure cooker of worries and fears, needs, responsibilities and ever-present grief. Shelbie articulates her thoughts about this time in her life: "I truly believe stress does enormous things to our bodies . . . and I believe that's what happened to Joshua." On January 16, 2002, baby Joshua is delivered prematurely. At only one pound, he is just too small to survive. After only a moment, and one heartbeat, Joshua is gone – his birth date, now also his death date. Only weeks later, Hunter falls into a coma and anguished parents can only be close as he passes on March 2, 2002. Within a month and a half, Jeremiah has lost two little brothers and Shelbie and Vic, their two youngest sons. Profound grief descends like a thick curtain over the family.

In the fall of 2002, Shelbie and Vic find that they are again pregnant. Deep in grief and steeped in legal issues and depositions for the lawsuit, family life remains extremely complex and difficult. Becoming pregnant after losing her sons moves Shelbie into another level of fear: ". . . every minute of every day is terrifying when you're pregnant again." And though they are still living in Wyoming, to help relieve some of that fear, the couple sets in motion details to make certain they will be delivering this next child in Denver. When Shelbie is twenty-nine weeks along with daughter Madeline, she is deeply embroiled in depositions for the lawsuit. Something goes wrong. Shelbie believes that the overwhelming responsibilities of the depositions cause her to go into premature labor and a Flight for Life airlifts her to a Colorado hospital where she stays for the next two months.

Madeline is born just shy of thirty-six weeks on June 5, 2003. Shelbie recalls her first feeling – one of utter terror – right after the birth: she didn't hear her baby cry. But all was well and Madeline is deemed a healthy, and quiet, baby girl. It seems that an ethereal Hunter is also present for his sister's delivery. A nurse who was part of the medical team working on Hunter during his time in Denver, is now also on the team at a different Denver facility when Madeline is delivered. This nurse and Shelbie recognize each other, and as this special person from Hunter's past also holds his new sister, she is able to connect sister and brother by sharing with Shelbie how "exactly alike" Hunter and Madeline look. It is as if he is with them during this precious time. Happily, Madeline turns out to be an amazingly easy baby – one who sleeps well, rarely cries, learns to entertain herself, and even in time, sings herself to sleep. Shelbie says that God must have intervened; that God must have known she could not handle one more problem. And, though Madeline and Hunter never met, he has always been part of her growing-up years; Madeline, like brother, Jeremiah, feels the strength of Hunter's place in their family. Shelbie fondly recalls the time her young daughter was assigned to tell others about her family; Madeline, in tears, recounted the story of a little brother, Hunter, who she never knew, but who she knows has a very real presence in her family.

"Losing children ruins your life. . . . It just changes you forever. Joy is never quite the same . . . and I'm a different person." Shelbie recounts. "I tell people that, yes, I still have Jeremiah and Madeline, but . . . one kid doesn't replace another." Shelbie still lives on grief's emotional roller coaster. She names herself a probable PTSD sufferer. "I don't sleep," she asserts. Instead, she relives the experiences surrounding the birth and death of Hunter. Shelbie returns to the details of her lawsuit and the desire for her day in court. "I wanted everyone in that town to know what they (hospital personnel) did to my son." She continues, "I don't even care about the money; it's a joke. I just needed that trial. I wanted it and I needed it." But in the end, she and Vic say yes to a settlement. And before her final signature lands on any paperwork, Shelbie presses for some caveats to be included: she expects to be able to talk about the reasons behind, and the details of, the suit (except the settlement amount) whenever she wants; and she demands to be in the same room with the named parties so they have to face her as she talks to them. "I wanted them to know they killed my child and I wanted them to remember that until the day they died." She eventually gets her wishes and so signs the first of the two-part settlement in 2003, and then finally brings a close to the suit by settling the second part not long after.

Shelbie feels as if she was not able to start the process of grieving for years after Hunter's death. Even though he continued to be an important part of her life, she felt unable to really share the critical and tender experiences surrounding this son's life and death. There were no support groups near her and many friends and family members who did talk with her told her to "just move on." The statement, "It gets better with time," she calls "fingernails on a chalkboard" because "for me it does not. I still cry a lot." The hardest thing, says Shelbie, is that people, even some close friends and family members, don't even appear to remember Hunter. It often seems as if his life is only an afterthought to others and that feeling continues to chip away at pieces of her heart. "People just say the dumbest things," Shelbie shares, and with a sad smile she repeats one of the most difficult things said to her as Hunter's parent: "it must have been easier for you because you knew he was going to die." And it is pronouncements like that one which prompt her to continue educating her own Hospice staff. "You can do fifty things right but the one thing that's done wrong or that one thing that's said – that's the thing people remember. We teach people (that) it doesn't matter . . . I don't care if they have six kids and they lose one; it is no different" Shelbie knows that every child, just like Hunter and Joshua, are precious to their parents; all deserve to be acknowledged, to be remembered and to be cherished – intentionally and out loud.

Shelbie is living a different life now and healing is happening. She makes her home in Colorado, is remarried, celebrates having Madeline and Jeremiah close, and shares that there are places within her life that are both peace-filled and wonderful. Shelbie now participates with a support group for bereaved parents, 3 Hopeful Hearts. In 3HH, she can talk openly about her children's lives and deaths with others who truly understand and who don't expect her to "just move on." She now mentors other parents who have lost their children, making certain that they know someone who understands their grief and pain wants to help. "I've been there," Shelbie assures them; "You can tell me things and I'll understand." She believes helping others in this way honors Hunter and is an avenue to compassionately give back to others. Once a young parent asked her one of the single most-asked questions of bereaved parents: "What do you say when people ask you how many children you have?" And Shelbie, who has a passion for keeping all of her children as alive in the hearts and minds of others as they are in hers, answers, "I have four children – and two of them are no longer with me." Though not all are physically present, every one of Shelbie's four children will always be beautifully alive, tenaciously loved and deeply-held as precious within her.

Brian: He was my best pal

A woman with an open, engaging smile and a splendid brown hat comes toward me, holding out her hand in greeting. I'm meeting Lisa for the first time; she's come to tell me the story of Brian, her beloved, adopted child. We've chosen to meet in the library on a blustery Sunday afternoon in July, and settle on a small, quiet room on the second floor with a window facing west. The sky is uncharacteristically overcast and a green-leaved canopy outside our window moves with the wind. Intermittent lightning and splashes of raindrops join in at will, but our spot is protected and cozy – a safe place to unravel a lamentable tale of heartbreak. We sit adjacent to each other and as Lisa starts to collect her thoughts aloud to share details about her son's life and death, I begin to understand the strength of this thoughtful woman who lost her only child less than two years ago. We smile at each other and soon find a shared rhythm of conversation as Brian's story unfolds.

Brian was born on August 26, 1973 in Wyoming. Lisa and first husband, Kent, adopted him when he was only five days old. The couple happily welcomes the infant, their first and only child, into their life, learning what it means to be supporting and nurturing parents and watching him grow into a strong, healthy toddler. When Brian is two and a half, Kent and Lisa's marriage dissolves. The split up is, and always remains, amicable; Kent moves east, while Lisa keeps Brian with her in Wyoming.

Though Brian experiences various lifestyle shifts, as with this early divorce, he is always enfolded into a network of supportive adults that lasts throughout his entire life. Now a single mom, Lisa makes her living as a retailer in a specialty ski and summer sports shop in their Wyoming town. As Brian grows, mother and son do many things together – one of them is skiing – and eventually the athletically-inclined Brian learns to enjoy the sport. Springtime often finds Lisa traveling for work and, as often as she can she takes her son to visit her parents in California. They, like Lisa, have strong and proud northern Finnish roots. They give their grandson both a loving environment and some familiarity with the Finnish language.

When Brian is four, Kent remarries and provides his son a new, caring stepmother. The youngster visits his father and stepmother, another professional woman, and is introduced both to their "country club life," as well as the lifestyle of his stepmother's parents. They all become an important part of his growing up and adult life.

When Brian is eight Lisa remarries. She falls in love with a "working cowboy," Henry, and moves with Brian to a ranch. "We both fell in love with this man," Lisa remarks with a sweet smile. She remembers how happy Brian was to have Henry come into their life. Her son embraces the rural lifestyle as well as his new stepdad – the "big, burly man that had a huge heart." Not yet ten, Brian is encircled by a variety of adults who lovingly care about his wellbeing: two fathers, two mothers and two sets of grandparents. His travel and lifestyle experiences span across the country; he is a child of the urban east and the rural west.

Lisa describes her growing son as physically healthy and showing signs of athletic giftedness. "Nothing scared him," she remembers with a touch of pride and some concern. She talks about how Brian could test boundaries, all kinds of physical and behavioral limits, but before her worry became too great, "he did always come back." The year Brian is eleven Lisa and Henry say yes to fostering a young boy. At this same time in their Wyoming town, a child molester, someone known and familiar to families within the area, is reported and arrested. The couple is concerned that Brian may have been a victim since their family also knows the perpetrator, but Brian contends he remained safe. Their foster boy shares that he had been molested earlier in his life, before his arrival into Lisa's family, and as a part of the social services system, he had received counseling as a child of molestation. He relays some basic information to his foster family and Lisa finds it very helpful. After some time and more discussion, Brian finally admits to Henry that he, too, was a victim of the town's molester.

Lisa recalls that during that difficult summer, conversations with their foster child seem to bring Brian some comfort and she begins researching more information about the ramifications of sexual abuse. The couple provides both boys with counseling sessions throughout that year. Brian, Lisa shares, continued to move in and out of counseling situations for much of the rest of his life. Lisa's voice grows quieter as she calls to mind looking at old photos of her son taken before and during this complex and troublesome time: "I can always see when the expression in Brian's eyes changed. . . . He was wounded . . . and who wouldn't be."

The early to mid-eighties find Lisa and Henry loving and worrying about a son who starts to find his way into mischief. The three live in a rural Wyoming area where both parents are well known. Unable to fly under the radar, Brian begins to act out in resentment to the area where his family is so recognized by all. The verbal, athletic and well-traveled youngster tells stories that are easily checked by others who know the family and he is caught in lies; minor shoplifting and school cheating experiences also begin to point to a pattern of distressing behavior for his parents. As he moves into his early teen years, Lisa notes that her son must have felt his world was just too "small." The eighties wind down and times become even more worrisome for the family. Brian's trouble with alcohol surfaces. Right after he begins his ninth grade year, he is suspended for bringing alcohol on the premises. Lisa conjectures that the earlier molestation incident might well be at the core of her son's problem behaviors.

Lisa and Henry decide with Kent and his wife that Brian should have a change of scene; they collectively hope that a move to Kent's home in Cleveland will give their son a fresh start. But Brian's life continues to unravel while he is with Kent; using pills, he attempts suicide and is hospitalized for a time. More counseling and a stretch within a mental health unit mark this unsettling period in the troubled teen's life. Brian returns home to Wyoming and when he is sixteen, the family moves south to a ranch in Colorado. "This time was all very tenuous. He knew he had love with us but he had all this stuff he needed to work out," Lisa explains. And so, with a mixture of anxiety and hope, the family of three tries to move forward.

The eighties turn into the nineties and the worry continues. The entire extended family feels the grief of a beloved son beginning a walk down a very dangerous path and they, each in their own way, hope for a turn around. Brian is caught stealing money from another ranch in the area and Henry and Lisa decide they must call the police. This time Brian's risky behavior lands him in juvenile detention and a mental health facility. But it is here, in a small Colorado town, when seventeen-year-old Brian authentically shares with others his molestation experience. He tells Lisa that he finally feels some relief. Lisa visits Brian during his time in detention and sees a glimmer of hopefulness for her son's future. But as the nineties extend, so does heartache.

Brian seems unable to get his footing and he continues to slip farther and faster down a precarious pathway. Still walking the increasingly thin line between substance use and abuse as well as between misbehavior and outright criminal activity, he spends time back and forth between his Ohio and Colorado families. Shifting in and out of relationships and brushes with the law, Brian grows from his teens into his twenties. With a sad certainty, Lisa states, "He was always at risk; he was always a risk taker; he was always on the edge." Finally, Brian ventures beyond petty crimes and steals enough to land him into the adult prison system. With time served, he receives parole and transfers into a halfway house, but too soon he violates his parole conditions and is returned to prison. All the while Lisa and Henry follow their son, visiting wherever he is incarcerated, even traveling as far as Texarkana. His parents remain in contact as much as Brian allows. In 1997, Brian, now in his early twenties, finally exits prison on parole. Lisa and Henry agree that it is in their son's best interest to move to Cleveland to serve out the terms of his parole with Kent and his wife. Lisa calls his relocation to Ohio a hard but necessary step for everyone in the family. And it is then, still living with the consequences of past behaviors, when Brian begins to find his feet. He successfully adheres to the probation limitations, serving his time and finally exiting the penal system.

Brian relocates to New Jersey where his stepmother's parents, a couple he has grown to know and become fond of, also live. And though alcohol continues to be an ongoing problem, this troubled, yet accomplished young man finds work as a carpenter. In the early 2000's Brian meets a woman, a decade older, with a young daughter, and the couple commit to working toward a new life together. They have two more children, first a boy and then, thirteen months later, a baby girl. They make a home for a family of five: he, striving to live into new patterns of behavior, to create another fresh start within a different kind of family unit; and she, a recovering addict, hoping to build a life for her and her children with a man whose past and present behaviors she understands. Lisa shares that her son was at his most successful when he had structure;

the woman he chose had experiences with addictive behavior patterns and, according to Lisa, she controlled the situation fairly well. In 2006, she and Brian marry.

Unfortunately, the decade of the nineties, one filled with ever-present anxiety, chaos and grief for Lisa and Henry, eventually takes its toll on the couple's marriage. They divorce in 2002. And though they are apart, Lisa speaks of her ex-husband with gentle fondness. She shares they knew it would "add value to our lives if we continue to be friends and honor each other," and it is clear in how she speaks about Henry that they still do – both honor and have respect for each other.

Lisa reveals her son knew as a youngster of his adoption. She explains how, when he was little, she would talk with him using children's stories and clear, simple language to introduce the concept of adoption, being adopted, and how it connected to their family. And then she declares, "Brian always knew he was a gift;" he was told how much he meant to her and how important he was to their family. First a curious youngster, later a risk-taking teen and now a grown man in continual search of elusive answers to crucial questions, Brian decides to follow through with his wonderings about his birth mother. In 2006, the search he and his wife began earlier ends in discovery. Brian's mother is located in Las Vegas and she comes east to meet her son and his wife and children at their home.

During her stay, Brian learns a good deal more about his background, and though it may have satisfied his curiosity, much of it also wounds him further. A woman who struggled with addiction and abusive relationships, Brian's mother, according to Lisa's description, never fulfilled her own, full potential. She shares with her son that he was conceived in violence, by rape, and that she never knew his father. While she is with his family, she abuses a substance, and her son, wanting to protect his children, tells her she can't be in his home when she uses. She leaves to return to her home in Las Vegas, and sadly, eventually dies of a Heroin overdose. After hearing about the visit and what he learned, Lisa begins to even more clearly understand the challenging path her son has had to navigate, the biological limitations he has had to overcome throughout his thirty plus years. She states, "His road was going to be hard – no matter what." The visit leaves Brian – a man who so dearly wants to stand firmly and peacefully on solid ground – more aware of his background than ever before. His physical resemblance to a biological parent, his athleticism mirroring a possible football player rapist father, and a probable genetic predisposition to addictive behaviors combine to leave an indelible mark on Lisa's cherished son.

Though his family network still circles supportively around him in various ways, by 2011 Brian has seriously lost his footing. Finally able to admit to his alcoholism, he enters his first serious rehabilitation situation. "He always felt dark inside; . . . those demons . . . while he wanted to lick them, he couldn't." Lisa asserts solemnly. During the following years, 2012 and 2013, the slide with substance abuse continues and Brian experiences a series of addiction counseling sessions, hospitalizations, and rehab and halfway house placements. In 2013, he also endures the death of his first-known father, Kent, from a heart attack. In January of 2014, he enters a six-week placement followed by a move into a halfway house close enough to his family in New Jersey to be able to have regular visitations with his children. Lisa shares that unfortunately it is also during this time when her son decides to dissolve his marriage. In May, 2014, he and a woman he has met during their common rehabilitation time move in together. They are able to stay clean and sober until the fall of 2014 when they both fall back into their respective addiction patterns. Tragically, on October 19, 2014, they both overdose on Heroin.

After Brian's death, Lisa sought and found some comfort in grief groups sponsored by her local Hospice and the 3 Hopeful Hearts organization. She was able to share her grief and voice her truth with others who listened unconditionally. In time, her son's death prompts her to take a journey of discovery along varied pathways. A long-time feminist, she notes that the writings of the social and political activist and author, Gloria Steinem, led her down one path, helping her move forward as a woman in her sixties progressing, interacting and grieving within our 21st century's culture. A second shows itself as Lisa starts to notice obituaries tying addiction to suicides. She discovered the mission and works of the National Action Alliance for Suicide Prevention, and was drawn by its partnership with the Substance Abuse and Mental Health Services Administration. Due to her own personal introspection and study as she traveled down these new paths, Lisa has come to believe her son's death dose of Heroin was "accidental-intentional." The many and complex revelations of her son's life and death are leading Lisa down yet another path – one toward honoring Brian.

Lisa looks up and in a strong voice declares, "Brian was born on Equality Day, in the Equality State." Her dream is to give her son a gift. A committed feminist dedicated to equality, Lisa was struck by Julia Ward Howe's 1870's initiatives. Howe, the first drafter of the Mother's Day Proclamation, framed the document to represent her concern over the consequences of war as well as her hope for war's end and ongoing peace. Lisa's favorite words from the document mirror her own best hopes: "Let them meet first, as women, to bewail and commemorate the dead. Let them then solemnly take counsel with each other as to the means whereby the great human family can live in peace." Lisa's third path is leading her to write a proposal to bring women together in the Equality State in order to discuss how humankind can more humanely move forward – to take counsel with one another to identify healthier ways to live peacefully, one with another. "My dream (is) . . . to honor Brian," his mother states. And though we didn't talk specifics, I wonder if this mother of a beautiful but burdened son might craft language in her proposal to not only include the collective legions who war with others outside, but also the individual souls who are at war within. Perhaps Lisa will find ways to honor Brian through promoting conversations about the shaping of a better world for the whole as well as for the one; about the attainment of inner peace and a quality life for any and all who strive to find their footing but somehow lose themselves in the process – conversations about individual children in pain; conversations about Brian.

As Lisa thinks back over the life and death of her son, one of the words she attaches to her beloved child is "wounded." She continues, "He was a beautiful person . . . as loving as he could be . . . (but) he was killing the pain." She takes a moment to recall some of their face-to-face and phone conversations throughout the years as she and Brian brought each other up to date on family details, hopes and goals. She still remains in ongoing contact with her daughter-in-law and grandchildren as well as Brian's stepmother, taking joy in collecting and sending them pictures of a husband, a dad and a stepson who grew up in the west, in a different time and place. She wants her grandchildren to know the fullness of their father's life.

Favorite moments for Lisa were when Brian would call her, "Ma," because when he said it, it signaled to her he was feeling good, affectionate, even playful; it was a special bond they shared. With sadness, Lisa notes that "nobody can call me 'Ma' anymore." Then with a brighter voice, she shares that thinking of her son still brings a smile to her face; he was not only a person who lived life in large ways but was also a compassionate man, befriending people who had somehow been traumatized. She learned on one of her visits to New Jersey, from others who knew her son, that "in small and large ways he had given a lot of people comfort." Such details about Brian continue to also comfort her. With a small catch in her voice she expresses what she knows is true: "I did what I could. . . I have to let go." And as she works to move forward with her life, she also carries with her a wonderful gift: Lisa learned that her son was glad to have been adopted – that he believed he had been given a good life, and he was grateful. Shimmering tears of gratitude and grief surface: "I miss the knowledge that he is on this earth. . . He was my best pal."

Grant: Remembering through the whisper of wings

I've found Leanna's home early, giving me time to study the well-manicured lawn of this attractive house on a now-quiet corner. The late August day sports a bright blue sky and a pleasantly warm temperature. Summer's beauty and ease are still evident in Leanna's yard; flowers abound and the front porch – set apart by white picket fencing and a cozy, round table with two matching chairs – beckons visitors to join the family for conversation and something cool to drink. My eye travels just to the right of the porch where an interestingly-crafted birdbath rests. Its wrought iron legs display intricately-designed butterflies and dragonflies poised in flight and I'm struck by its playfulness – and its meaning. Both sculpted insects are powerful symbols in many cultures; they signal transformation, change, even resurrection. Aristotle is said to have named the butterfly, Psyche, meaning soul, while European legend tout the dragonfly as a reminder to all souls to dive more deeply into self-healing. So much symbolism – of adaptability, of a revitalized sense of inner life and purpose, of a return to joy within one's spirit and soul – all contained in the metal figures cradled so fittingly in the side yard of the bereaved mother I'm visiting with today. My interest growing, I move to the front door to meet a smiling Leanna. Soon we are deep within the process of laying out the puzzle pieces of the tragic death of her beautiful son, Grant.

Leanna is her son's greatest champion. Love and grief mix continuously as she fits together the picture of his death story. Born on November 8, 1980, Grant is a well-loved boy who grows to be active, fun-loving and challenging. His mom recalls a son who is an "outside-of-the-box thinker;" who enjoys the fast-paced energy of playing hockey; who loves to snowboard, hike and travel with his family; who appreciates shopping, planning, crafting and cooking with his mom to prepare for family occasions; who grows from a cute youngster into a handsome life of the party; and who brings enormous light into the lives of all who sit in the circle of his love. When he is about eleven, Grant's circle of support expands as Leanna introduces Tom into their family. "Tom is not Grant's dad, but he is Grant's dad . . . ." Leanna smilingly declares. This man who becomes Grant's stepfather holds a vitally important place in her son's growing and developing teen and adult years. From early on, Leanna's boy is enfolded into a close-knit, supportive and loving family – his mother, older sister, Shay, and stepfather, Tom.

A clever youngster develops into an intelligent, ambitious young man and Grant earns three higher-education degrees over the years following his high school graduation: one from the University of Colorado, Boulder, a second from the University of Arizona in Tucson, and finally a Masters in Architecture from the University of Colorado, Denver. He meets a woman as he is finishing his first degree at CU, Boulder, who he marries after their return to Denver for his Master's Program work. This bright and hopeful couple decides to settle in Denver where they both find work and begin to build a life together.

Leanna continues presenting the puzzle pieces of her son's story, moving closer to his death event. It's the springtime of 2012. Grant has been working as an architect for about five years and though he realizes this position is not his dream job, he perseveres; Leanna's daughter-in-law has begun travelling a lot – going back and forth from their home in Denver to St Louis, where her family lives. Leanna finds her daughter-in-law's frequent travel both puzzling and troubling. "I thought that was peculiar," she asserts, "so I knew something was up." But what, she wonders. About ten days before his death, Grant's wife comes into town to attend a professional conference and stays with Leanna and Tom. Grant is to join the family for the upcoming Easter weekend. While with her mother-in-law, the young woman shares her worry about her husband. Evidently Grant is drinking heavily. They talk, and finally Leanna tells her: ". . . sometimes people get themselves in a hole and they can't get themselves out on their own." Then she continues, "Maybe we should do an intervention." Grant's wife turns down that suggestion and with a razor-sharp edge to her voice, Leanna says, "well, interestingly enough, ten days later my child is dead – so that was a missed opportunity."

The Friday before Easter, April 4, 2012, Grant drives north from Denver to be with the family, and, according to his mom, he is "his darling self." Though the Easter holiday weekend seems normal, the earlier conversation with his wife and a growing change in her son's communication behaviors peak Leanna's concern. She shares that he doesn't return phone calls as he once did; he seems to be "missing in action," perhaps even socially isolating. And now she's also feeling confused and worried by his reported drinking. Leanna texts Grant with a loving query: "what's going on with you? I'm really worried about you. You can tell me anything. I'm always there for you." His text back tells her "that means everything to me, Mom. Thanks." But her worry-filled question goes unanswered. As the time of his death ticks down, important puzzle pieces needed to help bring clarity to a picture of what's really happening in Grant's life still elude his family.

On April 18, 2012, Leanna receives a call from her daughter-in-law telling her that Grant, who was to pick his wife up at the airport from her latest trip has not shown up. "That's not like him," Leanna asserts. "And, of course, I left work right away." Leanna's plan is to drive to Denver, but before she has gotten very far, she receives another call.

Before Grant's mother receives that second call, much has happened: after calling Leanna, her daughter-in-law's next call was for a cab to take her home where she discovers her husband in the garage; he has hanged himself. Her third call then goes out to the police, who are quickly dispatched to Grant's home to investigate the circumstances of his death.

With a voice full of emotion, Leanna shares that the second call she receives while on her way to locate Grant and offer help, is from the Denver police who ultimately deliver the horrific news of his death. Leanna stops driving and quickly contacts her daughter, Shay, and Tom to tell them the devastating news she been given – Grant is gone. Together, Leanna and Tom with Shay and her husband begin a different journey. They arrive at Grant's home the afternoon of April 18th to discover the Coroner has already removed Grant's body and the puzzle that is his death looms as a grief-filled jumble of heartbreaking, unanswered questions.

In his house, Leanna is confronted by several clues that help to fill in the picture that has become her son's lifestyle. On the kitchen counter she finds several personal items which she grabs to take with her – his phone, laptop, wallet and wedding ring. She also notes two large bottles, one of Vodka and one of orange juice, both almost empty. Eventually the grieving mom also discovers a prescription bottle of Ambien and, by counting the number of pills left and matching that figure to the script's date, can tell Grant has been self-medicating, in more than one way. Before the family, including Grant's wife, finally leave Denver the night of April 18, Leanna calls the Medical Examiner; she wants to know about her son – what's happened to him? where is he? who is taking care of him? Leanna speaks of the M.E.'s kindnesses with an emotional, but grateful lift in her voice: "She said, 'he's right here with me. I have him. I'm taking good care of him. He's safe.'" With these latest pieces of information, Leanna arranges the puzzle pieces into an order that she can make some sense of: "I knew he was impaired; he had to be." And though the family requests a toxicology report from Grant's autopsy, that particular piece of the still-confused picture is never received.

Grant's wife remains with Leanna and Tom as she waits for her own family to arrive. Grant's funeral looms, and Leanna talks of the awkwardness surrounding the situation. In a halting voice, searching for just the right way to describe the evolving events, Leanna articulates the complexities of how to best communicate with all the involved family members, how to best honor Grant, both a son and a husband. "What was peculiar was that I was put in a weird position because I'm his mother, but he has a wife. I have no decision-making power, really. . . . He wanted to be cremated, but I wanted him to have a memorial service at the church where he was baptized." After some discussion between the families, decisions are made. The weekend before Grant's memorial, Leanna and Tom are given the full responsibility of collecting things from both Grant's home and office. They meet and spend time visiting with their son's shocked and saddened co-workers as they collect individual work items. To gather Grant's other personal belongings, the pair goes to his home. Leanna reveals the shock she feels at finding her son's house filthy. "I was so angry, so mad," she declares, "that he lived like that. To me it was like he was neglected." And another puzzle piece drops into the unfolding picture. Leanna spends the next hours scrubbing Grant's home on her hands and knees – a way to bring order and give honor to the last place her son was alive. Grant's things, including his car, are packed and prepared for the return trip to their home.

Leanna creates her son's obituary, Tom makes all the necessary arrangements for the service, and Grant's memorial is held at his childhood church where Leanna delivers the eulogy. Together the couple both plan and host a reception for their son's family and many friends. Leanna pauses to share another decision she and Tom made to honor Grant, the son. Though they support his desire for cremation, Leanna also wants a physical place where the family can go to be with him. To that end, she and Tom purchase a cemetery plot in his home town where Grant's cremains now rest. Close by is a beautiful bench where all can linger and visit a cherished son, brother and uncle whenever they wish. Leanna pauses before she speaks about the unexpected lack of involvement of Grant's wife and her family during this tender, heart-aching time. In fact, though she tries to talk with Grant's widow about the collective grief they are experiencing, it is made clear to Leanna that she does not want to have any part in Leanna's – the family's – grieving process. Eventually contact is irrevocably broken between Grant's family and his widow: "That part of our lives is a closed chapter," Leanna states definitively.

Life moves forward; the family unit has shifted and those who are left search for their footing on the paths leading each toward their respective walk in grief. But there is still more to know about Grant's life, his choices, his death. Leanna says of herself, "I am the kind of person that I turn over every stone" in order to discover the full truth. Opportunities present themselves and Leanna takes full advantage each time one comes up. Since his death, she and Tom continue to have contact with some of their son's good friends; they attend celebratory functions, reconnect, and remember together the Grant who occupied an important role in their lives. Such times bring Leanna joy. She maintains, "I like to talk about Grant because he mattered. . . . And it makes me feel good if you say his name or share a story." These conversations provide a variety of information about Grant, the person and professional adult, helping to create a more developed look at his life before the suicide.

Leanna also contacts the psychiatrist Grant was seeing. Though she and Tom are unable to secure Grant's medical records, his psychiatrist kindly agrees to talk with the couple and during the visit shares with them how highly Grant thought of and spoke about his parents. But other statements are unsettling. On the Tuesday before his suicide, Grant called his doctor, crying. He is alone and drinking; he is in deep distress. Leanna's anger at a professional who neither calls to alert one of Grant's friends, or asks the local authorities to do a welfare check on her son, is palpable. Leanna's strong response carries with it a frustrated mother's heartbreak: "I've seen him drunk before but that really doesn't matter to me; but his crying matters to me!" New pieces settle and the picture they help create brings more clarity, but little comfort.

Leanna is still, and always, Grant's greatest champion and she continues to extend her high-powered support to others. A dedicated and client-centered Occupational Therapist, she takes a moment to reveal starling statistics she's discovered about suicide in 2012, the year Grant hangs himself. Skyrocketing suicide rates, especially among males, head the list. She goes on to think aloud about how the complexities that define a suicide so often leave those who remain with a myriad of perplexing questions: what triggers were tripped to lead their loved one to take his or her life? Leanna's personality, training, and now her own experience fuel her passion to help others discover answers.

She talks about the lack of federal, state and community resources, one's inability to realize and access what could be an available resource, limiting environmental barriers, and the presence of damaging societal expectations – all factors that can put people at risk. Her work leads her to clients, both youth and adults, who could easily experience, or are already living within, any of those risk factors and she treats them with the respect she knows every person, including her son, deserves. "We need to embrace humanity – the human condition. . . . I think people try to do the best they can. They cope in a way that maybe isn't in their best interest, by drinking or using drugs or whatever. It was an attempt to cope with pain (that) just didn't work out very well. . . ." Like the metallic sculptures – butterflies and dragonflies – that hover in her front yard, Leanna's life's work, her profession, keeps her poised to offer possibilities of change and transformation to others who need a revitalized sense of peace and harmony and purpose.

During their walk forward, toward hope and healing, Leanna and Tom discover and soon appreciate the services offered by 3 Hopeful Hearts, a local group that provides a variety of supportive opportunities for bereaved parents. The couple continues to participate and contribute in various ways with this caring organization that advocates for grieving parents. Leanna serves as a mentor for other parents, as well as a co-facilitator for a monthly, collaborative support group combining 3HH with the

Alliance for Suicide Prevention. Leanna leads a full-time life, one in which she is seriously and lovingly involved: she is Grant's mother and his memory-keeper; a mom to Shay; a grandmother to Ella and Hannah (who Leanna, with a big smile, refers to as "Grant incarnated"); a wife to Tom; an Occupational Therapist in an educational setting; a facilitator of psycho-educational groups for a mental health facility; a volunteer who helps other grieving parents; and . . . the list goes on. But even though she lives her busy life at full speed, giving to others is never a burden to Leanna. "I don't give advice; I'm just there because I know how they're suffering and they had to have something to hold on to because it's so easy to go down a rabbit hole and not get out. . . . I'm here to walk with others . . . and help them understand that they can survive." More than a survivor, Grant's mom finds healing in serving others and staying open to all that is possible – in our known world and beyond.

Leanna affirms that she has repeatedly experienced ethereal events, letting her know in profound ways that her son is always close, always bringing her gifts. Not long after Grant's death, Leanna began to hear her son's voice, feel his breath close to her. She recalls lying in bed and clearly hearing Grant playfully calling, "Hey Mom! It's me." Her dreams are vivid and regular for about two years after his passing; all of her senses are engaged during those dreams as she and Grant directly communicate. Over time the dreams morph and messages vary but they continue to bring him close. She keeps a journal during this time of exceptional dreams and remembers that once her son told her, "Mom, our bond can never be broken. . . . I'm always with you." In one particularly interesting dream, she talks of seeing an angel figure who transforms into butterflies that fly free. Leanna is so struck by the clarity and beauty of the vision that she finds healing through painting and then framing it to hang in her home. Over the four years since Grant's death, his mother is certain he has been a real and sacred presence in her life . . . and not only in her dreams.

Just recently another event reminds her that Grant is ever-present. She sets the stage by sharing how she and Grant loved to watch meteor showers together. In August, 2016, Leanna and Tom are looking forward to watching a predicted, fantastic meteor shower. Unfortunately, that night they note that thick clouds have gathered and believing there will be no way for them to enjoy the celestial show, they go to bed instead. In the early morning, the couple is awakened by a clatter from another room and when Leanna checks, she discovers that a photo book has "fallen" from a shelf. But it is as if the book has been plucked from its spot and dropped purposely on the floor because all of the photos in front of and close to the book remain in their places, undisturbed. And it is then that Leanna recognizes her latest gift from Grant – the noise that awakens her to discover a beautifully clear sky. She and Tom go outside to enjoy the brilliance of light streaking across the horizon and celebrate the wonder and joy of Grant's presence with them.

Being presented with a completed, fully-understood picture of any life may be too much to ever expect, no matter how long or hard we search, but discovering how to be at peace with what we are given is an incredible gift within our grasp. Butterflies and dragonflies, harbingers of self-healing and resurrection, serve as gracious reminders that souls, spirits, like that of a treasured son who has passed, are never really lost, but instead, lovingly transformed. When we invite quiet, listen closely, and let the moment speak, we can hear the delicate whisper of wings prompting us to understand that our only guarantee is that love abounds – that it exists to be shared intentionally and lavishly, that healing is available when we find ways to sit in its circle with others, and that anything is possible when we wrap ourselves in its arms.

Johanna: An exceptional, loving force

I climb the road toward Daniel's home and discover that it's nestled within the folds of the foothills just to the west of town. A hairpin turn and unpaved lane take me the final way to reach a house rising skyward from the surrounding rock-face. When I exit the car, noting the slope of the road behind me, I'm awe-struck at where I've found myself for this interview. A three-sixty turn gifts me with remarkable views. Dan graciously greets me and after pleasant introductions, we climb up and back to one of the decks of his home. I have a few moments to look around and gratefully soak in the majesty of this newest panorama, welcoming the freshness of a gently-sweeping breeze as it moves from the rising mountain range to our west, up and over the tree and boulder-rimmed reservoir below Dan's property. Right here, right now, life stands still; it is calming being encircled in such stunning beauty. And though I'm in no hurry to leave such a gorgeous scene, I am well aware of why I'm here and the importance of the next quiet hours, so we move inside. Dan begins our conversation: "This is totally new territory for me though it's been seven years. There is no way I could have done this a few years back. The grief process for me is to do this and I know she (Johanna) is totally in support of it." The timing is finally right to take the opportunity to talk about the daughter he calls an exceptional human force, his beloved Johanna.

Johanna Emilie was born on November 19, 1987, to two family physicians. Johanna's mother, Ingrid, and Daniel were divorced when their daughter was not quite three. Consistently in contact with parents, grandparents and extended family, Johanna grew up knowing she had intersecting, loving family circles enfolding her. Dan describes his daughter as an "old soul." At her birth, she just looked all around – never crying, but instead surveying what lay before and around her. He continues crafting the picture of a daughter who flourishes as she matures: she was "wise beyond her years," a straight A student and avid reader, in love with poetry and all forms of music, who grew into a "caring, loving, strong woman . . . committed to helping the underserved."

Johanna loved travel and was unafraid to independently discover the world. Dan shares how much his daughter delighted in exploring the people, food, art and music of new places. She especially celebrated the times when she was able to combine the joy of personal travel with volunteer opportunities to serve others. Traveling to San Francisco to stay with her uncle while volunteering for Planned Parenthood, assisting at a Lakota Indian reservation in New Mexico, helping teach English at a rural school in Guatemala and marching in Washington D.C. for women's rights and non-violent conflict resolution are examples of Johanna's generous, fearless and selfless spirit. This was a young woman who relished living life fully and understood that serving others made it all the sweeter. With love and pride in his voice, Dan calls his daughter an "amazing human force. . . . She was just extraordinary."

Johanna's considerable academic gifts are encouraged and developed throughout all her schooling, beginning with her attendance at the Montessori Children's House. After spending the early and middle years within the local public school system, Johanna transfers during the second semester of her high school freshman year to Westtown School in West Chester, Pennsylvania. Westtown, a Quaker, coeducational, college preparatory day and boarding school, provides the stimulation Johanna needs to excel even more. *Dan takes a moment to reveal that Westtown School is a family tradition. Both Johanna's mother and maternal grandmother attended the school and it was always an expectation that Johanna, as well as her offspring, will do the same.* Dan continues to share that, though he knew Johanna would thrive in the Pennsylvania school, he missed her terribly. Their relationship, while father and daughter had lived together, was one of mutual love and respect as boundaries and familial expectations are tested and established. "She accepted me for my follies . . . accepted me unconditionally," Dan smiles; "She never let me down."

After graduation from Westtown, Johanna moves on to Wesleyan University, a highly-respected, private, liberal arts University in Middletown, Connecticut. She spends almost three years growing more beautiful, both inside and out, making her mark as a double major in English and Spanish, demonstrating a strong commitment to social justice, and preparing to move toward her goal of earning a Master's in Public Health. Additionally, Johanna seemed to have found the mature relationship for which she had long searched. "She wanted to love and be loved so much," Dan states. "She met and fell in love with a nice man. She was in love; she was happy." And even more wonderful news follows. As Johanna is ending her junior year at Wesleyan she discovers she has been accepted for an upcoming summer internship at the National Organization for Women in DC. Life is joyfully unfolding for Johanna – she's found love and purpose and can see the light of her dreams dancing just ahead. With a catch in his voice, Dan reflects, "She was thriving in every possible way . . . . She had no knowledge of what was going to happen."

It's May, finals week at Wesleyan, and Johanna is at work in the University bookstore/coffee shop. A young man she knows from an earlier time enters the coffee shop; shots ring out and Johanna falls. The story behind this horrific scene is complex and heartbreaking. Softly, as if retelling a nightmare, Dan begins to unravel an unimaginable chain of events. The summer before Johanna enters college she meets a young man, also from Colorado, in an NYU summer class. He becomes smitten with the lovely Johanna, but she learns early on that he is unstable. She rejects his advances. Hoping for her attention, he doesn't give up trying, and in time his pursuit turns ugly – into unreasonable fear and antipathy. Hateful anti-Semitic emails follow and eventually Johanna needs to involve the New York City Police as well as the NYU campus police. The young man stops emailing and seemingly disappears from her life, but behind the scenes he continues to stoke the fires of irrational, fear-filled hatred toward Johanna, her family and her Jewish roots. For some time he stalks Johanna and eventually, through social media, finds she is attending Wesleyan. He contacts her again but Dan is unaware of how and when because Johanna never shares that information with either the authorities or her family. Then, on May 6, 2009, in disguise and carrying a gun, Johanna's stalker comes face to face with her at her workplace and carries out his plan to shoot her.

Dan receives a call from his daughter on the evening of May 5th. They talk as usual, neither aware that this is to be their last conversation. The following day, Dan receives another call from Johanna's phone. The person on the other end of this call reveals that his daughter has been hurt at work, and then passes the phone to a police officer who tells Dan his child has been shot and taken by ambulance to the hospital. The stunned father is given a number to call. Dan's voice becomes softer, a little tentative, as he continues to retell the unthinkable details indelibly etched in his memory. He uses the number given to him and reaches the Emergency Room at the hospital to discover that the doctor working on Johanna is doing CPR, that she was shot multiple times but that she is holding on. But before long, terror turns into abject heartbreak as the doctor returns to the phone to break the news to Dan – his daughter is gone. Still at work in his own doctor role, Dan somehow wraps up things at his practice with the help of his office staff. Now as the father, he tries contacting Johanna's mother to share the horrifying news of their daughter's death, but his efforts are unsuccessful. Next he tries reaching out to other family and close friends but to no avail. He is totally alone in the swirling chaos of thoughts and feelings, the horror of this inconsolable loss.

Before the evening ends another call comes in. A detective from Middletown is hoping Dan can give him names of anyone who could have wanted to harm Johanna. The shooter, who flees right after the crime, is not yet in custody and police are looking for clues to his capture . . . but Dan can offer no help. *It takes two interminable days for authorities to finally find and arrest Johanna's killer.* Quietly, Dan reveals that he's used to being in control, used to being able to decisively help: "It's what I do; I make decisions for a living." But now, he's found that he can't even imagine what might come next. With a kind of awe in his recalling, Dan repeats the grief-filled mantra that takes over his life for weeks to come: "I don't know what to do. I don't know what to do."

Johanna is killed on a Wednesday and by Friday the family is transporting her body home from Connecticut. The burial is Saturday and by Monday, only five days after Johanna's murder, Dan is back at his office. He talks of the professional drive to serve his patients as well as his personal need to have a purpose – a reason to go on living. Steeped deeply in pain, he's unwell – emotionally and physically. Eight days after his daughter's death, Dan drives himself to the emergency room and undergoes successful surgery to repair a health issue, and again, taking little time off for recuperation, he returns to work. There is no rest. Unfortunately, for many weeks the national and local media attention surrounding Johanna's murder is staggering. Family, friends, acquaintances and patients are all touched in various ways by the overflow from the pressure cooker that has become Dan's life: "I'm a dead man walking; I felt like I'd lost the most important reason for living." His focus becomes simply finding the strength to put one foot in front of the other, to keep going, to continue responding to his professional and personal responsibilities.

He shares that he did feel nourished and loved by supportive family, special friendships and many of his patients. Still, the pain is overwhelming: "For three years I didn't want to live in spite of everything." Thankfully, in time he is able to promise his parents he won't take his own life. Dan remembers his father's words: "If you kill yourself, her memory . . . goes with you. You need to stay alive to continue to memorialize her." "And he was right," Dan asserts. "Now I live for her." He thinks of all the joys and pleasures, the service opportunities and adventures his daughter can no longer experience and he tries to do them for her. "Every time I do something good for others, I feel like I do it for her; I honor her life."

Dan calls himself gifted in compartmentalizing. "Being able to compartmentalize keeps me going," he smiles; being able to shift focus "saved me." The ability to modify his focus "like changing a channel," serves as a vital survival skill when he travels to Connecticut in the winter of 2012 to attend the trial of Johanna's killer. Armed with a network of loving friends, both his and Johanna's, and his family, Dan leaves for the east coast. The group rents a lovely house next to a lake, stocks it with provisions, and prepares – physically, emotionally, mentally and spiritually – to endure the unimaginable feat of reliving Johanna's death. Dan sits in the courtroom day after day, listening to the pertinent details and timelines of his daughter's death, only leaving the proceedings when details of her autopsy are presented. He hears once again that after the perpetrator is caught, authorities discover he is the same young man who Johanna met and rebuffed at NYU three summers earlier, and that not only his daughter, but his entire family had become this man's target. Diagnosed as a Paranoid Schizophrenic after capture, the killer has been awaiting trial in the Connecticut State Hospital. The ugly facts of his intentions and planning, the deranged reasoning he uses to justify his actions, and his dangerously malicious anti-Semitic communications pour out into the courtroom until finally Johanna's death is labeled a hate crime. The young man, now a convicted murderer, is returned to the state hospital, committed into the highest level of security. "We were traumatized but we survived it," Dan says quietly.

He returns home, channeling his focus toward his professional and personal life, and on making certain Johanna's murderer stays tightly and securely locked away. Every two years Dan writes a letter to the Psychiatric Security Review Board of Connecticut stating his recommendations for the man's future. He asserts his worry that Johanna's murderer will receive permission to move into a lowered security level which he believes would mean more privilege and a better life. Johanna's father clearly doesn't want such a move to happen: "I would like him to live a very long life, but I don't want it to be a very pleasant life."

With a slight smile, Dan voices his truth: "My daughter's life continues to have meaning. . . . There are times I've just kind of felt her presence – like this little shimmering light that I can perceive and feel and see. There are times when I feel really connected. . . ." His extraordinary daughter remains alive, connected in spirit, and through legacy bestowed freely and lovingly in the form of simple and complex gifts. One example resides in Kibera, Kenya, where a twelve-grade school and accompanying clinic have been built and staffed to serve young girls, teens and women. The health facility carries the name *Johanna Justin-Jinich Community Clinic*, honoring a young woman whose short but memorable life continues to influence others to work toward becoming their best selves. Though Johanna was gone by the time the school began, she was a part of its dream, a force behind its ambitious purpose. Close friends who were inspired by her dedication to service and her love for causes that highlight the health and safety of girls and women, carried Johanna in their hearts as they breathed life and put flesh and bone into the buildings that have become a haven for others. "It's a thriving organization," Dan declares with pride; it is an amazing dream-turned-reality community that is helping to transform lives by fulfilling the promise of a better future through access to education and health care.

Another of Johanna's gifts grew from a decision to spotlight her Jewish identity using her wit, maturity and intellect to serve the cause of transcending misconceptions and discrimination. Johanna wrote and illustrated a children's story highlighting ways to overcome differences and promote tolerance when she was only fifteen. Julia's Star, according to her father's words in its prologue, was written to help teach others about "the injurious effect of intolerance, and how curiosity, friendship, knowledge and trust can overcome prejudice." After Johanna's death, Renate, her maternal grandmother and a Holocaust survivor, wrote an epilogue to the story including words from Johanna's 2006 college essay: ". . . we long for hope, hope that tolerance, humility, and life will surmount the despair of death, prejudice, and destruction throughout the world." Sonia, Johanna's paternal grandmother, spearheaded the actual publication of Julia's Star and helped it find its way into elementary classrooms in California and Connecticut, where it is still used as a teaching tool to aid understanding and combat prejudice. She took on this monumental project as a way to memorialize her beloved granddaughter. Tears shimmering in his eyes, Dan remembers during that dark time in Middletown, as he endured the trial, he was able to visit a classroom where Julia's Star was being used. Listening as fourth graders reenacted the story and talked through what they were learning, he was able to witness first-hand the impact Johanna's loving and courageous spirit had on others. Dan still receives thank you notes from young children who read and learn from her book. He gently unwraps to reveal one set of colorful notes written by youngsters, all shaped like open hands whose fingers, palms and backs are full of messages of hope and good will; Dan spreads them out, a riot of bright joy, and what is possible in a world filled with tolerance, openness and love is laid out before us.

"Johanna had a full life in her short years and the greatest tragedy is the loss to this world of this amazing human being." A thread that weaves throughout the story of Johanna's life, death and legacy is her love of service and authentic caring for others. When I asked Dan to talk about what his daughter might be saying to him today, he first acknowledges the strength he feels from her. Her ethereal visits remind him that living fully means staying open and mindful in interactions with others, and that great joy comes from connecting with all living and non-living beings. Just surviving is not good enough; there must be something more for a life to be well lived. Dan talks and I listen, noting how he has responded to the call of life's opportunities since Johanna's death. Those responses draw me to Victor Frankl's (<u>Man's Search for Meaning</u>) words about finding meaning in our grief. Frankl attributes his survival and eventual liberation from the death camps at the end of World War II to his realization that *we can endure suffering as long as we have a reason to endure it.*

On the surface these words may appear a simplistic, one-dimensional thought, but below the surface is an invitation to become profoundly aware of who we are, who we want to be, and what we long for at our core. Why should we endure the aching, chaotic space to which grief can tie us when we've experienced irretrievable loss? I hear some of Dan's thoughts on this question throughout our time together. Enduring with hope allows one: to remain open to, as well as learn from and revel in what is offered from beyond what we know; to invite who and what we love to join us in service to others; to find love in all interactions; to welcome and celebrate the simple joy, beauty and peace of nature's bounty; and to keep the loving connection between father and daughter gloriously alive.

"She visits me periodically. . . . She has focused my spirituality and has given me the greatest gift of all, knowledge about the interconnections of all things and insight into the indivisibility of our Spirit as we journey beyond our mortality. I know. . . that sometime after I pass on I will meet up with her again." But until that day, Dan gratefully celebrates the gifts Johanna gives him daily as he moves forward, creating a life beyond suffering: "She gives me the strength to endure, to grow, and energizes my commitment as a physician to care, truly care, for others."

Lyla: She is always with us

The sky is a perfect blue and the air, both crisp and soft, a combination reflecting autumn's beginning and the tail end of late summer. Shirt-sleeved neighbors and the sounds of playing children dot the landscape of this neighborhood. Dion opens to my knock; we greet each other and he leads me into the kitchen area to set up. I place myself at the table so that I can look outside through the kitchen's patio door because I'm drawn to the fenced-in backyard – a place that appears designed for laughter, running, climbing, jumping, and playing with the two, big, gentle dogs who also call it home. But what really catches my eye is the tall, two-storied wooden playhouse, built against the back fence. It sports tri-cornered flags, hung the full length of the peaked roof; a sweet, blue birdhouse with a yellow roof dangling from one corner of the larger roof's overhang; a great climbing ladder on one side of the structure with a slide on the opposite side; and a rectangular wooden planter attached to one of the front handrails. It seems such a perfect place for children to flex their energetic and imaginative muscles. Clearly this home belongs to its children. I turn to see Taia's lovely, welcoming smile, and hear that their daughter is playing at a neighbor's, while their two sons are upstairs napping. Soon we three settle in to the business of talking about a beloved daughter lost in 2008, Lyla Hope.

Taia takes a few moments to set the stage for our conversation, sharing that she and Dion have not had a smooth road to parenthood. She continues that their earlier difficulties have never dampened their gratefulness for the four children who touch and brighten their lives every day. In total, they've experienced ten pregnancies: six miscarriages; Lyla's stillbirth; and the live births of their three other children – Millie, six years old, Torin, three, and Trygve, who turned one just a few months earlier. "We wouldn't change our life or the way we've gotten to our family," Taia declares and then turns to smile lovingly at her youngest son who, having abandoned his nap early, has joined us at the table. She reveals that Trygve is their only baby who was not preceded by a loss; "He was a surprise and I think that it was the universe saying, 'Look, this is what it can be like.'. . .we could have a normal pregnancy." Without a break in the conversation except for a wink or smile or a quick phrase here and there for the toddler, our discussion shifts from the children who now physically complete Taia and Dion's family, to center on Lyla's story.

"When we got pregnant with her (Lyla), it was following a very traumatic time for us. It was devastating to lose our first baby." Taia talks of the worry she experienced during her first pregnancy. "I feel like I have a very good mother's intuition." She continues by saying she felt strongly something was wrong throughout. Unfortunately, her insight proves correct; when the expectant couple goes to their appointment, at just over eleven weeks, to hear their child's heart beat for the very first time, they are saddened to learn there is no heartbeat.

Thankfully, less than a year later, in April, 2008, Dion and Taia are again pregnant. Though their doctor tells the couple he is cautiously optimistic about their second pregnancy, Taia finds herself much more cautious than optimistic. "The whole time I was pregnant, I physically felt ill. . . . I never stopped feeling sick." Taia recalls again those intuitive feelings: "It was like this sixth sense that I think every mom probably has." On August 12, 2008, Dion, Taia and her mother who has joined them, go for the twenty-week ultrasound appointment. Again, Taia feels something just isn't right and no matter what anyone else says, she is unable to shake the feeling. After the ultrasound, the tech tells the family that the doctor will be right in, and Taia knows she will only believe all is well when her doctor says those words. But when he walks in, she can tell by the look on his face her intuition is right again. Something is terribly wrong with this baby.

Their OBGYN tells the distressed parents that the ultrasound indicates unexpected abnormalities. The next day, Wednesday, August 13th, they drive to see another doctor in Denver and are told that Lyla most probably has Turner Syndrome. TS, also known as 45, X, is due to a chromosomal abnormality when all or part of one of the X chromosomes is missing or altered. While most people have forty-six chromosomes, TS females, the affected gender of this disease, usually have forty-five. The Denver physician suggests they be admitted immediately to terminate Lyla. "I couldn't do that . . ." Taia says, emotion filling her voice. The couple needs time to think and process this new and heartbreaking information. Returning for more discussion with their local Obstetrician, they learn that in his thirty-five years of practice he has never seen a baby like their Lyla – one with so many and such large cysts within the soft tissue, primarily around her neck area (Cystic Hygromas). Ultimately, he suggests they deliver Lyla. Dion and Taia take necessary time to visit with their families, sharing what they've learned and listening for understanding and guidance. Ultimately, Lyla makes the decision; Taia quietly recalls some of that grief-filled time: "The last time I felt her move was Friday morning. And then we called and said, 'OK, I think she's ready to be born.'" They are admitted to the hospital on August 16, 2008.

With a small lift in her voice, Taia affirms how she will never forget the gentle kindnesses of her OBGYN, who she calls amazing. "He switched his on-call schedule so he could be in the hospital and deliver her for us." Eventually, after several difficult laboring hours that take the delivery into the next day, the doctor returns to the hospital to deliver Lyla, stillborn, on Sunday, August 17, 2008. The doctor and his nurse stay with the family while Taia, holding her new daughter, Dion and Taia's mother begin their loving good byes to the infant. The doctor was wonderful, she maintains; he offers a blessing for Lyla and the memory of that tender time still brings her to tears. "It was special." The couple takes their time holding and loving their new baby. And it is during this period that a warm-hearted photographer arrives to capture poignant memories of the three of them. "It was the most amazing (time)." They tearfully say the final goodbyes to their baby girl and leave for home, arms empty, to face the next series of decisions: how to honor their daughter's life.

"We don't practice a specific religion, but . . . I believe we are spiritual people. . . . I believe there is something higher, bigger and better than us." While at the hospital, the couple meets and talks with a chaplain who not only helps them think about options for memorializing their daughter, but also eventually assists them in planning the service. The parents know that they want to celebrate their daughter's life outside, in nature, and so plans begin to take shape. Lyla is cremated; Taia recalls that picking her up from the funeral home was terribly difficult but, "once we got home, I just had this sense of peace, like she was here with us." That sense of peace sustains her as the details of the memorial continue unfolding. Dion and Taia decide to have the service at Steven's Gulch in a beautifully forested area, close to the Poudre River, located in Colorado's Front Range. A month after Lyla's delivery, on September 20, 2008, the couple's family and invited close friends join them to honor the spirit and ongoing presence of Lyla Hope. All surround a table set with displayed pictures, Lyla's cremains, her teddy bear, and a tiny outfit, especially knitted by Taia's mom, the only grandparent able to meet and hold the tiny girl. The hospital chaplain attends and helps to facilitate the service by delivering a homily. The parents read a letter they've written for their daughter, and everyone participates as rose petals are reverently cast into the river. The beautiful natural setting and love-inspired ceremony fit perfectly the desire to celebrate and honor a daughter within something "higher, bigger and better."

Rituals are important to Dion and Taia and each year Lyla's life force is celebrated through various observances.

One family tradition is to travel into the vast beauty of the mountains, to Zimmerman Lake, and scatter a few of her ashes to acknowledge and honor her delivery date. Tears shimmer in Taia's eyes as she recounts this ritual that continues to keep her first daughter alive in their hearts. "We love being in nature. We thought . . . because (then) we hadn't had any children we got to keep, that we wanted part of her there because we knew that would be how we would raise her; she would always be there when we would go there. . . . She will always be in nature with us."

The parents also establish a time to hold a celebration for friends and their children that centers around laughter, sharing, ice cream and birthday cake. "We created this little ritual where we have friends come over and their kids (say) 'Oh . . . we get to celebrate Lyla's birthday.' And they know who she is." Taia continues that these observances are also teaching moments – because as children and adults grow in awareness about the inherent nature of loss, they can pass their understanding on to others: ". . . you can talk about it (death/loss). It's OK to ask questions; people want you to; people don't want you to ignore the fact that you have a child nobody can see." All the opportunities created to keep Lyla a very real presence continue to help her parents teach their own family and friends what it means to support not only them, but also others who live within the transformational time of profound loss. "I think creating those rituals we have around who she is in our family, and how she completes our family, will continue to help let her siblings know about her."

"We totally believe she is with us here today," Taia declares with a smile. Millie, her oldest, and Lyla seem to share a special bond. She recalls Millie's twenty-week ultrasound check with a kind of awe. First, Taia reveals, she could feel Lyla in the car with her and Dion as they travel to another ultrasound, this time for Lyla's unborn sister. At the hospital they find themselves in the exact same room with the exact same tech and the exact same doctor as two years earlier, but this time there is a very different outcome. This daughter is thriving. Another example is a story Millie reports to Taia that "just stopped me in my tracks." She and her daughter are returning home when Millie says, "Mommy, I've been here before." After some questions, it becomes clear to Taia that her two-year old isn't talking about a street or their neighborhood, but about something much larger and more important. Millie tells her, "No . . . I came here before and you named me Lyla and then I came back and you named me Millie." The spiritual nature of this conversation is both comforting and stunning. Taia continues that Millie also remembers that Lyla visited her as a baby to tickle her and make her laugh. Now, six-year old Millie is most happy to tell anyone about her big sister. The ethereal, the normally unexplainable, accepted and shared clearly and simply by Millie is an ongoing reminder to Dion and Taia that Lyla's spirit is an ever-present reality in their family circle. "She is with us," Taia states with simple eloquence.

Taia surveys the wisdom she's received from living with not only Lyla's physical loss but also her still-present energy, through both personal and professional lenses. As a parent she acknowledges that Lyla has "given us an awareness and an understanding to be empathetic and compassionate in lots of different areas." She goes on to add that Lyla taught her and Dion to be more than individuals, making the best of each of their lives, but to be parents who "cherish life and everything it throws at you." Taia continues with another smile, "she teaches us patience." That quality shows up in Taia's professional life as well. A teacher, she believes her daughter has given her the right words at the right time to help students feel welcomed and at ease – most especially those in need. As a bereaved parent in a teacher role, Taia is able to share a unique understanding with children who have suffered losses. "Lyla gave me words I needed to help those students, especially those who have loss, helping them to know those they've lost are always with them."

Both parents share that talking with others who live in profound grief from loss is a tricky business. Dion believes it many never be possible to know the right words to say to others who grieve. This couple is all too familiar with those times when others, who mean well, spout platitudes because they don't know what else to say. What is helpful and important according to Taia and Dion? Holding the belief that your loved one remains with you; carrying empathy for others with you; being mindful of the words you choose; exhibiting compassion; practicing patience; and cherishing life and family, including "everything it throws at you."

Like the playhouse, sturdy, interesting, available and inviting, Dion and Taia have created a gathering place, a home where loss is authentic and shared, where transformation is possible, and where love always abides.

Negatives can abound when a couple loses a child, but Taia affirms that it has strengthened her relationship with Dion. "It's taught us a lot about people and about life, and how you can make the choice to let something break you down or build you up." She fondly recalls talking with her mother, asking the questions most all bereaved parents pose at one time or another: *Why me? Why us?* There is no one answer for these questions borne of such tender, despairing heartache, but Taia's mother's response has helped this couple find one life-affirming answer: someday you will understand why something so horrific has happened, and as you grow and learn and time passes you will have the choice to use that experience, the people with you, and those who have past to help others. "I've always hoped . . . that I could just help somebody else through their journey of grief and use that for good in the world." Taia knows that the pain may never leave but we can learn how to live in a different way with its presence and its wounds – with Grace – a way that builds rather than destroys.

Isaac: Our child in heaven

These last two months I have been driving to my interviews with parents, encircled within a sense of contradiction. I know I'm going to be hearing stories depicting the darkest time in parents' lives, yet I'm traveling to hear those heartbreaking narratives through landscapes that are truly awe-inspiring. The sky has been its most clear and brilliantly blue; the turning leaves boast breathtaking hues of gold and orange; the air is wonderfully soft; and the lively sounds of playing children greet me most every time. I'm struck by life's beauty surrounding each home I've entered, even though I know death has visited before me. Surely this dichotomy must have some meaning; perhaps I'm to remember that even in the most grief-filled experiences, grace and hope await, circling patiently, just outside.

Today, the glorious weather again ushers me toward a neighborhood that rests under a gloriously azure sky, where children's voices ring out and pumpkins relax in yards, waiting for their big night. I walk up to Patrick and Erin's front door, and before I knock I feel myself smiling and my shoulders relaxing, because just ahead a sweet sign tells me this family, once rocked by inconsolable loss, has welcomed a new baby. The couple, together, welcome me into what I learn is their new home. Erin is carrying their month-old daughter, Gabrielle, who is contentedly snuggled into her mom's arms. I'm lead the way to the kitchen table where we all get comfortable. Today I have the honor of hearing the story of the loss of their third son, Isaac James.

The three of us talk a few minutes about what they can expect during our time together, and quickly Erin focuses our conversation by setting the stage. The time is August, 2014; the family: Patrick, Noah, aged 9, Maddox, aged 6, and Erin, who is twenty-four weeks pregnant with Isaac, are on vacation in Ouray, a spectacular area located in southwest Colorado's San Juan Mountains. She begins their story by sharing her early concern for their unborn child: "I just couldn't get it out of my mind that he wasn't moving as he normally did . . . because he was an active little person." The family travels back home on a Sunday; the following Tuesday was to have been Erin's next midwife visit, but because of her uneasiness, she changes the appointment and goes in the next day, Monday, August 11th. Patrick is at work and she has Noah and Maddox with her. The office visit is tense – though earlier her baby was pronounced perfectly fine, today his heartbeat can't be found. Her midwife sends Erin to the local hospital for an ultrasound. With the boys in tow, Erin has the procedure and returns to the office for the results.

By this time, a very worried and confused Erin has contacted Patrick. He remembers that call well: "You called me and you said, 'They can't find the heartbeat' . . . and my boss, who works in the same room, stood up out of his chair and yelled, 'Go home now!' I was in shock." With tears in her eyes, Erin recalls, "By the time I got back to (the midwife's) office, I knew for sure it was not good news because all of the patients were gone . . . and the whole staff was waiting for me. And I started crying." Patrick arrives and the family realizes the devastating news – a son, a little brother, has passed away. They return home, shocked and dismayed by the unexpected, inconsolable loss. The family is joined at home by Erin's mother and sister and they all take the necessary time throughout the next many hours to process the still-inconceivable news, make some vital, pressing decisions, and rest before taking those next dreaded but inevitable steps.

Erin calls August 13, 2014, "the worst day ever." The boys are in Erin's mom's care and the couple go to the hospital. In the hospital's parking lot, Erin notices a pregnant woman who appears ready to deliver. She is sensitive to the fact that the two of them are going to the same area, and is caught in the sad and uncomfortable understanding that their two deliveries will most surely end very differently. This is just a foretaste of what Erin will feel as a bereaved parent who must find ways to balance the weight of her loss with the happiness of pregnant friends and new mothers in her life's circle. Patrick and Erin are taken to their room and discover they will be cared for by a nurse they call "wonderful." She settles them in for the upcoming induced delivery and then stops to take the precious time to cry with them. Her kindness and support help the parents to survive this bleak day.

The day unfolds and by evening, Isaac is delivered. "He is perfect." Erin softly shares, tears again filling her eyes. "I remember thinking I had only ever seen . . . two dead people in my life and they were so hard to look at. I remember thinking before he was born, 'can I even look at him?'" With a small smile Erin notes, "as it turns out, that's all we did." They look at him, hold him, love him. During this time, her two other sons, who have been brought to the hospital room by Erin's mother, join Patrick, Erin and the midwife, to meet and hold Isaac. Patrick and Erin had earlier made the decision, after much consideration, that Noah and Maddox should meet their baby brother while they can, to see "he is a real person." They share that during the evening a generous photographer, meets with the whole family – the parents, their three boys and Erin's mom – in order to take an array of photos, creating unforgettable memories to mark this tender occasion. And it is Noah's question, while he is holding Isaac, that makes the inevitable finality of their time together a stark reality: "When do we get to take him home?"

Erin thinks back to that poignant moment: "I'll never forget how everything in that room went quiet; every person in that room had tears in their eyes." And though she has already explained to her sons that Isaac is no longer living in the earthly body they are holding, but is already a soul in heaven, she gently clarifies again that Isaac won't be going home with them because he is already in his heavenly home. "The hardest part was leaving," Patrick remarks quietly. Erin continues, "We stayed the night with him and it was the hardest thing we've ever done." Eventually the parents must leave though it feels as if they are abandoning Isaac. Walking away from their tiny new son is the final act that truly defines this August time as the worst ever.

Still, questions remain. Patrick shares that they don't really understand why Isaac had to die. Theirs had been a normal pregnancy up until that time; the twenty-week ultrasound reveals no reason for concern. The prevailing theory becomes that there is a clot in the cord, making it impossible for the baby to get nourishment. Sadness and frustration darkens Erin's voice as she relives the heartache: "You can do everything right . . . but have a horrible outcome." Nothing critical to their baby's health and safety was left undone, yet it didn't seem to matter. The random unpredictability of life intervened and hearts were broken open. Yet, there is no time to quietly process the desolation of Isaac's loss, or to begin dealing intentionally with the unique grief journey each family member now begins because the opening of a new school year is only days away.

The family gears up as best they can: there are school clothes to purchase, nursery items to lay aside, schedules and materials to prepare, children to ready for the first day . . . and the list continues. Only days after Isaac's delivery, Erin finds herself having to do some school shopping for the boys. She vividly recalls the dreaded question coming at her, cheerfully asked by an unsuspecting but interested cashier: how many children do you have? Unprepared, startled by the question's power, Erin remembers the tears that immediately begin to fall, and her inability to find the words to respond. Her mother steps in to answer for her daughter, and later, with Patrick's help, the family's answer to this inevitable question becomes, "we have three children, and one is in heaven."

Erin identifies herself as a Type A person, well prepared, competent and in control of details that need attention. What she discovers is when one is immersed in the grief of profound loss all those usual expectations of oneself just no longer apply. As time goes on, the parents begin to realize that Noah and Maddox are also experiencing changes. Patrick and Erin take some time to express a few of the surprises and concerns they've had watching the boys struggle with their little brother's death. Though quiet about their feelings most of the time, each son demonstrates in unique ways that the event has touched them deeply. Grades fall, details at the hospital are remembered and shared in surprising ways, a teacher is told about a mom who cries a lot – and the parents, now aware of how affected the boys are by the family's common heartache try to help each to process grief's inevitable sadness and confusion. Losing a son and a little brother is not "something you just get over." As fall turns to winter and beyond, the family searches for the balance needed to move toward a new normal, a lifestyle to not only remember Isaac, but to also listen for and respect the very real hopes and needs of each family member.

In time, the couple establishes ways of honoring Isaac, both close to his due date, December 6, as well as near his August delivery time. They plan a balloon release, filling each balloon with a message of love for their little son. They arrange to take pictures to memorialize the event. With a kind of awe, Patrick and Erin share that each of these pictures contains a little green blip of light – light that wasn't there when the image itself was photographed – and reflect on the ethereal presence of their son, not physically visible, but still somehow with them. Their summertime trips to Ouray continue and now are also used to commemorate Isaac's life. The family's cabin is not only an important get-away but is also a meaningful setting for Erin and Patrick. It is there the couple's boys express their joy in family, fun and nature; it is there immediate and extended family members reunite; it was there Erin first felt her concern for Isaac's health; and now it is where those who join together lovingly remember and find ways to honor family who have passed before them. Erin tells the story of being at the cabin during summers after Patrick's father, James, died; each visit they were treated to the beauty of a rainbow. She smiles as she reports on the family's first trip to Ouray after Isaac's loss: a double rainbow decorated the sky. "I remember thinking if that is not a sign that he is happy up there with his Papa, I don't know what is."

"To be honest," Patrick reveals, "if you don't have faith, I don't know how you can go through this. It is so hard." Erin continues, "God put . . . people in our path that He knew we were going to need." After highlighting the kindness and help of Patrick's boss during this difficult time, the couple talks more about the importance of their Christian faith and their church home. Though they are fairly new to the church when they lose Isaac, the congregation richly blesses them with an outpouring of support. "Our families are wonderful," Erin asserts, "but I could not have imagined going through that without our church family." They talk about the friendship and compassion they each encounter, both before and after Isaac's death, emphasizing the fact that parents in this congregation have also lost children. As a group, they appear to more easily identify with and understand the couple's grief. Erin shares her experience as a volunteer during the church's Vacation Bible School. Pregnant with Isaac, she says yes to helping the committee but expects to do her volunteering activities from home. She soon discovers she is on the schedule to work at the church rather than from her house. "This was not my plan," she laughs, but continues that it turns out to be a wonderful time. Those friendships she nurtures as a volunteer still serve as a cherished support system for the entire family.

Early in 2016, Patrick and Erin learn they are again pregnant. They recall this pregnancy as an "amazing emotional roller coaster." Erin calls herself a little crazy during this time and remembers her many calls to the midwife's office to unload yet another of her list of questions and concerns. Every day they feel pricked by the pins and needles of anxiety and worry. She asserts that any pregnancy after losing a child carries with it a whole new set of heightened emotions for expectant parents to navigate, understand and process. But with thankfulness and guarded anticipation also comes some guilt. Erin recalls: "I felt really guilty when I did get pregnant with her . . . that I think people are going to forget about Isaac now." She voices that she did not choose this new baby over her lost son and, in dark moments, wonders if "maybe I gave her something I didn't give him." Thankfully, the concerns give way to joy as this pregnancy results in a healthy child, one with a very intentional and special name.

After Isaac's loss, Erin shares with Patrick a name she believes should be given to their next child – Gabriel. Though she and Patrick generally struggle over names, this one immediately seems just right to them both. The biblically historical angel, Gabriel, whose name means "God is my strength," serves as a messenger from the Lord. Erin and Patrick feel the promise, strength and hope of their chosen name and are told to expect baby Gabriel to join the family in September, 2016. Erin expresses to all involved her reticence in returning to the same hospital where Isaac was delivered stillborn; too many memories await her in that place. She and Patrick consider finding both another midwife for this next birth as well as a new birthing place. After some soul-searching and input from trusted others, they finally decide to deliver at the familiar hospital, with the same midwife in control. "We did go and it was wonderful," Erin says with joy coloring her voice. Though they were originally expecting a Gabriel, the new parents are delighted to welcome a baby girl, Gabrielle: "Having Gabrielle has been very healing," Erin reports with a soft smile. With her birth, the couple feels as if they have come full circle and are gratefully calling the experience a beautiful type of closure.

Erin and Patrick reflect on some of their feelings and certainties regarding the loss of their beloved boy. They have learned that it seems more comfortable for others to pretend that a baby's death never happened, to simply not acknowledge it out loud. Erin believes some might feel guilty for bringing it up because such a loss seems so unnatural. She goes on to show she understands: "It's not natural to be pregnant and have to decide what funeral home you're going to use." Still, these parents want to talk about Isaac; they want others to understand and accept the truth that they have four children – even though one cannot be seen. Erin continues, "People who have lost children all get it . . . they don't think it's weird that we talk about him." Unfortunately, they still get careless questions and hear hurtful messages from well-meaning people. Sometimes consistently insensitive encounters mean that old friendships must fall away so new ones can be forged with those who understand the realities of life after the death of a child: there is no timetable for grief. The couple's best piece of advice is: "You can give encouragement and offer comfort, but don't try to give advice unless you've gone through it - whether you have good intentions or not." They are equally certain about one more thing; Erin explains: "I know that heaven is a real place and I know, because I'm a Christian, we'll be there one day and so I feel like we have a unique hope." Patrick adds that "it is not fair; we will always wonder why it happened to us. And I don't think we'll ever know but I know he's being well taken care of." He continues that his belief has "gotten me through."

"Everything happens for a reason. It's made us and our faith stronger, and our family closer." Patrick and Erin realize that their irretrievable loss has changed the ways they now empathize and sympathize with others. Patrick's shares, "I know one day we'll be in a position to help someone come through this type of thing; we will be able to give them comfort because we know uniquely how this feels." The couple stands ready and willing to provide support to others whenever and wherever it may be needed. Steadfastness surrounds the core beliefs these parents voice throughout our time together. Hearing their story and their strong beliefs unfold remind me of an old, traditional hymn, filled with absolute trust, hope and resolution: *Great is Thy Faithfulness.*

Erin and Patrick are assured their separation from their third son is not permanent and that he is truly in that better, safer place where they, too, will dwell when they and Isaac are together again.

Ella: *Where love blooms*

A gorgeous early November day finds me searching for Josh and Lindsay's home. I make a turn to the west and slow a bit to drink in the view ahead, a panorama of layered foothills with wispy clouds rising into an azure sky. It's not far now, their neighborhood should be just ahead to my left. Their house, I discover, sits in a cul de sac of lovely homes and is fronted by white rose bushes, now pruned for the winter ahead. I head toward a classic red door sporting a beautiful, seasonal wreath and note two small bikes leaning against the left side of the porch. There must be children close by. Before I reach the door to knock, it opens and two little guys pour out onto the front area, heading into the wonderful afternoon weather with a babysitter in tow. Josh and Lindsay are close behind and, as they send their sons off to play, they also graciously welcome me into their home. I learn later that the boys aren't surprised to run into me, a stranger at their door. They've been told I'm the lady their parents are going to talk to about a sister they've never met; the one who will be listening to a story that can still make Mom and Dad sad. I'm the one who has the honor of retelling details and memories of a beloved daughter, Ella Elizabeth.

Seated at the dining room table in a room flooded by afternoon light, the three of us settle into the discussion ahead. Lindsay admits to feeling anxious about painful memories she will be sharing aloud during the next hour or so. It has taken her time to make the decision to talk about Ella for this project, but she and Josh finally decide that it might somehow be helpful as they continue toward healing. Still, now that we are together, ready to actually relive details of their experience, there is silence. Tears begin to shine in Lindsay's eyes and Josh leaves to get the Kleenex. Lindsay tries smiling with trembling lips and I get my first glimpse of the ongoing pain she carries from Ella's loss. When Josh returns, he places the box on the table, looks at Lindsay and gently asks if she wants him to start. But, with a breath that propels her into the past, she begins with an explanation of the exciting promise attached to Ella's birth. The couple, indeed much of the entire immediate and extended family, is thrilled to know a baby girl will soon be a part of their common life.

Ella is to be the couple's second child, conceived when older brother, Jackson, is four. Their first pregnancy was relatively uneventful, "normal" by all standards; he was right on time, delivered on his due date by the same doctor who is now overseeing Ella's safe development and eventual delivery. For the most part, Lindsay recalls, this pregnancy is also smooth. Ella appears to be developing at a normal rate; still, Lindsay is bothered by a kind of fearful foreshadowing which begins to weigh on her. "I had this woman stuck in my mind from when I was a child. I thought I remembered going with my mom and my sister, dropping off a meal because I had thought her baby had died – her baby was stillborn. And I had never thought of that until this pregnancy." Lindsay recalls this memory as she begins to detail the weeks before her daughter's delivery. The thirty-six-week check-up seems normal though the baby is measuring small for the first time. The parents are told not to be concerned. Two weeks later, Lindsay and Josh go to the hospital with false labor and though they are eventually sent home with assurances that everything is fine, Lindsay's concern only grows. "All of a sudden at the end of my pregnancy, I had this overwhelming urge to get this baby out of my body." At their last appointment, a week later, she voices her fears to her doctor: "I was just panicked," she recalls; she pleads with the doctor: "You have to induce me, please!" The doctor tells Lindsay she can be induced on her upcoming due date, May 11, 2011.

The day before the scheduled delivery Lindsay and her mother take Jackson on an adventure. Realizing that this is the last chance she has to spend special time with her toddler while he is still their only child, the three set off for the Denver Zoo. Wiping at the tears that again begin to fall, Lindsay shares, "I remember walking the zoo and the last time I felt her kick inside of me was when we were by the carousel. And I didn't say anything. I kept it in for a long time." Home from the zoo, Lindsay's mother offers to watch her grandson so that Josh and Lindsay can go out for a final, unhurried dinner before tomorrow's scheduled delivery. When the couple returns from dinner, Lindsay finally unloads the burden she's been carrying since the afternoon – the baby isn't moving. And though her mother and husband try to soften her anxieties, she reports not sleeping at all that night. The next morning, May 11, Lindsay still can't feel her baby move. She calls the doctor's office and eventually convinces them she has already done everything they suggest to lessen any concern. She is given an appointment, one that is just hours earlier than her already-scheduled late afternoon delivery time. Frustration hardening her voice, Lindsay maintains that as she communicates with her health professionals, she hears no sense of urgency about Ella's safety and no sensitivity to a mother's intuitive sense of imminent danger. She is trapped within a fear-filled maze of questions, but those she counts on for answers don't appear to be listening.

Lindsay and her mom are kept waiting at the doctor's office for almost an hour. Finally, a nurse brings them into a small room, moves the ultrasound in place and turns its screen so that Lindsay can follow the testing. The room is quiet, the nurse silent, until finally Lindsay asks for information. The nurse's answer comes: "I'm looking for the heartbeat." Her worst fears confirmed, Lindsay is now terrified. "I was such a mess . . . how every mother is when they find out their child could be. . . ." As her voice quietly trails off, her tears flow with the heartbreaking memory. She continues, "It was such a shock. I think I just started screaming . . . crying . . . and all they said to me was 'You have to go to the hospital and have your baby out.'" In the meantime, Lindsay's mother contacts Josh at work. Tears in his eyes, he relives the shocking news: Ella has no heartbeat and he must get to the doctor's office right away. He soon joins the others in that small room, where the news was first delivered, and their family grieving begins. They take time together, trying to find enough balance to make the first of many decisions to come – Lindsay's mother will drive them to the hospital.

The couple goes on to talk about the number of dark and demanding decisions they would have to make over those next horrific hours. The second has to do with the hospital room where they will labor. They are first led to the same room they occupied just days before, when Ella was still moving. The couple refuses that room and are shown to another where they settle in for the coming ordeal. Before long, a picture of a Columbine is affixed to the outside of their door, distinctly marking the room's purpose. The symbolism this flower carries includes the concepts of innocence and protection against evil; and now, in real time, the Columbine on their door signals a stillbirth waiting to happen.

The couple must now think through and then decide about delivery options – C-Section or Vaginal birth. Together they discuss their thoughts and feelings, while hospital personnel persist with a question that haunts them throughout all the hours to follow: *"Are you ready yet to . . .?"* Lindsay feels pushed to do something immediately but she and Josh, enveloped in inconsolable grief, desperately want time to make the critical decisions that will last as memories the rest of their lives. Frustrated by the seemingly arbitrary and insensitive time frames, they hold their ground, wanting any decisions to honor their daughter. "At first, I wanted a C-Section," Lindsay shares. "I felt like . . . just get this thing out of me. I felt like I had a dead thing inside of me; . . . It felt like we weren't even treated like we had a baby – we just had something to remove. I just wanted it gone; I didn't want to deal with it." After taking precious time, the parents instead make the call for an induced labor and natural birth. "The more we sat and just cried, we came to the decision we owed it to her to have her naturally . . . to go through the process." That settled, Lindsay is given drugs to start her labor and the waiting begins.

Lindsay's sister, Katie, joins the couple and her mom in the hospital room. They also are able to spend time with Josh's parents who come to the hospital to visit as Lindsay labors. And, all the while, the questions that must have answers keep coming: *Are you ready yet* to tell us if you want pictures? *Are you ready* to have us invite in a chaplain? *Are you ready* to tell us if you want an autopsy? *Are you ready yet* to tell us what you want us to do with your daughter's body – what funeral home to use? Have you decided about cremation? Burial? Enveloped in the crushing emotional and physical pain of laboring toward their imminent loss, Lindsay and Josh become only too aware that no pregnant couple should ever have to choose a funeral home, or wonder about the need for an autopsy . . . or hate the inevitable circumstances they face in a birthing room. Lindsay expresses her pain in a quiet voice as tears continue to fall: "It's the saddest thing to be in labor and know you're delivering a dead baby. When you lose a baby, you won't have any memories except bad ones . . . ." And when the time comes to do the final pushes the reality of her irretrievable loss washes over Lindsay. "I didn't want to push because I didn't want her to be out. All of a sudden she is not this thing that they were trying to take out of me." She is their Ella; she is the promised daughter; she is the one everyone's been waiting for.

"When the baby is born, it's so silent," Lindsay recalls. They discover Ella has her cord wrapped around her neck three times; the reason for her death becomes clear. When a nurse hands Lindsay and Josh their daughter to hold for the first time, Lindsay, in a voice tinged with both disappointment and anger, shares that Ella's skin is still blotched with amniotic fluids and the bloody residue of the birthing process. The nurse has wrapped her in a blanket without carefully and lovingly wiping her clean for her meeting with her family. It seems so disrespectful to the tiny infant. But the parents gratefully take their daughter, and with family close, she is held, sung to and loved. During their hours together, a hospital chaplain comes to the room to baptize and bless the infant, black and white photos are taken to commemorate this time with Ella, and the couple decides that there will be no autopsy. Not only do they know the cause of death, they don't want to put Ella through such an ordeal. Finally, the last and most difficult decision is made and all say their final good byes.

Josh and Lindsay opt to cremate their daughter. A few weeks later a memorial service is held for the baby girl at Katie and Ryan's home; Lindsay and Josh are still without a permanent place for a garden, so one is to be created at her sister's home, located not far from Colorado's stunning Flatirons. Family and a few close friends attend the ceremony, everyone honoring Ella by planting flowers and a white rose bush in the special space they name, Ella's Garden. The white rose becomes the family's acknowledged symbol memorializing the enduring presence of their little girl. Katie presents Lindsay and Josh with a story to commemorate this time:

The White Rose by Myrna Cox.

> "... A loving Father, spoke to the mothers, 'See the works of my hands, someday you will be the   mothers to these radiant spirits.' ...

> Once again the loving Father spoke, 'But who will take the white rose? These will return to me in purity and goodness, *they will not stay long in your home,* for I must bring them back to my garden for they belong with me ... I will personally care for them.' ...

> ... The Father spoke again. 'Oh blessed are you who chose the white roses, for your pain will be a heavy cross to bear, but our joy with be exceeding, beyond anything you can understand at this time.' ...

> And each mother who bore the weight of the white rose, would feel the overwhelming love of God."

Actual Sugar Moon white rose bushes now grace the gardens of Ella's family as beautiful, living and growing symbols honoring her forever place in their lives. Ella's Garden is both actual and symbolic – a real place to drink in nature's bounty and a reminder of the purity and innocence of one who is now in another's care.

Though her eyes are still wet with tears, they also flash with anger as Lindsay remembers her follow-up appointment with the doctor who delivered Ella. The obstetrician shows little compassion for the experiences Lindsay and Josh endured while in her medical care. Her words, "There's nothing we could have done to save her," carry neither empathy nor authentic concern for the feelings of the bereaved parents but they do serve to strengthen the couple's certainty they will never seek out this doctor's services again. Lindsay reaffirms the resentment she still carries from the insensitive treatment they received from both that doctor as well as other medical staff during the couple's labor, birthing and after-care experiences. But then, Lindsay goes on to tell of the man who meets them at the crematorium when she and Josh pick up Ella's cremains. They are aware they are meant to pay for the cremation but when they prepare to do that, the gentle person helping them says, "You have already paid the price." She and Josh are so moved by this gracious gesture that its retelling brings fresh tears. "I'll never forget that . . . there's the compassion." They walk away from the experience with grateful hearts and Ella's cremains held in both a treasured heart-shaped container and a lovely small box.

Though time and life's complexities continue to push them forward, the couple is caught in the detached, demanding and exhausting cycle of profound grief. "The world was still moving," Josh notes; he and Lindsay wonder how that can be since the world they live in seems to be standing still. "The sun was not supposed to rise," Lindsay adds. Josh takes several days away from work to gather private time for him and Lindsay to begin processing their devastating loss. Dismantling their daughter's nursery is a despairing task.

Its sadness adds another difficult layer to the grueling necessities of preparing for a move. They have recently sold one home and now face the many exacting decisions and predictable upheaval of building and moving into another. They move in with Lindsay's parents for a time while the house construction is underway. Lindsay recalls that her son is "bounced back and forth" between Katie and her parents; she and Josh see him mainly during planned visits. The grieving parents, each in their own way, go about the staggering tasks of designing and organizing the details for a new home as they try to navigate the turmoil and sorrow that defines their busy days and nights. They realize that their family is fragmented, that they are fragile, but there seems no time or energy to intentionally and gently deal with all the chaos continuing to surround them. So they keep going. "You just go. Somehow you just get there," Lindsay reports quietly.

Lindsay and Josh's spirits seem to lift when they talk about their *rainbow baby*, Reid. With this pregnancy, they look for a new obstetrician with whom they can form a trusting and comfortable relationship. And, to their relief, they find one. The couple is heartened, satisfied they have found the right person, especially when their new doctor tells them, "You will not lose another baby." The pregnancy is not without worry but Josh and Lindsay remain confident their doctor has an excellent plan for a successful delivery. Lindsay is induced at thirty-eight weeks and delivers Reid on June 30, 2012. He is a sick little boy at birth and spends time in the hospital's NICU as doctors work to unravel the puzzle of his illness. Happily, he ultimately rallies, and develops into a healthy baby. With a smile and a bit of awe in her voice, Lindsay reveals that she sees the first white bloom on Ella's rose bush June 29, 2012, the day she is sent to the hospital for Reid's birthing time. New life enters her family and Ella reminds everyone, beautifully, that she is as close as the garden.

Ella remains a presence. Some of Reid's unexplainable early comments make Lindsay believe her daughter is still close by. To keep Ella a real and growing part of their family life, Lindsay and Josh begin a Christmas tradition where each of the four family members chooses a present for her. Moving from baby to toddler gifts and beyond, each passing year's gifts are bought to match the age their little girl would be if she physically lived in their world. They imagine what their daughter and sister would love, and purchase it for another little girl to enjoy. The four gifts are donated to families who have little ones the age Ella would have been. Ella's parents keep her alive and growing within their hearts while passing on loving kindness to others and demonstrating generosity for their sons. A gift that also keeps Ella a true presence for her extended family are the beautifully-fashioned diamond and silver lockets Lindsay gives to her mother and sister. Inside each locket is the gift of Ella – a small amount of her cremains – a reminder that a precious granddaughter and niece need never be far away. For the parents, Josh's ring and Lindsay's necklace, each carrying the letter E, are keepsakes for the daughter who they will always hold as their ever-present cherished gift.

"Follow your intuition and push for what you think is right with your doctor," Lindsay declares with assurance. As a strong advocate of mother's intuition, she tells anyone who asks for her advice that when "you have this sense of urgency, listen to it!" It is clear that grief, with its anger, frustrations and sadness, is still a part of these parents' lives. And so is the very real feeling of empty arms. Ella's weight, felt when she was held for the first time by her mom and dad still leaves its impression, as a physical pressure, on each of them. Grieving, like healing, has no timetable and empty arms can still ache to go back, to hold her again. Still, each parent also knows that continuing to move forward into healing and grace is their healthiest reality.

Lindsay speaks of the relaxing, working and thinking time she spends in her garden. There, feeling Ella's presence, she can talk to her daughter. A smiling Lindsay also shares that "Ella sends me ladybugs." Josh calls Grey Rock, the natural space he visits in the northern Colorado foothills, his "special spot." He finds peaceful, meditative time as he also watches nature's landscape transform. Earlier ravaged by a wildfire, this once charred and quiet landscape has been restoring itself, becoming again what it is meant to be – a beautiful, nurturing home, teeming with life and growth. Like this reclaimed place, once devastated by circumstances beyond its control, Josh and Lindsay are also in the process of transformation. And, as they discover and follow new paths, they can be assured that Ella travels with them. She is alive – in the pure innocence of a blossoming white rose, the laughter of her brothers, the celebrations of a family, the serenity of her parents, the visits of ladybugs in a garden, a father's lovingly-crafted poem, the quiet meditation of contented hearts, and always, in the circle of gracious, unconditional love.

Carter: He made us parents and prepared us to love

It is a brisk, early December day. Thin clouds, a watery blue sky and patches of sun play tag above while bundled neighbors work to untwist some Christmas lights for decorating or exercise their dogs in the park down the street. I've found Chris and Emily's house and can see through their front window as I walk toward it, that their tree is not only up, but in full Christmas mode. The red front door holds a wreath, colorful and full of Christmas ornaments, and just beyond it come the sounds of children, laughing and playing in what must be the front room of the house. I ring the doorbell; it's answered by a smiling Emily who welcomes me inside. I'm quickly introduced to daughters, Clara, eight, who is standing close to her mom, and Abbey, five, who shyly peeks at me from around the Christmas tree.

All three usher me to a table where we'll soon be talking together. To my right, through an entry way into the kitchen, stands Chris who is mixing up something sweet for a holiday event later this afternoon. It becomes clear very quickly that this house holds an active family – one that is busy, engaged, lively, and happily involved with one another. Before I even sit down to unpack and begin our interview, Emily places a beautiful container on the table; it's a box designated to hold the special clothing and mementos she and Chris retained from the delivery of their son, Carter. Clara and Abbey start their questions to Emily about all the treasures Carter's box holds and each is taken out, shared and talked about as if Carter has just come home from the hospital. But he was never able to come home and that is why we are here today, together – to talk about a treasured son who never physically spent Christmas with them, but who has always played a very real part in his family's celebrations every year.

The story starts when Chris and Emily first discover they are pregnant with Carter. They talk about being really excited but also a little nervous because they suffered a miscarriage only a month earlier. They breathe easier after the pregnancy's first twelve weeks and everything going forward unfolds normally; the ultrasounds and checkups all go as expected. On Monday, July 16, 2007, during a routine appointment, Emily hears again that everything is fine, that her son is doing well. She works that entire week but near its end, she notices troubling changes. "I remember thinking Thursday and Friday that he wasn't moving very much; I remember asking people about it, and laying down in my office to see if I could feel him move. But I didn't really get worried about it. It never crossed my mind that he wasn't alive. You kind of convince yourself . . ." Emily says, her voice trailing off. Then she goes on, "In my head I assumed that when you're thirty-nine weeks pregnant your baby doesn't just die." On Friday, July 20th, she returns for another visit but this time the heartbeat can't be found. Their physician calls another doctor into the room to listen, but again, Carter's heart is silent. The couple is quickly sent to the hospital for an ultrasound. "It was a very quiet ride," Chris shares gently. At the hospital, the ultrasound tech silently completes the scan and then leaves the room. Chris positions himself to watch the monitor as she tests and realizes that what he is seeing on this day is different than in earlier scans; things aren't right. They wait. The tech returns and their doctor is on the phone. She delivers heartbreaking news, and their worst fear comes true: "She told us the baby is dead. . . ."

Emily, still on the phone, wonders aloud, "what are we supposed to do now." The doctor tells her they need to deliver Carter. She directs them to the Labor and Delivery area of the hospital and promises to be with them as quickly as she can. Emily and Chris move forward into the unthinkable. "I don't think we said any words to each other," Emily continues, "we just did it." Once admitted and settled into their room, Chris and Emily are joined by their doctor who gently begins to spell out the necessary steps to come. In order to keep Emily as comfortable as possible and insure a quicker delivery, she is given high doses of medication to begin her labor. As Emily's body prepares for the inevitable, Chris leaves the room to make the sad and necessary calls to special friends and family. In time, others begin to join Emily and Chris at the hospital. Close friends, Mark and Polly, get their call and leave immediately to help the couple by heading to their home, dealing with the needs of their dog and collecting the already-packed bag readied for Carter's birth, to bring to them at the hospital. Emily's mother, Marcia, and step-father, Richard, also arrive to be with them and eventually Richard picks up Emily's sister, Anna. Those three remain with the expectant parents throughout that Friday night and into the next morning when Carter is finally delivered.

As the hours tick down to Carter's delivery, Emily and Chris are asked to make decisions no laboring parent should have to consider. Hospital personnel, in an effort to focus expectant parents on their responsibilities for what is to happen to their baby after delivery, bring them a resource book with options – the choice of using the services of a photographer and/or a chaplain . . . or not; the choice of having an autopsy . . . or not; and the choice of which funeral home they would want to use. Chris shares, "I don't ever remember that conversation at all; I don't ever remember talking about pictures or giving permission for that. I just remember her (the photographer) showing up." The only thing he does recall from that resource book is that there were numbers and names of funeral homes and he and Emily had to make decisions about their unborn baby boy. Emily's voice is quiet, "It was a very weird time . . . we were just going through the motions."

Finally, the drugs and Emily's body do their inevitable work and Carter is delivered, stillborn, at 3:04 am on Saturday, July 21, 2007. The cord is wrapped twice around his neck. The couple decides after talking with their doctor, that an autopsy would help them rule out any other issues, genetic or otherwise, as causes of death. The results show that he is a "healthy baby boy" and the death is ruled a "cord accident." Emily and Chris remain in their room for the next several hours loving their tiny son. Marcia, Richard and Anna, still present, also hold and share their love for Carter. Sometime during those hours as Carter stays with his family, both a chaplain and a photographer visit the room. And though there is scant memory that they had asked for either, the parents are grateful for each. The photographer is especially appreciated. A thoughtful professional with a "perfect demeanor," she was both wonderfully appropriate and tenderly respectful of their feelings, and of their son. Carter's time, shared with the five members of his family present in the room, is now memorialized through precious pictures. Emily shares that though she couldn't imagine wanting pictures of this devastating time, she can now call them, "the best gift we have."

A hospital chaplain also visits the room. His peaceful presence and gentle words of comfort as he baptizes Carter brings the reality of their tiny son's death even more profoundly into the room, and Chris, Emily reveals, cries his first real tears. As the time nears when the grief-stricken parents will need to put their son into the hands of others, Chris remembers holding him: ". . . he was getting cold . . . and (a nurse was) coming to take him. I remember putting him in their (the hospital's) bassinette and her walking away." Eventually Carter will find his way into the hands of funeral home professionals for cremation. Their doctor arrives later that Saturday morning to check on the couple and after some discussion, discharges them. Chris and Emily leave the hospital close to twelve hours after their unanticipated arrival . . . with broken hearts and empty arms.

Emily takes a moment to look back and share both a regret and a laugh from that tender time surrounding their son's delivery. She is sorry that she didn't invite Polly and Mark back to share time with her, Chris and Carter. Concerned with how they might feel about seeing her baby dead, she opts to let them leave without an invitation to return. Now she wishes she had shared some of those life-changing moments in the company of her dear friends. That quiet laboring time also created a family story where smiles and laughter continue to this day. Chris, who admits to using sleep to cope in tough times, falls asleep as Emily and family members continue to await Carter's arrival. It was late, moving into Saturday morning and all was quiet and dark; "The next thing I know, Chris is sawing logs," Emily says with a laugh. Chris continues the conversation, "It's my defense mechanism. It's how I deal . . . I go to sleep."

At discharge, Emily, both physically and emotionally depressed and raw, talks about how uncomfortable she is entering her home without her baby. Carter's nursery stands ready, already wonderfully completed, just for him. "My biggest memory of being home right after is telling Chris, 'I just want to get rid of everything.'" Emily goes on, "He said, 'No, let's just leave it for now and let's think about it.' So we closed the nursery door . . . and let it be." Chris longed for the mindless, needing to somehow be out, active and purposeful: "I just wanted to mow the lawn," he remembers. And right as he finishes the job, Mark shows up to check on him. Chris admits that he did something then that he's never done before – emotions overflow, and he cries on his good friend's shoulder.

The week after Chris and Emily come home from the hospital moves forward quickly. They decide that they want a memorial service for their son and give themselves one week to organize it. Their decision calls for managing a lot of details . . . and handling the unexpected. Chris mentions the bewildering appearance of his long-absent father, Gary. After hearing about Carter's death, Gary surprises the couple by coming to town and contacting them. His stopover is short and he leaves before the memorial. During this same week, the couple makes visits to the funeral home to answer legal questions, do some planning, and pick up Carter's cremains. Emily shares her feelings about one surreal moment the day before the memorial service when they return to the funeral home for their son's ashes and she realizes, "I don't have my baby but I have this box." Later, she and Chris gently place Carter's ashes, for this one night, in the crib and nursery meant just for him.

Thankfully, family and friends do lend a hand to help the couple create a ceremony to honor their son. On Saturday, July 28, 2007, seven days after his stillbirth, Carter's ashes are interred at the church where Emily and Chris were married. A simple and thoughtful outside service with family and invited close friends is held. Chris' mom, Cindy, comes in from Oregon to be with the family for the memorial. Those who attend are handed cards on which to write personal notes to be placed in a beautiful book Emily prepares commemorating the service. Everyone is also given a sunflower to hold as the pastor shares a short homily and Emily's sister sings, "Jesus Loves Me." Afterwards, the sunflowers are collected in a vase and left at the church for others to enjoy. Emily remembers looking at them, observing their beauty . . . "like a ray of sunshine." The couple then asks for privacy and together they place the box with their son's ashes in the church's Columbarium, noting where his plaque might later be placed on the memorial wall. As a final tribute to each other, and their son's forever place in their lives, they fasten cross necklaces, one on the other. Soon after Carter's service ends, his parents leave town. Taking this time for the two of them to escape, to camp within the essential and surrounding beauty of nature felt like just the right way to mark this important milestone in their grief journey.

The couple takes another path in their story to share the particular way they found just the right cross necklaces for each other, and the significance of sunflowers to the family. Emily and Chris discover they are pregnant with Carter on Thanksgiving Day, 2006, and before long they are calling their unborn baby, Lil' Turkey. As they search for just the right cross to represent their son and this unforgettable time in their lives, they finally discover what they believe is a sign. They are in yet another store with crosses in front of them; handling one, they turn it over to find a tag with the word, "Turkey," displayed. They know their search is over; they've finally found the right one. Carter's mom and dad still daily wear this special sign of love for their first child. Another sign representing their boy is the appearance of sunflowers. "Sunflowers are Carter's flowers," Emily states. They have been present at many occasions where Carter is a strong presence: at Emily's baby shower; during Carter's delivery week when wild sunflowers dotted roadsides and fields in the area; and at his memorial. Every year since his death, sunflowers bloom right before his delivery date. It feels to the family as if nature is celebrating and honoring Carter's continued existence. Emily indicates that there is usually a large vase of sunflowers sitting on the floor between the kitchen and their dining area. Not only are they happy, bright and colorful, they are reminders of a son who is always around. "He's watching us," Emily declares; "he's ours."

Emily asserts that for months after Carter's death she had "never felt so uncomfortable in my own house or in my own skin." She felt lost. Each of the parents talks with gratitude about their bosses and different co-workers who handled the communication of their loss to their respective clients and colleagues. "We definitely had the right people in our lives at that time, just what we needed to try to somehow manage." Emily takes two weeks off of work to physically and emotionally recuperate and is actually ready to return to her job responsibilities, finding them easier than continuing to move aimlessly around the house.

Summer turns toward Fall, one of Emily's favorite seasons. She shares that her head and heart are still in July and moving forward seems impossible. Good friends, realizing her mood and also knowing how much she enjoys decorating for the Fall season, come to the rescue. Their support helps remind Emily of what she still finds lovely and lovable. They stay with her, decorating her home, reminding her of the beauty of the present. This time helps her realize she can do more than "just go through the motions of being alive." In October of 2007, Emily's grandparents give the couple the gift of a Bahamas getaway. The timing is perfect and the trip helps the bereaved pair physically and emotionally disconnect from the daily maze of grief's reminders. This gift takes them into the unfamiliar and the beautiful. "Things changed," Chris states and Emily smiles at the profound truth of that simple statement. The couple is able to rest, relax, renew, remember joy and reconnect. Not long after, in November, they discover with surprise and delight they are pregnant with their next baby.

As 2007 turns into 2008, the couple names the year they are leaving behind a really tough one – a very long year. Family grief, no matter how close or distant the family members have grown, carries with it especially intense, emotional burdens; each loss makes even more profound the power of the next. Chris' journey leading up to his son's death is particularly difficult. In March, just four months before Carter is due, he loses his brother, Nick, in a single car accident. Chris unexpectedly is able to talk with him when Nick accidently dials his brother's number looking for information. He is grateful for their long conversation, reliving some family stories and updating each other, because it is the morning after that unanticipated phone call when Chris receives another, reporting Nick's fatal accident. He spends two weeks in Georgia trying to unravel the details of Nick's death, all the while knowing how anxiously Emily is awaiting his return.

During the months following Carter's death, each of the grieving parents searches for ways to navigate all the chaos that accompanies deep grief and move toward the balance of living beyond simple survival. Emily shares the unexpected ways grief continued to visit her. "There have been a lot of times where responses or feelings have been very different than I expected . . . ." Though she understands the coming new year is meant to bring a fresh start, she also discovers that she doesn't want to move forward. "I thought I was going to be so relieved that year was over . . . but then was so sad 2007 was over. We were moving past to next year but our son wasn't here." She and Chris now face, with mixed feelings, the reality of having another child in the summer of 2008. Emily describes her emotional roller coaster: "it was kind of like reliving the last year of your life with a different baby."

Carter's nursery is still set up and Emily feels comforted spending time in the room and talking with her son. As her new pregnancy progresses she tells Carter that he has a job to do – he needs to watch over his unborn sibling. "I remember feeling that Carter was watching over us. This baby had (a) little angel in heaven . . . it was going to be ok this time." Though the pregnancy has some rough patches, Emily is at peace, believing the outcome will be very different than before. After all, their family doctor, the same one who delivered Carter, is "awesome." The couple call her a "huge blessing" in their lives, someone in whom they have ultimate trust. She is also, according to Chris, very understanding. "We had A LOT of ultrasounds," he shares as Emily smiles.

Springtime arrives and Cindy, Chris' mom, visits again to spend some time with the couple before her next grandchild's birth. It's finally the right time to convert Carter's room to a nursery for a new baby girl and Cindy helps. They repaint the room, do some redecorating, and finally fold and lovingly box all the things in Carter's layette. New baby Clara's room is created, her layette is assembled and the family looks forward to new life. Spring turns toward Summer and Emily's due date looms ahead. All along Chris and Emily have been reliving the milestones of this pregnancy, only one year apart from those of their lost son. It is especially uncomfortable and stressful for Emily. "There is no way I am going to be pregnant on Carter's birth date!" she declares to both her husband and her doctor.

Though their second baby is originally due after Carter's July 21st birth/death date, the doctor understands Emily's concerns and agrees to induce her early. New baby, Clara's, due date is set for July 15th. A week before the baby is due, issues with Emily's blood pressure send her back to the same hospital's Labor and Delivery area to be monitored. The couple calls those unexpected hospital hours a blessing. They were able to be in that same space where they lost their son, to process feelings and put to rest some fears – all before undergoing the normal stressors of delivering a new baby in a place of heartbreaking memories. As it turns out it was good they had the opportunity to wipe some worrisome memories clean, because Clara's delivery brings with it another set of unanticipated pressures. During labor the baby's heart rate drops and a timely delivery is critical. Things are very tense; both C-section and NICU teams are standing by. But in the end, all is well and Carter's new sister is born on July 15, 2008. Chris rushes to see his daughter, to find that she is safe and perfect.

Emily recounts the range of the emotional roller coaster of her daughter's birth. She is so thankful, yet incredibly sad; relieved, but also grief-filled. Carter did the job he was asked to do – Clara is safe. And though she presumed she would feel total happiness in her daughter's birth, Emily notes that any joy has to share the stage with her ongoing mourning. "I want them both." The entire first night both mother and baby cry.

The first anniversary of Carter's stillbirth is shared by the new family together. At 3:04 am on July 21, 2008, Chris, Emily and Clara all happen to be awake and out of bed at the same time. Looking at the clock, the parents note it is the very same time as their son's birth. Later that morning, the three attend "Carter's church," where his ashes lie interred, to commemorate his ongoing place in their growing family. Though Emily worries that the day will bring more sadness than peace, Chris shares that "it was actually a very good day." After church the family travels into the foothills together to picnic, play and soak in the natural beauty around them. The couple knows they want to continue to celebrate their son's presence in their family and decide on a yearly balloon release. In 2009, they begin the ritual of adding one more balloon each year to match the age Carter would have been. As Chris and Emily's family grows, adding Abby in September of 2011, so do the balloons the family of four use to pay tribute to a son and big brother who continues to grow in their hearts. Nine balloons, released by Clara, Abbey, Emily and Chris with love and laughter, dot the 2016 July sky.

Chris and Emily articulate some of the ways their lives have changed over these past nine years. In 2007 when Carter died, there was no dedicated support organization for bereaved parents in the area. "We felt like we were the only ones in the world that had ever lost a baby like this. We felt so alone," Emily recalls. For a time, the couple lives within that lonely reality. By 2009, Emily and Chris are involved with others who have also lost children. They discover a Candlelight Vigil is being held for bereaved parents to honor the lives of their children. After helping to publicize the event, they attend and commemorate Carter in a new and public way with others. They find comfort and healing in the company of parents like themselves, within a community of true understanding and mutual support. And things continue to change. Emily can still recall when she first noticed herself feeling differently. "I remember the first day I was laughing and had a good time at work and I felt kind of normal again and then all of a sudden . . . I felt like . . . Oh wait! Is it ok to be happy and laughing? And then you realize your son would want you to be happy and not be in this weird place forever." Over time, the couple pays forward the love, comfort and support they've received. They champion the organization, now called 3 Hopeful Hearts, through board membership, mentoring other parents, speaking at support group meetings, attending and organizing events and co-facilitating groups. Emily pauses and then gently shares that in these last few years she has been able to finally accept the past with a more grateful heart.

This afternoon, we are sitting in a thankful home: it's Chris and Emily's home; it's Clara and Abbey's home; and it is Carter's home. He is remembered through words, through family stories and memories, and within family pictures where he is represented by "Carter Bear," the teddy chosen for him that first Christmas in 2007. Emily proudly maintains that her daughters know their brother. "Neither Clara or Abbey met him yet in their hearts he is just as much their brother as they are each other's sisters." They can and do talk about him openly and comfortably. He is a real presence, an integral part of the family. "We have a brother in heaven." I'm told by Carter's sisters. Their brother's place in this family is secure and understood. With a sweet smile, Clara shares, "I say I'm the middle kid" . . . born after her brother and before her sister, Abbey. A grateful family of five, Carter's loved ones embrace how the spirit and presence of their first born continues to shape them.

"This is Carter's story," Emily affirms strongly. "Carter made Chris and I parents, and prepared us to love Clara and Abbey to the fullest. Losing him has certainly shaped our family into what it is today; we love deeply and treasure our time together. He will always be our son and for that we are thankful." Another year begins and the depth of love and assurance clearly continues to grow and thrive within Carter's family.

Angela: Love one another like it's your last day

I'm early. I want to unpack my writing materials and take a quiet moment to focus my mind on the upcoming interview with Veronica. I've secured a room in the public library for us; the room is quiet and has a bank of windows on one wall. I spread out and choose a seat at the table with my back to the windows; I want Veronica to be able to face them, to see the light and life outside as she tells me about the tragic loss of her cherished little girl, Angela. I don't have to wait long. Veronica soon joins me, armed with Kleenex and an unquestionable belief that her daughter's life and death continues to strongly influence her own. Though we start quietly, the depth of emotion this mother feels and then expresses through brief details of more recent losses of others dear to her, often by unnatural and violent means, soon rise to the surface – as do her tears. Funerals are on her mind and in her heart. "When my daughter died, my son used to say that we're cursed. Everybody around us dies and it's kind of feeling like that to me now. . . . So many who are kids to me are gone now. It's taken a toll." And so begins our conversation, setting the stage for the complex and unimaginable story of the death of sweet Angela, a lively and engaging five-year-old who earned the title, La Reina De Barancas: Little Queen of Barancas.

Veronica begins to detail the life story of a daughter who "from the day she was born til the day she died until now," is very much alive in her family's life. In the early 90's when she and her husband, Guillermo, decide to have another baby, they carefully plan for its safety. Veronica quit smoking and drinking for a full year before they try to get pregnant. The result, born on March 14, 1993, is Angela Gaucin, a truly treasured gift. Veronica affirms, "After she was born . . . it's like God really talked to us through Angie." A child lovingly planned for, her life is expected to be special, filled with significant events.

Even the very young Angela fearlessly believes in her own bright future. "Angie was the only one of my kids that really had a plan in life." Veronica continues to say that her little girl knew what she wanted and who she wanted it for. Angela was so excited to look ahead to that time when she would be Quinceanera; she wanted it for her whole family, especially her father. She planned to celebrate her fifteenth birthday with Guillermo walking her into the reception and dancing that traditional first dance with her. Her brothers would be close behind and her mother would help her find that beautiful, deep purple dress of her dreams – a dress fit for La Riena De Barancas. Another dream of the five-year-old was to become an Olympic ice skater and bring home the gold for her mother. "'Some day, Momma, I'm going to bring you home the gold medal.' And, I really think she would have," Veronica affirms, tears shimmering in her eyes with the memory. But regardless of the dreams and plans, Angela is never able to take ice skating lessons or celebrate her fifteenth birthday because before she turns six, life turns upside down.

Veronica's story shifts throughout when she recounts events she believes were premonitions of her daughter's death. "The signs were there; we just didn't see them." She continues, "We wouldn't have believed her if she had told us directly." One example she gives is that during the year before her death, Angela is randomly featured in the local paper. Her mother regards Angie's surprising "fifteen minutes of fame" as a worrisome sign. In both June and December of 1998, the little girl's picture appears, once even on the front page. Neither of these public events where her daughter is highlighted are planned and Veronica wonders if the unexpected focus on Angela is a sign. The last sign Veronica reveals happens not long before Angela's death. Veronica, Guillermo and the four children drive to a small town close to Guillermo's family Rancho. While there they visit a beautiful, local church. At first Angela fights the idea of entering, but eventually she does join her mother inside the church. Veronica remembers the two questions she asks: "Mom, do you think God is going to take good care of me?" "Will I be all alone?" Veronica reassures Angela that God will always care for her. Though her daughter couldn't explain why she reacted with such dread at the church door or why she needed to know the answers to her questions, Veronica now believes Angela was wondering about her own future. Still today, Veronica considers that her daughter, a burst of happy light, bright and full of loving energy, might have somehow felt she was going to die young. Wiping tears from her eyes, she admits she might not have understood it then, but now she thinks Angela "was trying to tell us good bye." A short time later, her daughter is dead.

It is January, 1999. Guillermo's father passed away on Christmas Eve, 1998, and Guillermo and Veronica decide to go to Mexico to make certain his mother is alright. Veronica's mother is expected to stay with the children, but things change and the parents find they must take four of their children with them. Jose', fourteen, stays in Colorado, but Kristina, ten, Ejay, eight, Kimberly, four, and Angela, five, are packed into the car with their parents, and all head south to Guillermo's family Rancho in Barancas, Mexico. Thankfully, they discover everyone is fine when they reach Barancas on January 28, 1999. The parents decide to stay awhile and treat their children to some extra days of family time. On February 4th, Guillermo takes his family of six and his mother to Sain Alt'o, a small town not far from the Rancho, to enjoy a day of shopping. The main downtown street is not only lined with stores, but also has vendor tables set up with souvenirs, food, clothing items and traditional gifts. The street-market tables are organized for walkers and customers to move among them, shopping and visiting together throughout the day. Veronica and her mother-in-law shop with the kids, buying clothes, shoes and gifts. She and Guillermo go their separate ways; the town is small enough that no one is very far away from each other. Family members enjoy the freedom of safely shopping, eating, visiting and playing. It is during this joy-filled family time that the inconceivable happens.

For some reason, even though Angela has her own new clothes, she wants to wear pieces of her brother and sisters' clothes instead. Concerned that Angela will mess up her siblings' new things, Veronica says no – that Angela can just wear her own new clothes. But Angela insists and before long is wearing shirt, pants and socks that aren't hers. The little girl heads off with ten-year-old Kristina to find and then try on some shoes from another vendor's table. Veronica stays at a separate table with other family members while Guillermo is off finding food.

Veronica recalls that she looks up and notices that a truck is driving toward the market area. "I remember that truck coming down a street and (it) turned where all the tables are." She knows the truck driver realizes he is not supposed to be on that street; he begins to slow and swerve to avoid things. Veronica believes that the driver sees her daughter who is now sitting on the ground, near the table, trying on shoes. He tries to miss her by turning, but the back of the truck "took her." Veronica, tears streaming, shares the horrific scene: "And I actually thought of the man that hit her before I even thought of her. It's like I saw it all happening . . . but I didn't. I was outside myself. I remember people running, things flying, shoes everywhere. And then I see this little girl lying in the road and I look at this man and think, oh my God, what he has to live with for the rest of his life. I look at the little girl and I just want to walk away and I turn to walk away when I remembered the pants and the shirt and the way I yelled at her to not mess up those clothes. And I turned back so fast because then I knew it was her."

We pause for a moment as Veronica wipes at the tears that refuse to stop. She continues her heartbreaking story sharing how she raced to pick up her daughter. ". . . her head was just back and she had all this blood gushing out of her ear and I'm trying to hold it in." The distraught mother's hands show how she cradled her daughter's head, trying to stop the blood. "I couldn't stop the blood!" These last words are like a cry and Veronica lowers her head, reaching for another tissue to wipe eyes brimming with tears. Veronica believes Angela is still alive; her head is moving back and forth and her eyes are rolling. Trying to catch her own breath to continue, she repeats the anguished words she said on that day, "God, let me feel her pain. I don't want her to feel all this pain." Still aware that Guillermo is not beside her at the scene, Veronica leaves everything behind but her daughter. She takes off running with Angela in her arms to locate a doctor, hoping that her other children and her mother-in-law will follow. The doctor she finds looks at Angela and tells Veronica there is nothing he can do. And all of a sudden Guillermo is there. He picks up his daughter, rushes to a waiting truck and speeds away with her, leaving Veronica, his mother and the three children wondering what to do next. They hurry through the streets of the small town, trying to find where Guillermo and Angela might be. Finally, they come upon another doctor's office but instead of being welcomed in, Veronica, her mother-in-law, Kristina, Kimberly and Ejay are locked within a room, away from Angela.

Veronica, her eyes still wet, but now flashing in anger explains her experience of being kept from her daughter. "I had a lot of hate at that minute. Why didn't they want me to be with my daughter? I'm her mom! I hated that I wasn't with her." *In Mexico, Veronica notes as an aside, women have no rights. She is told that as a woman she is not strong enough to be there, with her daughter. Though she* pounds on the door to get out and find Angela, no one helps. Veronica tries different ways to get out of the room – needing a bathroom, a cigarette, reminding the nurses she is a US citizen, demanding to see her daughter – and eventually the door is opened. Veronica moves out into a hallway and past another open doorway where she sees a doctor who invites her to come into his office. This doctor tells her again that her husband is with Angela and then reveals that "they are coming for her." Veronica angrily asks what that means and finally realizes that Angela is dead. Because she was locked away, unable to be with her child during this important time, Veronica says, "I went psycho!" She starts to throw and break things in the office and is then finally taken into the room where Angela lies. She finds Guillermo there and is surprised to also see two of his sisters who have somehow gotten there from Barancas and been allowed in the room. She focuses on Angela, goes to her, and finally is able to hold her.

Veronica learns that Angela actually died while in the truck with her father as he raced toward the doctor's. Though she felt robbed of the privilege of being with Angela at her passing, she is thankful that at least Guillermo was there at her end. She calls her husband "one of the richest men ever;" he was given the gift of being with Angela when she took her last breath. The parents mark this day, February 4, 1999, as the death date of their little girl.

It is still February 4th and though the hours are passing by, time is standing still in heart-aching ways for the parents. Where they are, now, in Mexico, the expectations, preparation and burial practices are unfamiliar. Veronica experiences more and more confusion and frustration at what she is expected to know, understand and do in those short, rushed hours after Angela's death. Angela's body is taken in one direction from Sain Alt'o to be autopsied and embalmed, and the parents are told to go in another direction, to a different town to meet local police and complete paper work about the accident. But before she and Guillermo can make that trip, his sisters insist that Veronica shop for Angela's burial clothes. There is anguish in her voice as she relates this unexpected shopping time with her sisters-in-law. She is taken through the same streets where she held her mortally-wounded daughter only hours earlier: "I just wanted to kill myself and they want me to pass by the street, and they want me to pick out clothes, and they want me to drive and do statements, and drive and see my daughter . . . and I didn't have anything in me. And they each . . . had an arm dragging me down the street."

Eventually, with burial clothes purchased and collected in a bag, Veronica is finally free to travel with Guillermo to provide the necessary information to the police authorities. Veronica voices how that particular experience is both irritating and painful as the officials continue to look toward her husband, the man, for the important details of the event even though she, a woman, was the person actually present at the scene who needs to recall it all again. In time the statements are accepted from the parents, and they leave, backtracking to where their daughter's body is being embalmed. The address they have been given turns out to be a cemetery. Veronica gives her husband the bag of burial clothes because she can't bear to go into the mortuary. She waits for him in the truck. And time stands still.

Veronica takes another turn in the story to relate how the next event impacts her and Guillermo in ways beyond the immediate tragedy. Guillermo, alone, observes the completion of Angela's embalming. He then dresses her, forgetting nothing. He comes out of the mortuary carrying their daughter and walks down the sidewalk toward Veronica. She names this time as one of her most enduring memories: "He looked like an angel." She is so proud of her husband during this time. Strong and capable, he tenderly cared for their daughter's body, handling all the necessary details. "He thought of everything." Then Veronica takes the conversation to another time and place . . . to another pain-filled memory. After Angela's death, the couple continues to struggle with the persistent grief, anger, guilt and frustration surrounding the loss of their daughter. They both had been living with pieces of the experience in Mexico they hadn't yet told each other. Their struggle grows worse. Eventually Veronica asks Guillermo, "What's wrong with you? Since she passed away you don't talk to me." Then she adds, "It became this thing that we blamed each other. We didn't know what we were going through. He didn't know what I had gone through. I didn't know what he had been through . . . and the truth comes out." Guillermo is finally able to share the horrible picture he witnesses when he entered where his little girl is being embalmed: a man, trusted with their Angela, has laid her, naked, on a cement floor; with one hand he holds a tube to drain Angela's blood from her, while his other hand is on her "privates." As she relates this atrocity, Veronica's voice rises in pain and anger, and the tears flow.

Just as Guillermo exits the building with Angela in his arms, a hearse arrives. A woman gets out of the vehicle and moves to the back to pull out an infant-sized casket. It has been brought to hold Angela, but it is much too small and the parents refuse it. Instead, Angela's body is lain across the laps of those in the truck while they follow the hearse to a funeral home where Guillermo chooses a different casket that is more fitting. This particular coffin is designed so that when the left, upper part of the separated lid is lifted, glass still covers the face and chest of the resting body. Others can see but not touch the departed. Veronica describes it: "She was covered like a queen."

With Angela's body now resting in a more suitable place and dressed in her beautiful white clothes for burial, the parents set off for Barancas. Veronica remembers that she begins to cry as she thinks of Angela, alone, bouncing around in the casket, so they stop the truck and the parents go back to lift their daughter's body out and hold her tenderly the rest of the journey. They arrive at the Rancho and discover Guillermo's family has been preparing a place for Angela to be laid out. A white sheet and surrounding candles await her little body. Though they weren't expecting to display a coffin, family members find a way to rearrange the area so Angela, in her casket, has a place to rest.

As Veronica describes the scene when she and other family members look at their little queen, more anger surfaces. She remembers in awful detail the lack of care given by the medical professionals charged with caring for Angela's body: she has never fully been cleaned, either after the accident or from the embalming process; her hair is in disarray; and her body is still smeared with fluids and her own blood.

Before long people begin to arrive to sit with the family in their grief. They are mostly unfamiliar to Veronica; she recalls that she is in a "state of numbness . . . there, but not there." Before the night is over, she decides to shoot a video of the visitation at the Rancho to commemorate that time. Veronica also realizes Angela's body is deteriorating and wants to have pictures of her for their Colorado family before that happens. The nightwatch progresses; family, friends and caring others pass the hours together. February 4th turns into the 5th as daylight brightens the horizon. Veronica is told, "its time." When she asks for what, a sister-in-law reveals that Guillermo's nephews have been working at the cemetery all night to be ready for this morning. It is then when Veronica discovers what most everyone else seems to know – Angela is to be buried, in Mexico, now. And the next part of this tragic story starts with a mother's declaration: "You are not burying my daughter here!"

Veronica reveals that those who are in charge of having Angela embalmed admit that they are not good at the process. According to the Mexican Health authorities, bodies are expected to be buried within twenty-four hours and burying a body after a forty-eight-hour period requires a permit from the Mexican Health Department. Her family is operating under these understood expectations, but to Veronica it means saying good bye too quickly, and then committing her daughter to a place too far away. She begs Guillermo not to let his family bury Angela in the grave, just dug, next to his own father's gravesite. Preparations for burial stop and the parents head back to Sain Alt'o to find a phone and call

Veronica's parents who still haven't been told either about the accident or their granddaughter's death. Veronica not only needs to give her family the horrid news, she is also hoping for guidance.

Veronica takes a moment to note that when she dropped her purse and all of her packages in order to pick up Angela and run to a doctor, most everything disappeared – new gifts, clothes and shoes as well as all of her money are stolen. Nothing remains but an empty purse with their identification documents still intact. During the call to her parents, Veronica relates the accident and, though she doesn't remember how she did it, tells them their granddaughter is dead. Distraught, feeling helpless and thinking only of her little girl, she tells her parents they should "sell the house, sell the cars, sell everything, keep it, I don't care. I'm not going home. I'm not going to leave her here." After her father hears the story of the family's last several hours, he strongly agrees with Veronica's wishes. Angela should be brought back to Colorado to be buried, where her mother and father can always be close to her. Knowing that her Mexican family is prepared to bury Angela, this very day, she tells her father, "I don't know how to bring her home."

It's February 5th and the first twenty-four hours are ticking away. Veronica and Guillermo understand that they cannot transport their daughter's body back to the United States unless it meets certain health requirements. In order to buy more time to create a possible path for taking Angela's body home, Veronica goes again to the mortuary and asks a woman in charge to embalm her daughter a second time. The woman agrees. Then the parents spend hours talking with others, checking regulations, asking questions – all the while searching for ways to transport Angela back to the states. Options are few and obstacles are many. Cremating her was never an option for Veronica, and the specific regulations surrounding driving out of the country with Angela's body are considered but marked off, one by one, as impossible. Time slips away and Veronica returns to the mortuary asking for a third embalming. Their little girl's body again receives the procedure and the parents continue to search for an answer to their dilemma. Veronica affirms, "Every door was closing." And then the situation begins to turn a corner . . . toward the answer.

Veronica's father in Colorado gives his daughter the name and number of someone to call who he believes can help them. Veronica, who has been trying unsuccessfully to get the funeral home to honor their business promise of providing air transport for the deceased to the states, returns to the funeral home. This time she makes a call to her father's contact – someone who works for the American Embassy. She reaches a man who is aware of her name and some details of the situation. After asking her some questions and assessing the difficulties the couple faces, he talks with the funeral home representative. Eventually, he directly tells them that if he must, he will come to Mexico and bring Angela out himself. The woman at the funeral home rethinks her position and tells the family she will honor their promise to transport the body. Veronica begins to believe that the closing door might stay open just long enough for them to send her little girl home.

As details unfold for the transport, more problems surface. The legalese and growing red tape wind tightly around the situation and the parents now wonder not only how they will get Angela, but also the rest of the family, out of Mexico together. Having little money, since most of it was stolen at the scene of Angela's accident, and facing new paperwork complications surrounding transport and citizenship issues, the couple senses the door begin to shut again. Their contact from the American Embassy makes another call to see how things are going. An anxious Veronica details the latest unreasonable expectations and again he asks to speak to the funeral home representative. This time he uses the power his job carries and the family's position as US citizens to untangle the bureaucratic, punitive paperwork. His words work and the family finally watches the door open fully. Angela's casket is put on a flight to Denver on February 6, 1999, two days after her death; it lands just hours later. After making certain Angela is on her way to Colorado, a relieved Veronica calls her father to let him know that his granddaughter is on her way to him. Then, she and Guillermo say their goodbyes to their Barancas family, load the children in the car and begin an almost non-stop drive home.

Angela's body is met at DIA by a mortuary located in Denver as well as by the Embassy representative who promised to help them bring their little girl home. She is held in Denver as her body is re-examined and re-autopsied. After another embalming procedure and all medical considerations are met, a funeral home from the parent's hometown collects their daughter's body, bringing her the final way home. Veronica, Guillermo, Kristina, Ejay and Kimberly arrive on February 7th, only one day after Angela lands. Thankfully the Colorado family is together to take possession of Angie's body when she is finally released by health officials and transported from Denver to Fort Collins. All the arrangements for a family viewing, the special Blessing and her rosary service, have been made by her family to commemorate the life of a beloved little girl. The Little Queen of Barancas, in her long, white dress, white shoes, jewelry and crown, is finally laid to rest on February 11, 1999.

Veronica reveals that she has held close many things of Angela's over the years. "I saved every piece of clothing she ever wore, toys and clothes she got for Christmas (right before her death), every paper she brought home from school and I still can't let go of the clothes from her accident. I just feel like if I throw them away . . . all her blood is on them; that's the last of her life. It will just go in the trash, like nothing. I just can't bring myself to do it." Veronica shares that she is now ready to give some of her daughter's things — those last Christmas presents and toys that she was never able to play with — to someone who will treasure them.

Veronica and I move toward the closure of our interview as I ask her about the passionate feelings she still holds concerning the accident and the circumstances of Angela's death. She thinks a moment and describes that she feels a kind of "grudge" against the truck driver who hit Angela. Though he was held by the police directly after the accident, before the parents could deal with the case the driver bought his freedom and fled the country. According to Veronica and members of her family, some form of justice needs to happen: this man must face Angela's whole family; he needs to admit to what he has done; to say he is sorry, that he didn't mean to take their cherished daughter, granddaughter, sister and niece from them. "Basically my daughter's accident turned to murder when he ran away," Veronica declares.

Veronica gives me a small smile when she says of Angela: "I have to talk to her a lot . . . to tell her about what's new and what I wish she could be here doing . . . and just everything. I told her I hope you know that we loved you." She continues, "God told us from the beginning . . . this is the one that's not going to be here long." Still, Veronica believes that Angela is always here, around her; she is love. She is present in the laughter, the special smiles and the bouncing energy of family – especially through (Guillermo) Junior, the younger brother Angela never met. In closing, Veronica shares important and grace-filled wisdom she has gained from her grief-filled loss: *"Every day is a gift. Love one another like it's your last day."*

Postscript

I cannot end this book without talking directly to my son who has been my mainstay throughout its conception and final creation. Because of his ongoing presence in my life, I am able to offer hope to the grieving heart.

"Grace is the central invitation to
life, and the final word.
It's the beckoning nudge and . . . mercy
which urges us to change and grow,
and then gives us the power to pull it off."
Tim Hansel: <u>You Gotta Keep Dancin'</u>

Before Matthew died, I sent him Tim Hansel's book, <u>You Gotta Keep Dancin'</u>. I thought the writer's journey with chronic pain would somehow speak to him, perhaps lead him to reflect on commonalities and differences between his journey and the author's. I had read the book fully and deeply. It was important to me then. And still must be. As I look at it again, right now, I am startled to note that there are more than two dozen red marking flags, attached to pages, sentences and ideas that I believed were profound and might speak to my son's astonishing intellect and gentle heart. I don't know if he ever read it. I hope he did and was somehow comforted by Hansel's discussion on the richness of life when things are far from easy. Statements like this that could set up a conversation: "I've survived because I've discovered a new and different kind of joy . . . a joy that can coexist with uncertainty and doubt, pain, confusion, and ambiguity." I was praying that Matt could find, or perhaps had already found, that kind of joy. But, I never knew; we didn't have that conversation before his death.

After he died, I wrote <u>Letters for Grace</u>, a memoir of a mom who had survived her first born and was fighting to understand why. In the book I composed letters to him, filled with wonderings and questions about my life, both with and without him, longing to somehow hear answers that would bring us together through the peace of Grace moments. This final letter, a compilation of those old and some new thoughts, is for you, Matt.

My son,

My time thinking about the place grace has in my life has morphed and grown in complexity over this tempestuous journey since your death. I have had time to learn from your loss: years of searching and readjusting, of crafting one and yet another vision of a life journey, of crying when your sweet face comes to me unbidden, and smiling when that same vision is wrapped in hope and expectation. Asking you questions granted me the wisdom to understand that dwelling in the quiet of my own soul, available to hear answers as well as generate new questions, can empower me to most safely and productively propel into the fireworks of reality – a reality surrounded by possibilities and moving to a rhythm independent of my control. You've been an exceptional teacher.

You continue to be in my life, my waking dreams, my best hopes, my best self. How much and strongly I love you continue to feed me. I feel your arm around my shoulders, your infectious grin is a presence just over my right shoulder and I believe if I turn my head ever so slightly I can be lost in its loving, grace-filled light. I don't know what is next for us, but I know grief no longer holds me captive because you are with me.

You are Grace, always present in me.
You are forever my boy, as I am ever,
your Mom.

Reading Group Discussion Ideas

1. How do you define grace? Explain why and how you have come to your definition.

2. In her essays, the author treats Grace as if it is a living character. Discuss how your understanding of this idea fits or conflicts with your own beliefs about grace.

3. On the last page of the first essay, "the call of Grace," Nicolet writes the following by Eckhart Tolle: "Acceptance of the unacceptable is the greatest source of grace in this world." Does this quote have meaning in your life?

4. Share your definition of paradox. How does Neils Bohr's idea – that a paradox can contain two absolute truths – mesh with your own understanding of paradox?

5. Explain the *Paradox Gap* (found in the final essay) to another? Describe a situation of loss and/or grief in your life where you believe you moved into that gap and discovered something new.

6. Do you believe, as the author writes, that grief and grace are both readily available within our hearts? Share your position and then talk about the experience that has taken you to that belief.

7. " . . . the truth is that once profound grief takes up residence in you, time is meaningless; there is no returning to that accustomed place before it." Does Nicolet's quote ring true in your life? In what ways?

8. In the third essay, "finding Grace in the mystery," the author quotes Brian McLaren (<u>We Make The Road By Walking</u>) as saying: "Maybe a vision means seeing into what's more real than anything else." What does this statement mean to you? How might believing it impact the way you live your life?

9. What do you think of the author's belief that one cannot truly begin healing until he/she intentionally lives fully present, in the *Now* of time?

10. In her essay about standing in stillness by others as they grieve, Nicolet provides a list of best hopes written from the perspective of the griever. Which in this list do you believe are the two or three most helpful for you to remember as you support another? Which two or three would be your best hopes from another if you were grieving?

11. Which of the eight essays in <u>Finding Grace</u>:
    - ✓ *helped* you better understand how interconnected grace and grief impact your reality? Describe any new perceptions.
    - ✓ *gave* you the most to think about as one who is either now living, or has lived, in grief? Explain one idea you will consider more fully.
    - ✓ *provided* you with the most surprises? What one idea from that essay startled, dismayed or helped you think differently?
    - ✓ *gave* you something new and valuable to consider? Explain one useful idea you are considering.

12. The author provided quotes throughout to help her readers pause and process the material being presented. Were there one or more quotes that you found especially interesting and meaningful? Share one and its importance to you.

13. At the end of the last essay, "beyond grief: moving through the paradox," Nicolet shares 10 ideas for becoming intentional as one works to move beyond grief. Of those 10, which one or two resonate most deeply with you?

14. Of the 19 stories included in the Addendum, which demonstrate the idea of grace after grief most clearly to you? Find an experience or a quote within that story to illustrate your belief.